Stronger Than Dirt

Stronger Than Dirt

A Cultural History of Advertising Personal Hygiene in America, 1875 to 1940

Juliann Sivulka

Humanity Books

an imprint of Prometheus Books
59 John Glenn Drive, Amherst, New York 14228-2197

Published 2001 by Humanity Books, an imprint of Prometheus Books

Inquiries should be addressed to
Humanity Books
59 John Glenn Drive
Amherst, New York 14228–2197
VOICE: 716–691–0133, ext. 207
FAX: 716–564–2711
WWW.PROMETHEUSBOOKS.COM

05 04 03 02 01   5 4 3 2 1

Library of Congress Cataloging-in-Publication Data

Sivulka, Juliann.
    Stronger than dirt : a cultural history of advertising personal hygiene in America, 1875–1940 / Juliann Sivulka.
        p. cm.
    Includes bibliographical references and index.
    ISBN 1–57392–952–2 (paper : alk. paper)
        1. Advertising—Soap—United States—History. 2. Advertising—Social aspects—United States. I. Title.

HF6161.S62 S58 2001
659.1'6313—dc21   2001024571

Printed in the United States of America on acid-free paper

Cleanliness is, indeed, next to godliness.

—Reverend John Wesley
"Sermon XCII—On Dress," 1788

Most of us want the good and beautiful and worthwhile things of life. Soap and water alone cannot give them to us, but we know they can help.

—Grace T. Hallock
A Tale of Soap and Water, 1928

Contents

7. WHITE SOAP AND BLACK CONSUMER CULTURE 251

AFTERWORD 291

A WORD ABOUT SOURCES 305

NOTES 309

BIBLIOGRAPHY 343

INDEX 357

Acknowledgments

This book would not have been possible without the assistance of a host of people who were a tremendous help to me, whether they know it or not, in the research and writing of this book.

Carl Holmberg at Bowling Green State University gave an extraordinary amount of time and effort in helping me to write the book I wanted to write. His close reading of the manuscript has challenged me as a writer, even as his enthusiasm has kept me going. The manuscript has also benefited from readings, in part or whole, by Marilyn Motz, Don McQuarrie, Susan Kleine, and Phil Terrie. I would also like to thank Keith McGraw and Jason Ayer, who provided the many photographs for this project. Thanks to my colleagues at the College of Journalism and Mass Communications at the University of South Carolina for their encouragement and for allowing me the time and the resources to complete this book. I must also thank my family and friends, who sustained me through the long period of research and writing.

I am grateful for financial assistance for research from the J. Walter Thompson Travel Fellowship, I also thank the Hagley

Museum and Library, who welcomed me as a visiting scholar for one summer. In the course of researching. I received capable and enthusiastic assistance from many archivists and librarians, especially those at the Archives Center of the National Museum of American History; Bowling Green State University Popular Culture Library; the Hagley Museum and Library; New York Public Library; State Historical Society of Wisconsin; Winterthur Library; the University of Delaware Library; and the J. Walter Thompson Archives in the Manuscript Department, William R. Perkins Library, Duke University. In particular, Ellen Gartrell greatly assisted my research; her respect and appreciation for the treasures under her care inspired me to see those archival materials used and to encourage both the preservation and the study of vintage advertisements.

Finally, I must gratefully acknowledge the contributions of my editor at Humanity Books, Eugene O'Connor, whose wise counsel and endless patience are most appreciated. Thanks also to associate editor Meghann French, Chris Kramer, Jacqueline Cooke, and the other talented staff who were involved in the production of this book. I appreciate their capable assistance and enthusiasm.

1
A Culture
of Cleanliness

In 1919, the Lever Brothers Company of New York City made an announcement about Lifebuoy, an antibacterial bar soap. It told readers that "[f]or the first time in history soap is part of a soldier's equipment, and every man in the U.S. Army is *compelled* to use it." The ad, which had much the same look as other magazine ads, explained that one of the first rules for keeping well in the army was to "bathe once a day. The clean soldier, the Army General Pershing is quoted as saying, is more courageous, never discouraged—he is brimming with energy." The rest of the advertisement concentrated on the product's advantages, telling readers that casual washing with water alone does not cleanse the skin, but Lifebuoy Soap cleanses thoroughly and keeps your skin healthy (see Fig. 1.1).[1]

The 1919 advertisement for Lifebuoy Soap may be understood as an artifact of a culture in the making, a culture of cleanliness founded on new technologies and structured by new economic forms and new consumer rituals. Well into the late nineteenth century, the privilege of washing with soap had been a special prerogative of the well-to-do, and a bath was some-

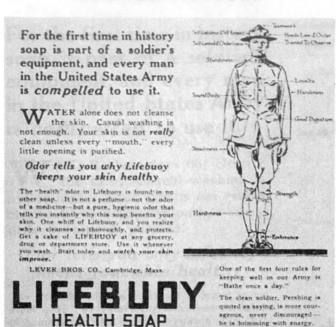

For the first time in history soap is part of a soldier's equipment, and every man in the United States Army is *compelled* to use it.

WATER alone does not cleanse the skin. Casual washing is not enough. Your skin is not *really* clean unless every "mouth," every little opening is purified.

Odor tells you why Lifebuoy keeps your skin healthy

The "health" odor in Lifebuoy is found in no other soap. It is not a perfume—not the odor of a medicine—but a pure, hygienic odor that tells you instantly why this soap benefits your skin. One whiff of Lifebuoy, and you realize why it cleanses so thoroughly, and protects. Get a cake of LIFEBUOY at any grocery, drug or department store. Use it whenever you wash. Start today and *watch your skin improve.*

LEVER BROS. CO., Cambridge, Mass.

LIFEBUOY
HEALTH SOAP
Copyrighted, 1919, by Lever Bros. Co.

One of the first four rules for keeping well in our Army is "Bathe once a day."

The clean soldier, Pershing is quoted as saying, is more courageous, never discouraged—he is brimming with energy.

Fig. 1.1. Lifebuoy Soap, advertisement, 1919. Courtesy of J. Walter Thompson Archives, John W. Hartman Center for Sales, Advertising, and Marketing History, Duke University Rare Book and Special Collections Library.

thing to avoid. A hurried rinse at the backyard pump was enough for most farm folks, while a splash of water and quick scrub with a sponge or cloth sufficed for most city dwellers. In World War I, however, soap went along in American soldiers' knapsacks and officer kits as an army requirement, an event that marked the beginning of the transition of soap from the status of luxury to a ubiquitous necessity. By the 1920s, it became not merely fashionable, but also normative for Americans to wash their hands, frequently bathe, and generally use large quantities of soap.

The transformation of soap from a luxury product to a staple necessity of American life marked a sea of change, not only in rituals of personal cleanliness, but in conceptions about the body, about inhabited space, and about social groups. As cleanliness rituals became more elaborate, specialized places devoted to the care of the body were created, and domestic interiors became more complex. At the same time, this dynamic affected spaces other than architecture. The subsequent demand for water required reconstruction of cities, both above and below ground.

Today's cleanliness, then, should be understood not as a natural progression from a prehygienic age to an era of cleanliness based on scientific rationale, but in terms of a psychological process caused by the phenomenon of consumption. In a new industrial America, people's status changed from colonists to workers, citizens, consumers, and eventually pleasure seekers. For people experiencing these social changes, cleanliness denoted far more than that one was clean; it also provided a system of meaning that helped men and women navigate the changing conditions of modern social experience. Advertising imagery, too, writes historian Roland Marchand, offered up "havens of security, intimacy, and simple pleasures [that] would compensate for, and make tolerable, the anonymity and competitive insecurities of urban complexity."[2] Similarly, the images and rhetoric about personal cleanliness that appeared in literature of advice, as well as in films, novels, and magazine stories, helped Americans assume gender roles and construct their own life stories for a new world.

The Lifebuoy Soap ad appeared near the end of a major transition in American marketing, advertising, and society. Many historians have described the forty or so years on either side of the beginning of the twentieth century as a period of major change, a new stage of economic development. During this time, the United States completed the transition from an agricultural to an industrial society, while modern systems of business organization, production, and distribution transformed industry itself. Countless new products—some of them packaged versions of goods people had used for centuries, like soap; others completely new, like indoor bathrooms—may be understood as material representations of that shift and its effect on American life.

Perhaps no other standardized, packaged good furnishes a more useful case in point for this period of major change than soap. In this study, then, soap is defined as a cleansing agent for washing the hands, face, and body, which is manufactured in bars or liquid form. Brand-name packaged soap became one of the first nationally advertised goods, along with cereals, baking ingredients, and foodstuffs. Many small businesses became enormous ventures, with annual advertising expenditures skyrocketing from several thousand dollars a year in the 1890s to multimillion-dollar sums in the following decades. The needs of soap companies like Procter & Gamble, Colgate-Palmolive, and Lever Brothers reshaped the advertising business, creating new demands for advertising vehicles like magazines and for agency services such as art, copy, and layout to execute their marketing strategies. Just as a century ago the largest advertisers of nationally advertised consumer products were Procter & Gamble, Colgate-Palmolive, and Lever Brothers (now UniLever); the same companies still rank among the top ad spenders in the United States.

Mass production and mass consumption in American society is so pervasive at the dawn of the twenty-first century that many people tend to take it for granted. Ads told—and still tell—Americans the right soap to buy, the right clothes to wear, and the right car to drive. The practice of evaluating how affluent people appear with how many goods they appropriate has become the norm. Yet the consumption ethic is a relatively recent phenomenon of American culture. The basic values of a society geared toward production and mass consumption are a cultural and social construction that voluminously increased the demand for goods, a demand that could no longer be met by methods of hand production in the nineteenth century. By 1875, American enterprise and inventiveness were at work to create the foundations of new manufacturing, marketing, and advertising systems.

SOAP AS AN ARTIFACT OF CULTURE

One definition of material culture suggested by anthropologist Melville J. Herskovits that proves particularly useful for investigating bars of soap, bathroom fixtures, and other objects that function as artifacts of American culture. It suggests that material culture can be thought of as a totality of objects in a culture that are used by humankind to cope with the physical world, to facilitate social intercourse, to delight their fancy, and to create symbols of meaning.[3] Even the most common mass-produced goods can take on meaning. For example, household objects embody both the relationships and routines of private daily life and the social relationships of production and distribution. Though both may be used to wash or clean, a chunk of soap made by hand from wood ashes and animal fat is an artifact distinct from a commercially produced bar of Lifebuoy or Ivory, packaged with an identifying wrapper and sold at the grocery store.

New ways of relating to the objects of everyday life, such as bars of soap to wash the body, developed along the way and exemplified changes in the material culture of American society. During the decades around the turn of the century, brand-name, packaged bars of soap came to represent and embody the new systems of production, distribution, and advertising, as well as the social relationships that brought people the things they used. Household routines became less involved in making things such as fireside soap and became more involved in purchasing commercially made products like packaged bars of soap; consumption became incorporated into household work as more Americans became consumers. This change amounted to nothing less than a major cultural transition that entailed new kinds of human needs which affected customs, ideas, attitudes, social organization, and material resources—in short, the elements of culture.

As personal cleanliness rituals changed, so did interpretive communities. Some people needed perfumes and clean linen to cover up an unwashed body in the nineteenth century, while others used Ivory and, later, Lifebuoy soaps. In the culture emerging in the twentieth century, a culture increasingly organized around the mass production and marketing of consumer goods, new needs surfaced in tandem with new products and with the new ways of life that characterized urban society.

The corporations that made and distributed mass-produced goods did not necessarily set out to create needs. Procter & Gamble made Ivory Soap in order to sell it. The firm put most of its marketing efforts into producing a demand for the particular product, not a need for the product itself. There was also no distinction between hand soap and clothes-washing soap. Soap was soap. Sometimes manufacturers did create needs among markets, as Lever Brothers did in advertising Lifebuoy Soap with its disinfectant properties. The firm exploited new fears of how germs were spread by coughing, sneezing, and shared public facilities to promote its product as the health soap. Still, even the most powerful marketers had little control over changing ideas, habits, technology, demographic trends, and the many facets of culture; instead, they concentrated their efforts on perceiving and taking advantage of these changes. Despite the size of their advertising budgets, their efforts were limited by ethnic, regional, and personal preferences.

Cultural shifts did not evolve at a steady, predictable rate, but rather at an uneven one, with new developments interacting in complex ways and exhibiting many ambiguities and contradictions. Some of these ambiguities and contradictions of American society were expressed in objects of everyday American life. Even an everyday object such as soap embodied many of the central issues that occupied American society at the turn of the century—issues of power and power relations, the distribution of wealth and resources, gender roles and expectations, and enforcement of appropriate beliefs and behaviors, as well as continuity and change. Cleanliness became an indicator that some individuals were morally superior, of better character, or more civilized than others. It also served to differentiate larger numbers of Americans, especially as society increasingly became more middle-class and white-collar.

The foundation for the rapid transformation that accompanied mass production of soap after 1875 had been laid over a long period of change. Americans had been living in filthy circumstances until the mid–nineteenth century, but when it was discovered that the lack of proper sanitation often brought germs, disease, suffering, and death with it, Americans came clean. Health reformers, nurses, and social workers pressed for more sanitary conditions; public sanitarians and public works engineers built a system of public utilities that Americans now take for granted. Proponents of the new gospel of germs built on traditional methods of preventing disease advocated by earlier sanitarians, such as disinfection, water purification, ventilation, and plumbing. Soap makers began to take advantage of these new needs, producing milder soaps for use on the face, hands, and the body as more people adopted lustration rituals. As running water became available and bathrooms moved indoors, it became even easier for people to clean themselves. By the 1920s, it had become normative for Americans to wash frequently and generally use large quantities of brand-name, packaged bars of soap.

In any case, consumption choices simply cannot be understood without considering the cultural context. Culture is the lens through which people view the world of goods and which determines the overall priorities and meanings people attach to activities and products. This study, then, deals substantively with the cultural factors that paralleled changes in advertising and personal cleanliness rituals over time. In particular, it examines the production of domesticity along with sweeping changes in domestic architecture that created a specific area devoted to cleansing rituals, the bathroom. Gender was also a vital part of the production of cleanliness, particularly since cleanliness came to be modeled as women's role.

At the same time, four strategic unities emerged that formed specific mechanisms of knowledge and power centering on personal cleanliness:

(1) the evolution of women's clubs from the Civil War to 1920; (2) the settlement movement from 1890 to 1920; (3) a proliferation of literature of advice, ranging from etiquette books to popular magazines such as *Godey's*, *Ladies' Home Journal*, and *True Story*; and (4) the development of the advertising industry. Together, these cultural factors focused attention on middle-class standards of cleanliness and promoted a powerful message: that keeping clean was not only healthy, but it was important to the country's standard of living, social welfare, and economy. In the new industrial America, personal cleanliness rituals ensured order and advancement; they also disciplined, built character, and created new customers for an emerging consumer society.

Thus, this study examines advertising strategies used to sell packaged soap from 1875 to 1940. Beginning with the advertising message, the study sketches out advertising content quite specific to a particular culture in terms used in the study of popular art forms, including myths, icons, heroes, stereotypes, rituals, and formulas. This historical interpretation interprets advertisements as artifacts that evoked consumer rituals that occur when interacting with the variety of ritual artifacts associated with personal cleanliness as opposed to centering on a theory of cleanliness.[4]

With this in mind, the research questions in this work are as follows: (1) What do the advertisements for personal cleanliness products tell us about the change in beliefs and values of mass society from 1875 to 1940? (2) What are the visible expressions of these beliefs and values in terms of myths, icons, stereotypes, heroes, rituals, and formulas? (3) What rituals of cleanliness are portrayed as socially necessary? (4) What types of advertising conventions developed as reliable formulas for success?

DEFINITIONS: MYTHS, ICONS, STEREOTYPES, HEROES, RITUALS, AND FORMULA

While most of the terms used in subsequent chapters should pose little difficulty, a few terms used in the study of popular art forms and exemplification require discussion, because they are used variously by diverse writers and scholars. The terms are as follows: *myths, icons, stereotypes, heroes, rituals,* and *formula.*

Used here in a broad sense, *myths* essentially express deeply held significant cultural beliefs and values, while *myth-narratives* are "stories" that explain nature, history, and evil in the universe. Myth-narratives that achieve immense and long-lasting popularity are especially important as story formulas in selling messages, because they tap into vital myths of society. The ads may take the form of allegory, a device in which each character, object, and event symbolically expresses a mythic expectation or a moral or religious principle. In *Advertising the American Dream*, Marchand identified a number of myth-narratives that he termed "great parables" of the 1920s and 1930s, including the "democracy of the goods," "first impression," and "captivated child," among others.[5]

In soap advertising, a number of myths present themselves. Using the advertised product, for instance, may invoke the mythic expectation of romantic love, particularly in preparing for a date. As one version of the romantic-love myth spins, for each individual there is one perfect partner, who, once found, will make life complete. The logical extension is the myth of the nuclear family. That is, the continued use of the product will not only magically bring romance, but also will eventuate in marriage replete with children and a well-appointed home. Soap ads also suggested the material success myth: In America, a clean appearance would provide an advantage in the scramble for success and lead to good fortune.

The word *icon* from the Greek *eikon*, meaning "image," is used to denote religious objects developed in the late medieval times of Eastern Europe to communicate significant beliefs and values to a largely illiterate audience. The icon as an image itself is not only a sign, but is itself also the object; the image may in itself be taken to be sacred. "Thus, a symbol of holiness that reaches beyond the icon itself and is invested with sacrality beyond itself . . . is not just a representational sign," explains popular culture scholar Carl B. Holmberg. "Thus, in popular culture studies, an icon is an image that carries a set, if not system, of assumptions behind it, a magical aura that calls to mind other images, concepts, memories, and feelings identified with the aura."[6]

These observations suggest how brand names and trademarks also fundamentally work as icons, a sign of not only the object, but also a bundle of values. Inferences about a product's "personality" are an important part of building brand equity, which refers to the extent to which a consumer holds strong, favorable, and unique associations with a brand. For example, a brand name may represent a well-established firm or an assurance of uniform quality, which could give customers a reason to choose a particular product instead of a competing brand. To build such a brand image, admakers attempted to create an iconic connection by placing the product in close relationship with another object or showcasing it in a certain setting, highlighting that they share some quality such as integrity, function, or prestige. An outstanding example is early Palmolive Soap advertising; the ads associated the emollient properties of oil from palm leaves and olives with luxurious images of ancient beauties, well-appointed baths, and Mediterranean scenes. Today millions of dollars are invested in image building for brand-name products.

Stereotypes are most easily understood as a standardized conception of a specific group of people. They represent one way in which advertisers view people and define different cultures. If people are to appear in an advertisement, their race, sex, age, class, status, and occupation must be selected. The clothing and body postures must also be specified.

Stereotyping provides a useful function as well. It allows the advertiser to reach a significant group of people who are perceived to share a common mindset. These images have some basis in reality as direct expressions of beliefs and values. This means that stereotypes are especially useful in tracing the evolution of popular thought. American attitudes toward women in society can be easily marked by the changing nature of the popular stereotypes associated with them. Such portrayals varied from housewives concerned with a well-stocked and well-run home to the independent flapper of the 1920s, the young working women with an entirely different set of needs.

The concept of *heroes* involves those men and women who embody myths associated with mainstream America, the traditional values of the community and nation. This study examines the profiles of the pioneering people behind many of the products and companies that shape our lives. Among the citizen heroes, there were: William Colgate, who founded the Colgate Company; Harley Procter and James Gamble of the Procter & Gamble Company; Benjamin T. Babbitt of the Babbitt Company; and Madame C. J. Walker of the Walker Manufacturing Company, who became the first African American millionaire. Likewise, there were the creative personalities who helped to remake the face of advertising, namely, Claude

Hopkins of the Lord & Thomas Agency and Stanley Resor and Helen Lansdowne Resor of the J. Walter Thompson Company, among others. Of course, persons depicted in advertisements can themselves be endowed with heroic status, from the mother who protects her children by keeping them well scrubbed to the infantryman who uses soap.

Rituals are special activities that have a number of repeated parts. In this study, the primary focus is on personal cleanliness rituals. They are sometimes performed mindlessly, and thus they may be conceived as merely habits with ritual overtones, but when they are purposely performed at preordained moments, like washing hands before a meal or taking a shower in the morning, they are clearly activities that can be conceived as rituals. The study of soap illustrates the full range of ritual elements and practices associated with cleansing of the body, including ritual artifacts, shrines, symbolism, and scripts. For example, the ritual artifacts that accompany bathing rituals include various accessories such as soap dishes, washcloths, bath towels, and candles, and ceremonial garments such as the bathrobe. These consumer products are often integral to the total experience. Package designs help transform brand-name products into ritual props or icons, by incorporating ritual names, colors, and motifs, such as white for purity. Likewise, advertising jingles may be read as ritual incantations.

Then there is the certain area in the home that is viewed as more ritually indispensable than others—the bathroom, arguably a sacred place for lustration rituals, a shrine. Anthropologist Harold Miner made this connection between bathrooms and shrines in the famous essay "Body Ritual Among the Nacirema":

> While each family has at least one such shrine, the rituals associated with it are not family ceremonies but private and secret. The rites are normally only discussed with children, and then only during the period when they are being initiated into these mysteries. . . . The focal point of the shrine is a box or chest which is built into the wall. In this chest are kept the many charms and magical potions with which no native believes that he can live without . . . . Below the charm box is a small font. Each day every member of the family bows his head before the charm-box, mingles different sorts of holy water in the font, and proceeds with a brief rite of ablution.[7]

Stereotypical ritual scripts guide the use of various artifactual materials, prescribing the artifacts to be used, in what sequence, and by whom. Some scripts may be casual, like a quick morning shower, and allow for spontaneous variation. Other ritual scripts, such as the evening bath, can be more involved affairs. Extreme cases employ a highly codified, ritual script, such as religious purification ceremonies like corpse washing. Finally, soap-and-water rituals may also be aimed at a larger audience and integrate major social functions like communal bathing.

The basic assumption of a *formula* recognizes that, like story patterns in popular literature, whenever a certain formula appears to work, the formula is constantly duplicated until buyers stop responding, since the form is assumed to ensure commercial success. This study is centered on an attempt to identify and define the elements that a large number of soap advertisements share, which can thus be assumed to help account for their popularity over a period of time.

Finally, this account of advertising and personal cleanliness rituals suggests that the demand for health and beauty might be considered an enduring American consumer characteristic, even though cleanliness has only recently become a virtue. However, this interpretation must be treated with caution. We still know relatively little about consumer decision processes or the meanings before the twentieth century people attached to the things they bought. Since our understanding of contemporary consumers is based on a number of assumptions with potentially limited validity, we must be doubly careful when trying to understand past consumers. Nevertheless, historical research gives a depth to current issues on advertising and consumer rituals that should not be ignored.

What follows, then, is an account of the relationship between advertising and the changing nature of personal cleanliness rituals between 1875 and 1940, which found expression in the beliefs and values of ordinary American people. But the consumption of soap and its relationship to modern American bodies cannot be understood without understanding the prior ideals and practices of hygiene, domesticity, and manners centered on the body. The next chapter traces ideas of cleanliness from ancient times to the nineteenth century to establish a foundation for a more detailed examination of personal cleanliness rituals over the sixty-five-year period.

2
Cleanliness, Not Always a Virtue

ost soap looked pretty much alike in the nineteenth century, if one used it at all. City dwellers could purchase their house soap from the local grocer, who received the product in huge blocks squared at four inches by a foot or more long.[1] The shopkeeper then chopped off an irregular chunk from the large cakes, charged by the pound, and wrapped the piece in brown paper for a customer. The soap itself came in various shades of translucent yellow, had no particular fragrance, and had to be kept dry. If a piece sank to the bottom of a washtub, it melted and soon disappeared, but it often lasted longer than the home-made varieties.

Farm families and those who lived in small towns made their own soap. It was an expected part of housekeeping and instructions were handed down generation after generation orally or written down in recipe books for household prepara- tions (see Figs. 2.1, 2.2, 2.3). Soapmaking was not particularly difficult, but the product was unpredictable—and it was a long and evil-smelling process. Frugal housewives kept the wood ashes from fireplaces, open fires, or wood-burning stoves in a

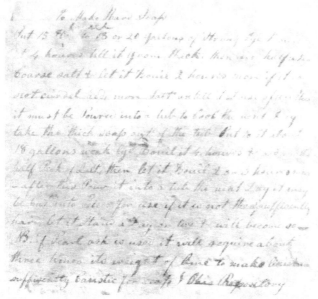

Fig. 2.1. One of a collection of "receipts" or recipes for making hard soap copied for Andrew S. Rappe, early 1800s. Courtesy of the Winterthur Library, Joseph Downs Collection of Manuscripts and Printed Ephemera, no. 74 × 116.

Fig. 2.2. Family soapmaking, from *Something about Soap*, Procter & Gamble, company publication, 1881.

backyard barrel, and at monthly intervals, they poured water over the ashes, which drained into a bucket beneath. By the time the runoff had gone through the ashes and was caught in pans or pails, it had become *potash*, or lye. They then heated the grease saved from the frying pan until it melted, adding the lye and a spoonful of salt at a time. What they got was a "soft soap," which never hardened and was kept in a tub. To get "hard soap," they salted it out with brine and let it stand. The soap mixture, being less soluble, floated to the top and cooled into a solid cake that could be cut by a heavy thread. Both soaps worked very well.[2]

The soap recipe captures much of what was distinctive about the soap trade before the rise of its mass industry in the nineteenth century. Until the industrial revolution, commercial soapmakers made soap basically the same way as people did on the farm. Following the instructions, housewives would have found all the ingredients but one in the kitchen—the salt or soda used sometimes as a solidifier, which a traveling peddler or a general store would have supplied. The problem, however, was that neither the housewife nor the soapmakers knew when the recipe would work, or precisely what the final product would be like.

One difficulty in making soap was in judging the strength of the lye.

Fig. 2.3. Homemade "hard soap" made with lye.

Recipes presumed a notion of proportions to determine "strong" and "weak" lye or the degree of heat required to simmer the mixture long enough to "to bear up an egg."[3] This process of conversion (saponification) was almost mystical. When it did work, what makers got was "soft soap," a clear kind of mush, which gave fairly good suds and did clean clothes. However, strong lye soap was notoriously harsh on the skin; thus, soap justly earned a negative association. Another problem involved the amount of each ingredient needed to make a batch of soap. It took about two bushels of ashes and eight pounds of grease to make a bucket of soap. This was enough for the family wash, which traditionally was done once a month; however, this amount was not sufficient for the weekly "Monday washday" that became a ritual after 1890.[4]

The nineteenth century was also a time when bathing was almost as rare as clothes washing. Even the washing of the hands, face, or body with soap was a relatively new concept, and not until the middle of the nine- teenth century did domestic manuals begin to advocate the practice. Bathing, as American people know it today, barely existed. An occasional quick rinse in cold or warm water from the waist up followed by a brisk rub with a towel sufficed to keep one clean; there was seldom mention of soap in the literature of advice. Doctors had stigmatized bathtubs as carriers of disease when filled with warm water.[5] With changes in advice and cultural perceptions, accompanied by improved sanitation, public utilities, and indoor plumbing, soap made its way into larger numbers of American middle-class homes by the end of the century.[6]

ONE THOUSAND YEARS WITHOUT A BATH

Nineteenth-century Americans inherited traditions of soapmaking and bathing, combined with a cultural disinclination toward cleanliness, that borrowed from a variety of sources and reached back through the centuries. The first common soaps appeared naturally in the wild as certain plants, probably species of the soapwort, while soap made by combining grease and alkali dates back at least two thousand years. The term *soap* comes from the Latin word *sapo*, referring to Mount Sapo near Rome, which was the site of a sacrificial altar erected before the common era began.

According to legend, rainwater would mix with ashes and the fat of sacrificial animals that washed down the hillside toward the Tiber River. Women who washed their laundry near this runoff found that clothes emerged cleaner with less effort. This soap was similar to the homemade soap produced on the farm in nineteenth-century America.[7]

The early Celts produced soap by heating a mixture of animal fats and plant ashes and named the product *saipo*, presenting an alternative etymology for the origin of the word *soap*. Soap made by the fireside remained an article of luxury for the Celts, however, as they primarily used the substance as a hair pomade to give the hair a gloss and reddish tint and occasionally as a medicament for wounds. In antiquity, both the Romans and Greeks used cleansing agents made from plants, while putrid urine worked as a laundry detergent, but they did not use soap to wash the body. Instead, the people of antiquity used blocks of clay, sand, pumice, and ashes, then anointed themselves and scraped off the mixture with a metal instrument known as a *stirgil* to "wash" the face and body.[8]

Although the ancient peoples found little use for soap, the major religions of the world did popularize taboos, or customs with strong moral overtones, that often proved to be the basis for health and well-being in a community. From these flowed norms or rules dictating what was right or wrong, permitted or forbidden, acceptable or unacceptable. According to anthropologist Mary Douglas, societies often placed cleanliness practices in such binary systems as sacred or profane to explicitly define norms for cleanliness, such as what one could eat and drink, and what was taboo.[9] Clean was pure, while dirtiness was filthy and polluted. In any case, people must be protected from pollution and from polluting others; hence their holiness must be protected and kept from indiscriminately contaminating others. Taboos thus prevented people from such transgressions. In a practical vein, however, avoiding unclean food or drink enabled not just the clean individual to live a longer and healthier life, but the family and possibly the entire community as well.

Traditional practices may actually have been the closest to modern hygienic practices. Since ancient times, bathing in many lands was regarded as a religious or social duty or a relaxing pastime, rather than a hygienic practice. For example, the sweat baths of Native Americans, the steamy *hammas* of Islamic nations, and dips in the Ganges were more of a spiritual purification than a physical cleansing. Although people from around the globe may have discovered the sensuous pleasure and healing powers of hot springs, the feat of heating water for the hot bath had its roots in central Asia where the practice originated, then spread, and eventually took hold. These practices suggest that attitudes toward dirt developed as a protection against noxious germs before infectious microorganisms could be detected by scientific means.[10]

Whether for cleanliness or health treatments, however, bathing has had an uneven history, ranging from periods of popularity to disdain. By the advent of the medieval period in Europe, all that was left of the public baths was the local well. Those who could afford it had buckets to transport the water, more refined bathing amenities did not exist. Not surprisingly, many people did not wash very often, in part because there was no running water. If they wanted to wash, either the water was going to be cold, or they had to haul it or heat it. "And if you lived in one room often with animals, the fact that you smelled didn't matter much," notes historian Ross Edman.[11]

The Crusaders, who had enjoyed the modified form of the Roman bath in Arabic-Islamic countries, brought public baths back to Europe for the first time since the Roman occupation. The communal baths, called "stews," also spread infection, especially the bubonic plague, which led to municipal and state quarantine as well as other preventive measures. Few cared to cleanse themselves when water appeared to be downright bad for health; it could cause sickness or even death. The Reformation and the rise of Puritanism dealt another blow to cleanliness via the communal bath, and after the sixteenth century, bathing again fell into disfavor. Nakedness had become synonymous with sin, and not surprisingly, the stews generated ecclesiastical disapproval.[12]

Thus, for more than a hundred years the public bath disappeared in Europe, until it emerged in a new guise as a strange, magical fluid that, if applied by a physician and used correctly, could cure a wide variety of ills. When communal bathing in mineral waters at the great spas arose in the late 1600s, the practice was said to promote health, wealth, youth, and fertility. Many people also found that they actually enjoyed it. Still, bathing for cleanliness remained rare, practiced principally by royalty or the wealthy, while commoners found the practice virtually impossible.[13] The English people of that era couldn't bathe even if they wanted to. There was still no running water; streams were cold, heating fuel was expensive, and soap was scarce. Well into the nineteenth century, soap was heavily taxed as a luxury item.[14]

Another factor that undermined the pursuit of cleanliness was inadequate sewage treatment as people crowded together in towns and cities. Before the water closet, the most common place to "go to the bathroom" was the nearest tree, hole, or river. To solve the cleaning-up problem, people made use of leaves or a clump of hay, grass, or straw, as toilet paper had yet to be invented. And to spare a trip outdoors, people kept a slop jar with a lid, often called a "chamber pot," which city folk emptied out their windows onto the street. The French warning that accompanied the dumping—"Gare l'eau" ("Watch out for the water")—may have inspired another euphemism, "the loo." In crowded cities like London, sanitation and water delivery systems paled in comparison with those in ancient Rome or Minoan Crete. Given this cultural disinclination toward cleanliness, these societies were dreadfully dirty by today's comparatively fastidious standards of personal hygiene.[15]

In a culture where people seldom bathed, how did the unwashed stand being around one another? One explanation is that they did not seem to be bothered. One can grow accustomed to even the most noxious odor. After a few days, the nose adjusts to the environment; then one must be absent from the odor for at least a week before it will be overpowering again. It is not the human body or sweat that really smells. The skin has more than two kinds of sweat glands, and the perspiration that comes from the abundant eccrine sweat glands is fundamentally clear and odorless. But common skin flora (several kinds of benign bacteria) feed off secretions and skin particles on the body and clothing and eliminate waste, causing the stench.[16]

The aprocine sweat glands, mainly found in the armpit and pubic areas, emit a very mild scent, particularly during times of anxiety and sexual arousal. In the animal kingdom, the accumulated chemical cues, called pheromones, are sexually provocative. This may also be true of humans, not necessarily at a cognitive awareness level, but on some subtle level of brain systems.[17] In Elizabethan times, about five hundred years ago, lovers commonly exchanged a different kind of love letter. They would keep a peeled apple in their armpits until it was soaked with sweat. This "love apple" would then be sent to the sweetheart to smell and treasure.[18] Sound pretty gross? Not to Napoleon; when he neared the end of a campaign, he sent a famous message to Josephine: "Will be home in three weeks. Don't wash."[19]

Josephine and other women of privilege during Napoleon's time may have been familiar with soap as part of their knowledge of grooming, the body, and household practices. Before printing became inexpensive enough to be prevalent, the mistress of the house kept vellum rolls containing dozens, sometimes hundreds, of recipes and formulas that dealt with the common household procedures of everyday life. Some dated back to the thirteenth century and were handed down to the eldest daughter, generation after generation. In these "recipe" books, women often compiled household hints, cooking techniques, medical treatments, and cosmetic preparations. At the same time, skilled craftspeople also recorded the secrets of their trade, including the knowledge and principles of soapmaking that were carried on in France, Spain, and Italy. Soap itself had numerous applications in pharmacy, such as pill making, lotions and liniments, dentrifices, plasters, enemas, suppositories, and poultices, in addition to veterinary products.[20] Printing eventually provided a way to record this important information on documents so people no longer had to rely on their memories or hoard vellum.

Early cookbooks, household manuals, and medical treatises commonly included recipes for household preparations, codifying formulas once circulated orally. One of the first printed collections of recipes written for the purpose of publication appeared in 1602. Sir Hugh Platt's *Delightes for Ladies* cataloged page after page of beauty advice, food recipes, methods of preserving food, and household hints such as how to take stains out of linen and how to keep teeth clean.[21] Platt also wrote how to make an excellent but "very cheape [*sic*]" hand water or washing water for the table: "Take a gallon of faire water, one handful of lavender flowers, a few cloves, and some orace powder, and four ounces of Benjamin: distill the water in an ordinarie [*sic*] leaden." The use of water basins at the table reflected a custom of medieval nobility to wash their hands routinely before and after meals, because forks were not widely used until the end of the seventeenth century.

NEW GENTILITY IN THE NEW WORLD

European immigrants brought their ideas of personal cleanliness and traditions of soapmaking with them to America, but the concept of washing the body with soap was slow to take hold. Colonists simply had little desire to use soap and seldom bathed. They also found printing equipment and supplies to be both expensive and scarce in the New World. With printing presses and paper rare in the New World, information primarily spread through word of mouth within families and between neighbors. All printed matter had to come from Europe, and even then, few colonists could read. Despite these limitations, household hints, cooking recipes, and soap-making traditions circulated in the colonies.

The soapmaking knowledge and principles of the colonists blended European housewifery with Native American, French, Spanish, and African traditions, which differed little in terms of materials and preparation from those of antiquity. Native Americans used indigenous plants to make their own form of soap, such as the amole, a member of the lily family with a white, tennis-ball-sized bulb covered in layers of brown fibers. The brown fiber was removed and water was added to a few layers of the white bulb and agitated between the hands to create a rich lather to take a bath, to wash hair, or to launder clothes. One of the more interesting wild soap plants was soapwort, which had a large taproot. To make soap, one first grated the root, added water, and then rubbed it between the hands to form a frothy lather. Both "soaps" could be dried and stored for later use.[22]

Other folk cultures borrowed from the European custom of compounding animal fats and lye processed from wood ashes to make simple soaps. Ozark natives, for instance, took lye water and boiled it with hot fat, skin and all, to make a heavy-duty cleanser. Commonly called lye soap, it was an all-purpose soap.[23]

By the eighteenth century, new personal cleanliness rituals began to surface in America that affirmed the adaptability of centuries-old customs to life carried on under later and vastly different social circumstances. For example, the custom of using water basins for hand washing at the table signified an enduring connection to Old World culture. When the upper classes began washing their hands again, they also adopted the laver, usually a bronze water container that hung on a hook in a niche in the wall where they kept a freestanding basin, so they could pour water over their hands. The laver looked like a teapot with no top on it; it could also be heated in the fireplace. Expensive porcelain basins and pitchers later came into use.[24]

As rituals of personal cleanliness became more elaborate, specialized furniture came to be viewed as indispensable for lustration rituals among the gentry. Washstands, a new furniture form, appeared in Thomas Chippendale's *Gentleman and Cabinet-Maker's Directory*, published in 1754, implying that washing the body merited a unique and elaborate furniture form in America. These new pieces of furniture had splashguards and often featured a cutout in which the basin could rest. Along with special shaving furniture, the male equivalent of accomplishing one's toilet, beautiful dressing tables also emerged as the upper middle class embraced gentility.[25]

Both washbasins and the new furniture forms reflected a similar upwardly mobile class and cultural orientation. The items also pointed to the growing importance of maintaining a good appearance in an increasingly commercial and cosmopolitan society. Clean hands, greaseless clothes, and attractive appearance required careful discipline. Indeed, concepts of personal cleanliness may have been strengthened in the eighteenth century as a movement among the colonial gentry emphasizing bodily regulation gained ground.[26] Yet the achievement of gentility could not be accomplished without effort.

The new colonial gentry erected houses with furnishings to stage social occasions like those of English gentility, learned appropriate conduct, and taught it to their children as they formed themselves into a polite society. Books, periodicals, and pictorial material were imported from Europe, and for those who could read, the texts provided a means to navigate the genteel social world by cultivating a well-groomed face and form. Americans in Boston, New York, Philadelphia, Raleigh, and so on learned the arts of genteel living and the duty to be clean, both morally and physically. These manuals included many rules for keeping the body immaculate: "Keep your nails clean and short, also your Hands and Teeth clean, without showing any great concern for them." Along the same lines, clothes were not to be "foul, unript [sic], or dusty" and to be "brush'd [sic] everyday at least."[27] The person who bore grease on a jacket and failed to keep clean invoked a certain mark of vulgarity, for which the individual paid the price in the loss of respect. Instruction for youth also found its way into print early in the eighteenth century. Eleazar Moody, a Boston schoolmaster, published one of the earliest American courtesy manuals, *The School of Good Manners*, in 1715. It admonished children at play to "make not thy Cloathes [sic], Hands or Face dirty or nasty, nor sit upon the ground."[28]

This heightened attention to the cleanliness and adornment of the body may also be seen in European recipe books, which began to circulate in the colonies. Women often compiled their own recipe books and passed them on to their daughters. The books of two eighteenth-century European writers, for instance, contained recipes touted as "common to the trade." Occasionally, a soap recipe appeared. Nicholas Lémery, in the 1711 advice book *New Curiosities in Art and Nature*, wrote down instructions for several such recipes. To perfume soap, Lémery suggested using the essences of orange flowers, rose petals, and almond blossoms or exotic spices such as cinnamon and cloves. Other recipes instructed how to make lemon or rose washing waters for the table and how to blend fragrant toilet waters for the body. The 1797 edition of *Valuable Secrets in Arts and Trades* illustrated the basic principles of metalworking, dyeing, and preserving food among others. It also included formulas to make a variety of soaps, including "Geno" or white soap from wood ashes, black soap from lime and olive oil, and a blue-marbled variety.[29]

The proliferation of such books and new pieces of furniture also suggested that by the end of the eighteenth century something more than the desire to be presentable was influencing personal habits. Modern ideas about bathing as a means of getting clean emerged only when another bodily system, the skin, began to be understood, as Richard L. and Claudia L. Bushman explained in their study of the history of cleanliness in early America.[30] By around 1724, a number of physicians thought that one of the tasks of skin was to rid the body of wastes through a multitude of tiny pores that covered the surface of the body, which constantly emitted perspiration.[31] Articles in Benjamin Franklin's newspaper, the *Pennsylvania Packet*, also affirmed the physicians' theory about the composition of the skin. According to one editorial in 1777, it was "a well known fact, that the perspiration of the body, by attaching itself to linen, and afterwards mixing with rain, is disposed to form miasma, which produce fevers." With this continual perspiration, attention had to be given to frequent changes in apparel, as well as to washing.

In addition to the emphasis on gentility and health, Americans' wish to be clean came from ideas associated with religion. Advocates of cleanliness drew on the long tradition of bathing, which went back to the ancient Roman, Hebrew, and Islamic washing rituals that linked moral and spiritual purity to bodily cleanliness. Methodist founder Reverend John Wesley made a similar connection with the famous line from his 1788 sermon on dress: "Cleanliness is, indeed, next to godliness."[32] Thus, the heightened attention to cleanliness occurred as notions of gentility, health, and religion gained popularity.

Changes in soap-manufacturing processes also reflected and reinforced this heightened attention to cleanliness toward the end of the eighteenth century. By this time, Nicholas LeBlance had developed a process for the commercial production of cheap soda from salt, which eventually replaced potash as the standard alkali. Another important development was the work of Chevreul, also a Frenchman, who discovered the chemical nature of fats and oils. Thus, the soap industry had the means to operate on a more scientific basis rather than by guesswork, making it possible to produce low-priced, abundant quantities of soap. Yet it took more than dirty skin, religious inspiration, and manufacturing know-how for America to clean up its act.

Well into the nineteenth century, Americans lived in dirty, smelly, and bug-infested surroundings and died of associated diseases. Whether on farms or in towns, Americans lived with human and animal fecal matter all around. The rivers were filthy. Clothing was infested with vermin. Disease ran rampant.[33] As for soap, it remained a seldom-used substance except for washing the finest articles of clothing. Still considered a luxury item, commercially made soap fit few budgets.

NINETEENTH-CENTURY AMERICA

America changed profoundly during the nineteenth century. The American frontier opened new horizons, and the nation's reaction to the rapidly emerging industrialized world had a significant effect on the nation's culture and standards of personal cleanliness.

The nineteenth-century urban population explosion was a key factor in the health problems that followed. Beginning in the 1820s, the risks of contagious diseases multiplied as cities multiplied and expanded. The last half of the nineteenth century especially saw an explosion in urban growth.[34] The circumstances of five or six people who lived by themselves on a farm were quite different from those of tens of thousands who lived in close proximity in a city. More people were crowded into tenement buildings, city water supplies were often insufficient, and sanitation was almost always inadequate. Public utilities and health care facilities could not meet the demands made upon them by overcrowding. Before antibiotics, diseases like tuberculosis, diphtheria, typhoid, and polio were a constant threat.

Scholars observe that advances in medical science such as vaccines and antibiotics were the major factors in turning the tide of America's health problems; they also credit nutritional improvements and milk pasteurization. Improved public sanitation, garbage collection, sewers, and delivery of potable water also played a major role. An often overlooked factor, however, was the dramatic change in personal and domestic hygiene practices, the benefits of which cannot be overestimated.

For people experiencing these changes, ideas of cleanliness versus filth entered deeply into their notions of the body, health, and judgments of other people. Still the use of soap for washing the body would not become standard in many middle-class American households until around the Civil War.

Advice to Nineteenth-Century Americans

By the nineteenth century, knowledge of methods of physical care had split into distinct disciplines of medicine, cooking, and grooming. Physicians and pharmacists claimed health care as their field, while hygienic and natural healing practices remained women's domain. But throughout the century, women's access to information increased as the publishing industry expanded in the United States. Indeed, women's authority in these areas may have been strengthened as popular ladies' guides and household manuals proliferated.

Literature of advice played an important part in the affirmation of personal cleanliness rituals as a foundation for health and an attractive appearance. Ladies' guides to beauty and fashion self-consciously addressed middle-class women and all those who aspired to that rank. Similar to etiquette books, these guides explained how to conduct oneself in the genteel social world by cultivating not only health and morality, but also a perfectly neat and clean appearance. Cheaper editions carried the message to women who worked in mills or as domestic servants, explaining how to move through genteel society with a well-groomed face and form.

Many guides affirmed the importance of personal cleanliness rituals. As early as 1831, the women's magazine *Godey's Lady's Book*, the arbiter of fashion among middle-class women, stressed the benefits of bathing. "It maintains the limbs in their pliancy, the skin in its softness, the complexion in its lustre, the eyes in their brightness, the teeth in their purity, and, the constitution in its fairest vigour."[35] J. Thomas offered a similar assessment of bathing, adding that it was people's duty to bathe frequently. In 1837, the ladies' guide *The Book of Health & Beauty, or the Toiletries of Rank and Fashion* stressed that everything connected with personal cleanliness "is a principal duty of all people, an unclean and dirty person is never in health and is always a loathsome and disgusting sight."[36] Certainly both the recipe books and the guides to health and beauty pointed toward the growing importance of maintaining a pleasing appearance in an increasingly commercial and mobile society.

Women's access to information about personal hygiene expanded even more with the publishing boom of the 1840s and 1850s.[37] By the end of the century, scores of manuals offered instructions on personal hygiene and house cleaning. Household encyclopedias contained information on everything that people wanted to know about maintaining their homes, from the arts of the toilette to managing household servants. The compendiums could be found in farming as well as urban, middle-class households. They proved to be a haphazard accumulation of knowledge, though cataloging page after page of recipes. For example, Marion Harland's popular *Common Sense in the Household* offered formulas for such sundries as cologne waters, dentrifices, and medical remedies among recipes for full-course meals. The compendium also included directions for making a "hard soap" that was much better for washing than "yellow turpentine soap," a "bar soap" made by cutting a large "box of soap" into small squares and laying them to dry before use, and a "soft soap" blended from grease, baking soda, and hot water.[38] *The Ladies Medical Guide* warned that soaps generally contained too much alkali to act beneficially on the scalp. Instead of soap, the guide suggested "boiling water poured on bran, left to stand until cool, and then well-strained off, washes long hair very nicely."[39] So could a woman use Queen Bess's recipe for a beautiful complexion and to remove freckles, suggested *Practical Housekeeping*: A "perfectly harmless" formula of powdered gum of benzoin, nutmeg oil, orange blossom or apple blossoms was boiled down and strained into one pint of sherry wine."[40]

In the face of opposition from medical doctors and scientists, some therapeutic traditions about health, hygiene, and beauty were discredited. In particular, many popular beliefs in the power of nature's cycles, astrology, and magic did not survive. For example, the ancient theory of humors or bodily fluids had maintained that different proportions of these kinds of fluids determine a person's health. The humors, in turn, produce human temperaments that reveal themselves in the appearance and condition of the skin. A good complexion thus was a matter of temperament, health, and spirit—not soap and water.[41] Other popular beliefs instructed readers to bathe their faces in May dew, considered the purest of waters, or to remove freckles by washing with virgin milk and the first juice of spring plants.[42]

Two old traditions, however, survived the new medical techniques and scientific discoveries of the Enlightenment: (1) the consequences of "bad air," and (2) the importance of hygienic regimen. Bad air was known as "miasma," so called because a noxious atmosphere was believed to cause disease. Miasma was an idea reminiscent of medieval fears of the vapors that were thought to generate spontaneously in prisons and dungeons. The 1850 sanitary lecture "The Mischief of Bad Air," for instance, described how "bad air really does poison us . . . *dirty* air—*foul* air, as it is often called." The pamphlet also emphasized that keeping the children well washed and as clean possible "outside" was only half the business, and that the homemaker must do all she "can to keep them clean *inside* too" by proper ventilation and by keeping the children and the rooms themselves clean.[43]

At the same time, the concept of bodily regimen became more popular when nineteenth-century America endorsed cleanliness, diet, and temperance as the path toward a sanitized, well-regulated body and beautiful complexion. Experts advocated bathing, vegetable diets, and exercise. For American health reformer Sylvester Graham, "the failure to bathe daily was one of the bad habits that prevented Americans from enjoying good health." Graham, who is remembered for the cracker named after him, remained largely unknown until 1832, when the United States's first cholera epidemic brought him into prominence. Since cholera attacked the gastrointestinal system, Graham argued against overstimulating the digestive systems with liquor or greasy food, encouraging people to abstain from caffeine, meat, and alcohol, to bathe frequently, and to live in well-ventilated houses.[44] If Americans acted in such a practical manner, they could avoid most illnesses.

Similar to Graham, domestic expert Catherine Beecher also had a strong influence on middle-class ideals. Beecher presented a vision of the labor-saving home for American women. In the 1841 book *A Treatise on*

Domestic Economy, for the Use of Young Ladies at Home and at School, Beecher offered practical suggestions on raising children, cleaning, training domestics, cooking, nursing the sick, sewing, and gardening. Beecher believed, as did most women of her generation, that women belonged at home. She especially encouraged women to devote more attention to cleanliness, economy, and comfort by carrying out their household tasks in a systematic and orderly fashion. But what set Beecher apart from traditionalists was that she advocated new roles for women. They should be educated for a "profession" as mothers, housewives, and teachers. Beecher's book also promoted domestic work as important to families and to the nation. She conceded, then, that no profession could be successfully pursued unless "superior" and "subordinate relations" between men and women were instituted.[45]

The writings of other health experts agreed with Graham and Beecher on the benefits of cleanliness. To persuade people to bathe, their advice books continued to emphasize the healthful effects of the practice. When properly used, warm-water baths "promote health and cleanliness," argued James Baird in *The Management of Health*.[46] *The Bazar Book of Decorum* also urged American to take "daily bathing in cold water" as a main requisite for giving health, strength, and grace to the body.[47] So did Marion Holland. In the popular book *Eve's Daughters*, Holland recommended at least a "daily sponge bath," although only to the waist.[48] This latter advice most likely considered that nineteenth-century Americans were reluctant to be seen unclothed.[49] And the periodical *Godey's Lady's Book* offered "Fifteen Rules for the Preservation of Health." Rule number one mandated fresh air, while the other rules urged moderation in eating; forbade "strong drinks, tobacco, snuff, and opium"; and advocated "exercise, sunlight, and cleanliness in the home."[50] This change of opinion regarding health, however, did not occur rapidly. Historian Suellen Hoy explains: "It took years for middle-class Americans to realize that they could act in practical ways to prevent disease."[51] Nevertheless, the literature of advice took two directions: toward an expression of the pure womanly ideal, and toward an elaboration of middle-class personal cleanliness norms and rituals.

The idealization of the domestic woman as the guardian of the home and primary agent of cleanliness occurred when the middle class began to define itself through gender roles and consumption. Women's authority, especially in the area of hygiene, had been strengthened as popular health movements emphasized self-help, prevention, and natural remedies. By the mid–nineteenth century, Americans perceived the home as the center of virtue, a separate and private place set apart from where husbands and fathers worked, and women were its guardians and protectors. Women's work transformed the house into a home, made it a refuge as well as dwelling, and produced privacy as well as intimacy. Domestic tasks like cleaning, doing the laundry, cooking, and caring for the children increasingly were seen as the sole and inherent province of women. Americans came to view cleanliness as being maintained in the family through the domestic woman and in the community through public boards staffed by leading males committed to the public interest. With a certain degree of cleanliness and tidiness, the emerging middle class associated these values and feelings with genteel living and respectability. These values distinguished middle-class people from the poor and the countrified.

At the same time, another language of cleanliness began to emerge. When urban middle-class Americans talked about being clean, their rhetoric focused on health, women's work and role, good social values, and the proper goals of social policy. Institutions for the deaf, blind, insane, and orphaned had been built or expanded during the mid–nineteenth century, giving Americans opportunities to become involved in social welfare efforts and networks of voluntary associations. These areas of community service and care of dependents were not fully within the realm of male electoral politics and formal government institutions or within the female world of home and family. Thus, the production of domesticity provided many middle- and upper-class urban women an opportunity to expand their ascribed spheres from the home to the bigger "family" of city and state.[52]

Women made their most visible contributions to the cultural discourse on cleanliness as founders of and workers in social organizations and as teachers. Such efforts were embodied in the women's club movement, which began with the formation of the U.S. Sanitary Commission during the Civil War. This commission provided models for the many large-scale, corporate-style associations that women would form in the postwar decades. Moreover, the work of these early promoters of cleanliness marked a turning point in American attitudes toward cleanliness.

The guiding light of many hospital staffs was Florence Nightingale, whose disciplined attention to cleanliness reduced the number of deaths from disease in the British Army during the Crimean War (1854–1857). Although Nightingale defended the popular but erroneous view that "miasma," or noxious atmospheres, rather than infectious organisms caused disease, these beliefs gave force to practical suggestions regarding sanitation during this period. Through the use of fresh air and the washtub, Nightingale dramatically transformed hospital conditions. Concerned not only about diet and supplies, she also focused on the cleanliness of patients' bedding, personal linen, and bandages.

With the outbreak of the Civil War, thousands of women in the North and the South offered their services to the Sanitary Commission, as both volunteers and paid nurses. Some twenty thousand women served the Union Army in all capacities, but only two to three thousand were nurses.[53] Even as nurses, however, these women spent the bulk of their time as housekeepers, expected to cook, clean, and do laundry for their patients. Still, their efforts contributed to the increased knowledge and principles of hygiene.

During the Civil War, thousands more women became directly involved in the commission, moving information and goods between households and the military posts. Wartime volunteers also produced items such as quilts, pillows, uniforms, and hospital gowns. In the Confederacy, women also organized hundreds of relief societies to nurse, sew, and raise money. But the South was unable to create a sanitary commission dedicated to the health and welfare of the volunteer army comparable to that of the North.

In the North, the U.S. Army issued soap along with rations of food supplies for care of the troops. Army regulations provided for four pounds of soap, to the established daily allowance for hundred people, which amounts to .64 oz. per person per day.[54] Notes on preparing stores suggested that best soap was composed of tallow, or lard, rosin and soda rather than inferior articles such as fish oil, skimmings of lard, and other kinds of grease. "Bad soap can be told by the smell," advised one army manual.[55]

Still, the idea of soap as something to bathe the body was a new idea to some recruits is well described by George Campbell of the 8th Minnesota. Although the description is of a Fort Ripley, it could equally well be any military mess hall of the period:

On the night in question, we were expecting a supply of butter and cheese from below and, as we took our places, one fellow says, "Ah! Our cheese has come!" and without waiting to be helped, he reached out and took a piece. He quietly laid it down beside his plate and then another took a piece. I noticed that they did not make any comments so I took but a slight taste, and behold it was soap.[56]

Many veterans apparently learned about soap and acquired better habits of hygiene as a result of their wartime experience. This new knowledge of dirt and disease, combined with the knowledge of wartime volunteer organizations, provided the foundation for the subsequent struggle to bring sanitation to American cities.

Unlike practical suggestions regarding sanitation, however, the introduction of bathing encountered difficulties. The scarcity of appropriate plumbing technology, the difficulties of bathing without hot and cold running water, and lack of easy drainage certainly dampened most people's desire to bathe. Not until the end of the nineteenth century would the bathroom move inside the house and make it easier for people to be clean. With no prototype for a tub available, people had to rely on their inventiveness. Since a tub for lying down might have seemed indecent, a tub for standing up was the answer. Typically a circular basin so shallow that the water barely reached to the ankles served the purpose, which was just as well, water being scarce. Even then, the best New York hotels provided only water for washing hands and face, but no fixed bathtub.

Just as nineteenth-century Americans met difficulties bathing for lack of facilities inside the house, "going to the bathroom" still involved going outside. But instead of going to the nearest tree, hole, or river, people now made a trip outdoors to the privy, often called an "outhouse" or "necessary." Although technology for indoor toilets, or "water closets," was known and occasionally used, many sanitarians considered outside privies more hygienic than water closets, because indoor facilities generated sewer gas and foul odors and caused disease.[57]

The outhouse was a small structure with no inside walls, insulation, or decoration. There was only a seat with a bench that had a hole in it, and the whole building was positioned over a shallow pit in the ground. Wooden ones could be easily moved to another location, and their pits filled in and planted over. Privies in the rear of the backyard were standard even in the large and expensive New York houses until the mid–nineteenth century. The units in crowded town lots were cleaned out periodically, much like the modern septic tank, and the failure to do so often resulted in a fine.[58] In the rural South, a crescent moon sawed into a privy door became the sign of the "ladies' room." Luna, the crescent-shaped figure, was an ancient symbol of womankind. A sun pattern sometimes indicated the "men's room." As only a fraction of the people could read or write, these symbols were necessary. Other people claimed that the sun and moon motifs primarily served as a source of ventilation and light in the windowless rooms. In the North, however, these cutouts were not often seen because even the smallest crack would admit a freezing blanket of snow.[59] The lack of indoor plumbing and running water remained a perplexing problem for many Americans, especially in the crowded cities.

The need to wipe oneself clean upon relieving oneself compounded the difficulty; toilet paper had yet to be invented. Until then rural Americans solved the cleaning-up problem with a form of a scraper like the corncob, a box of which would be on hand in a well-appointed privy. It was customary for town dwellers to grab a rag. With increased availability of manufactured paper, people cut up old paper bags, dress patterns, newspapers, envelopes, catalogs, and other uncoated scrap paper. People then threaded the sheets with string and hung them on a nail in the privy. When toilet paper came on the market in midcentury America, it was in the form of pads of medicated paper. Gayetty's Medicated Paper was marketed in 1857 as a "perfectly pure product," good for the "prevention of piles." Mr. Gayetty's name was watermarked on each sheet. Still, toilet paper manufacturers had to employ aggressive and persistent efforts to convince Americans not only that the product was cheap enough to throw away, but that it should be publicly sold.[60] Since nineteenth-century American society considered frank talk of certain bodily functions in polite company inappropriate, mentioning the "unmentionable" was taboo.

Taboos against mentioning things related to natural bodily functions appear to be peculiarly Puritan in origin, found principally in Britain and the United States, what Carl B. Holmberg in *Sexualities and Popular Culture* identifies as a "shame culture" that begins "in hiding nudity and perpetuating that concealment."[61] In the nineteenth-century shame culture, for example, bodily appearance, behavior, and certain discourse were carefully managed in the form of "horror of the body" taboos. During this arch-conservative period, prudery became a mark of refinement because Americans considered that their most natural functions and needs—nudity, sex, and eliminating wastes—evoked widespread disgust, shame, or even horror. Certainly, personal cleanliness rituals that involved washing the body were replete with fears, since nakedness was synonymous with sin.

Emerging from a Puritan shame culture, nineteenth-century Americans proved keen on not mentioning the unmentionable; thus the restrictive social conventions resulted in a proliferation of euphemisms. Americans used the substitutes "limb" for leg, "white meat" for chicken breast, "white-sewings" for underwear, "lavatory" for the water closet, and "necessary" for the privy, among other euphemisms. Mores also dictated that a proper person pretend that most bodily functions did not exist; the "right" thing to do was be silent on these matters in polite company. Thus, we inherited shame culture. But the code by which American society came to define hygiene and appearance was not of law; it was a matter of good and bad manners, another artificial social construction. This, then, was the scene into which early American soapmakers set out to make their fortune in the soap business.

THE COMMERCIAL SOAP TRADE

Commercial soapmaking began in the American colonies in 1608, with the arrival of several British soapmakers in Jamestown, Virginia. For many years, however, soapmaking remained essentially a household chore.[62]

Professional soapmakers basically made soap the same way as people did on the farm, but the commercial product proved better than the home-made variety in some ways. For instance, some manufacturers had replaced tallow or animal fat with all-natural vegetable oils, which would lather and moisturize more consistently than the fireside soap. The resulting manufactured soap often used little or no water, so it lasted longer than home-made varieties. Even then soapmakers often replaced lye with some other alkali to make a milder soap that would not harm the skin.[63] Finally, commercial soapmakers frequently added essential oils to create special scented soaps that were known as toilet soaps.[64]

A. *Boiling*

Fig. 2.4. Factory soap-making process, from *Something about Soap*, Procter & Gamble, company publication, 1881.

B. *Filling the frames*

C. *Stripping the soap from the frames*

D. *Cutting and packing*

The factory soapmaking process began in what was known as the kettle house. The boiling or blending process came first as the soapmaker cooked the ingredients under intense heat. The manufacturer then poured the soap out of the kettles, dropped the substance into metal frames, and allowed the mixture to stand for four or five days for hardening. When the soap mixture hardened, workers removed the frames and guided the large blocks through slicers that cut them into slabs and then into cakes. An assembly line worker seized the finished cakes, laid them in a box, and nailed the lid on (see Fig. 2.4).[65]

During the nineteenth century, the methods and machinery of soap production gradually but vastly improved, and the processes became more scientific. The small fire-heated kettles gave way to huge steam-heated vats. Pumps, mechanical agitators, and automatic stamping and wrapping machinery replaced manual labor. In addition to the new equipment, the introduction of steam power, interchangeable parts, and assembly lines to the large-batch production process enabled manufacturers to turn out commercially made soap at both a low cost and a uniform quality.[66]

Perfumers, too, played an important part in the toilet soap business. Requiring specialized knowledge of essences and distillation, perfumery was considered a skilled craft. Historically, the perfumer made toilet soap with expensive fragrances, elegant shapes, and decorative wrapping. Moreover, the production process involved more delicate processes of pressing, running poundings of shreds through machines, perfuming, coloring, and stamping out with dies. Essences of lavender, rose, jasmine, sandalwood, and other natural oils magically transformed the soap mixture into delicate, fragrant toilet soaps.[67] The fine soaps came wrapped in layers of tissue paper, then a stronger decorative glazed paper, and usually in a box. Toilet soap was associated with fine ladies' smooth skin, while the harsher grades were for laundry and scrubbing floors. The scented soaps, however, proved too costly for the average American consumer, since they were typically produced from expensive imported ingredients.[68]

With the increasing importance of personal appearance and cleanliness the market expanded for all types of commercial soap in the nineteenth century. Ironically, early American soap manufacturers found that their greatest competitor was the very person they targeted as their best customer, the housewife. The lye soap of the day was largely made in the home from the fats saved by the housewife. It was typically harsh, not too efficient, and not too fragrant. This last factor proved of great importance. The introduction of essential oils to scent soaps changed the business in a tremendous way, but soapmakers first had to convince the housewife that their soap was better and cheaper, and had a more pleasant scent than the homemade variety. Though soap was not a standard ingredient of American life, its profitability in larger city markets pointed the way to subsequent inroads into American society.

A Trio of Household Staples

Three of the most recognized American soapmakers established themselves in the nineteenth century: (1) the Colgate Company, (2) Procter & Gamble, and (3) the Babbitt Company. In 1806, William Colgate started the Colgate Company in New York City, where he worked as manufacturer, buyer, salesman, bookkeeper, and boss.[69] When Colgate began to advertise in 1807, he placed this newspaper announcement:

SOAP AND CANDLE MANUFACTORY
WILLIAM COLGATE AND COMPANY
NO. 6 Dutch Street, Second Door
From the Corner of
John Street, New York
Have for Sale on Best Terms
A Constant Supply of
Soap, Mould and Dipt [sic] Candles
of the First Quality
Orders for the Exportation
Executed on the Shortest Notice
N.B. The Highest Price Given
for Tallow[70]

Like most advertising at the time, the notice made a simple announcement that answered a few basic questions of the buying public: Has anyone got any soap and candles for sale? Where can one go to buy the goods? When would the stock be available for sale?

The Colgate Company flourished, becoming the first big soap company in America. In 1845, Colgate built a kettle for boiling soap that held forty-five thousand pounds in a single batch, though friends and rivals called it

Price List of Toilet Soaps.

No.			
Almond Soap (Fine).			
42.—Boxes of 6 cakes		@	$8.00 per gro.
Almond Bath Soap.			
3 W.—Boxes of 3 doz. cakes (wood)		@	$3.50 per box.
3 P.— " 3 cakes (paper)		@	15.00 per gro.
Almond Flower Toilet Soap.			
161.—Boxes of 3 cakes		@	$18.00 per gro.
Ambrosial Soap.			
148.—Boxes of 5 cakes		@	$28.00 per gro.
American Mottled Castile Soap.			
48 A.—3 oz. cakes, boxes of 4 doz.		@	$1.75 per box.
48 B.—3 " 1 "		@	5.25 per gro.
49 A.—5 " 3 "		@	2.25 per box.
49 B.—5 " 1 "		@	9.00 per gro.
American White Castile Soap.			
57.—Boxes of 3 doz. cakes		@	$1.25 per box.
Aromatic Vegetable Soap.			
66.—No. 1 size, boxes of 3 cakes		@	$30.00 per gro.
67.—" 2 " 3 "		@	20.00 "
Assorted Bath Soap.			
54 W.—Boxes of 3 doz. cakes (wood)		@	$3.50 per box.
54 P.— " 3 cakes (paper)		@	15.00 per gro.
Assorted Fine Soaps.			
(Honey, Glycerine, Brown Windsor, and Elder Flower.)			
96.—½ lb. bars, boxes of 2 dozen		@	$4.00 per box.
Assorted Toilet Soaps.			
1 A.—8 oz. bars, boxes of 4 doz.		@	$4.50 per box.
1 B.—8 " 3 "		@	3.50 "
1 C.—8 " 2 "		@	2.25 "
1 D.—8 " 1 "		@	13.50 per gro.
69 A.—4 oz. cakes, 8 "		@	4.50 per box.
69 B.—4 " 6 "		@	3.50 "
69 C.—4 " 3 "		@	1.75 "
69 D.—4 " 1 "		@	6.75 per gro.
9.—Cushion form, No. 1, boxes of 4 doz.		@	1.75 per box.
7.— " 2, " 80 cakes		@	2.00 "

No.			
Assortment "A" Fine Soaps.			
(½ doz. each of Brown Windsor No. 1, Glycerine and Honey, Medium and Sweet Brier Soaps.)			
165.—Packages of 1 doz. (4—3 cake boxes).	@	$14.50 per gro.	
Balsamic Soap.			
114.—Boxes of 4 cakes		@	$18.00 per gro.
Barber's Shaving Soap.			
56 A.—1 lb. bars, boxes of 2 doz.		@	$6.00 per box.
56 B.—1 " 1 "		@	3.00 "
21.—Boxes of 3 doz. cakes		@	1.25 "
137.— " 12 cakes (wrapped)		@	7.00 per gro.
Bath Soap. Almond.			
Do. Assorted.			
Do. Brown.			
Do. Palm.			
Boxes of 3 doz. cakes (wood)		@	$3.50 per box.
" 3 cakes (paper)		@	15.00 per gro.
Bath Soap (Perfumed).			
76.—1 lb. bars, boxes of 15 bars		@	$3.75 per box.
Bay Laurel Soap.			
110.—Boxes of 3 cakes		@	$24.00 per gro.
Brown Bath Soap.			
5 W.—Boxes of 3 doz. cakes (wood)		@	$3.50 per box.
5 P.— " 3 cakes (paper)		@	15.00 per gro.
Brown Windsor Soap.			
6 W.—Boxes of 3 doz. cakes (wood)		@	$2.13 per box.
6 P.—Packets of 3 cakes (paper), Eng. style		@	9.00 per gro.
47 W.—No. 1 size, boxes of 3 doz. cakes (wood)		@	3.50 per box.
47 P.—No 1 size, boxes of 3 cakes (paper)	@	14.50 per gro.	
73.—1 lb. bars, boxes of 2 doz.		@	4.00 per box.
95.—½ " 3 "		@	4.00 "
Brown Windsor Soap "C C C."			
(LARGE SIZE.)			
130 A.—Boxes of 3 doz. cakes (wood)		@	$1.56 per box.
130 B.—6 cake packets, boxes of 6 doz.		@	6.25 per gro.
130 C.—Boxes of 1 doz. cakes, (wood)		@	6.25 "
Cashmere Bouquet Soap.			
91.—Boxes of 6 cakes		@	$36.00 per gro.

Fig. 2.5. Pages from Colgate & Company spring price list, 1887. Courtesy of Hagley Museum and Library.

a folly. Soon the kettle was too small, and a larger one was built to meet the demand for the firm's soap products. Five years later, the company added toilet soap to its line of products, a practice other Americans left to the European manufacturers. Ads began to appear for Colgate's ever-wider variety of fine soaps of every description, ranging in size from three-ounce to eight-ounce cakes (see Fig. 2.5). Among the most popular soaps were Cashmere Bouquet, Almond Flower Toilet Soap, Honey Soap, Oatmeal Soap, and Olive Palm Toilet Soap.[71]

Other soapmakers located near meat packinghouses, where the basic raw materials for soapmaking were plentiful. Enormous amounts of fat were generated in the butchering of steer and pig carcasses. They were employed as lubricants and were an ingredient in cosmetics and dyes, but the most important fat-based products proved to be soap and candles. When candle-maker William Procter and soap manufacturer James Gamble started their business in Cincinnati in 1837, the city was known as the "Porkopolis" of the West.[72] Not only was the site close to local meat packinghouses, which increasingly became the firm's key source of fats, it was also adjacent to the Miami-Erie Canal, a prime route to markets in the north.

With the basic raw materials readily available at the nearby pork packinghouses, Procter and Gamble produced candles and soaps. In addition, they processed and sold lard; its secondary product, lard oil, fueled the household lamps that some people preferred to candles, and it was equally useful as a lubricant. The following year a newspaper ad announced that the firm had soap and candles for sale:

SOAP AND CANDLE FACTORY

Main street, second house north of Sixth street.

The subscribers offer their manufactures, warranted full weight, correct tare, and marked as the late City Ordinance directs—

No. 1 Palm Soap,
" 2 Rosin do [*sic*],
         Toilet and Shaving Soap,
         Pure Tallow Candles, mould [*sic*] and dipped.
                 PROCTER, GAMBLE & Co.

In the 1850s, the Procter & Gamble Company made two important decisions. First, it made a sizable investment to expand its soap production facilities, boasting two kettles, each of which could turn out around one thousand pounds a week. Second, the manufacturers chose to concentrate initially on star candles, a generic name for the products made from the stearic acid of lard. The basic raw materials for these candles were hog fats, readily available at the nearby pork packinghouses. Moreover, the residue produced by the star candle process, oleic acid—called "red oil" in the trade—especially attracted the partners' interest.

Red oil had become a key ingredient in Procter & Gamble making soaps better than the other products on the market. It was first used to make a hard, white soap with visible red mottles or marbling, which sold in one-, two-, and three-pound bars. Called "Mottled German Soap," the laundry product became a consumer favorite when thrifty homemakers discovered that the veined appearance meant that it did not contain an excessive amount of water (see Fig. 2.6).[73] The other red-oil soap that the company introduced was Oleine, a hard, roughly textured soap for general household

Fig. 2.6. Stamp used on Mottled German Soap with the "Moon and Stars" trademark, from *Something about Soap*, Procter & Gamble, company publication, 1881.

use. One of its ingredients, palm oil, gave the soap a pleasant violet scent.[74] Floating white bars of Ivory Soap came later.

Procter & Gamble also advanced the use of commercial symbols to mark its products so that distributors and storekeepers could identify them. Typical of the time, the firm packed its soap in crates for shipping and began literally to "brand" its products with hot irons that burned the maker's name (or brand) in wooden packages. This was hardly a new idea; since antiquity people had branded symbols or name's on livestock to mark ownership. Yet not all workers could read the brands. Hence, the Procter & Gamble emblem was put into use around 1851, when wharfhands painted a crude cross on boxes of star candles to help workers who could not read identify the boxes. Some time later a more artistically inclined wharfhand altered the cross into an encircled star, perhaps to symbolize star candles. William A. Procter added a cluster of thirteen stars along with a quarter moon drawn as a human profile in 1859; the famous "moon and stars" became the company's first standard trademark.[75] People who recognized Procter & Gamble's trademark knew its quality.

Among the American soapmakers who developed the mass market, Benjamin Talbot Babbitt emerged as the most innovative. Babbitt began his New York City operations in 1836. By this time, the soap business had

THE CONTRAST

Blest is the prudent man who keeps his mind alert

Against a bilious stomach and a fly-blown shirt,

Beset with all the joys that health and hope impart—

Bland friends, a livery liver, and a happy heart:

In life and linen so unstained, it is breath so marv'lous sweet.

Thousands attend his bounteous beard, his praises to repeat.

Through all his outward life as a spotless beauty lies,

So maidens "yield their hearts" and matrons "lend their eyes."

Pale, melancholy mortal, never seen to smile.

Racked by some crushing sorrow or some "rising bile,"

Perch "green and yellow sadness" and a yellow shirt.

Again, poor man seek heath, and hope, and high renown'

Rally to keep they temper (and thy victuals) down;

Aspire above the "great unwashed," and with unfaltering hope.

Try manfully to "make a raise," and you can get the "Soap."

Is thy "cake dough," thy bread depressed," with all its sacred ties?

Out with the "Soap" (and spend it right), and you can make it rise.

None with foul breath, or bread, or linen need be cursed.

Since "Babbitt's SOAP and SALERATUS" cures the worst.

Fig. 2.7. One verse of the "Poetry of Soap" from Babbitt's *Washing Made Easy*, Babbitt Co., company publication. Courtesy of J. Walter Thompson Ephemera Collection, John W. Hartman Center for Sales, Advertising, and Marketing History, Duke University Rare Book and Special Collections Library.

become extremely competitive, with products not only from the American market but also from several British soapmakers. In order to overcome this challenge, Babbitt followed the strategy established by the toilet soap companies. He packaged small, consumer-sized cakes of all-purpose soap with identifying wrappers and called it "Babbitt's Best Soap." Printed on the wrapper and stamped on the cake was the signature of B. T. Babbitt. Sampling offered consumers a free trial in hopes of converting them to habitual use. In 1870, for example, Babbitt distributed a free booklet with a free three-quarter-pound cake of Best Soap. The first page had a calendar, fol-

lowed by Babbitt's "great manufactory," "poetry of soap," letters from satisfied customers, and a list of grocers who carried the product (see Fig.
2.7).[76] Still, Babbitt had difficulty convincing consumers to switch from
their homemade soap or chunks of soap bought at the local dry goods store.

In order to interest consumers in the packaged soap, Babbitt turned the
wrappers themselves into valuable commodities; the campaign became the
first to employ premiums extensively in the soap business.[77] The term "premium" refers to an item offered for free or at a bargain price to encourage
consumers to buy an advertised product. As early as 1851, Babbitt encouraged consumers to save twenty-five wrappers from Babbitt's Best Soap and
to exchange them for one of the "beautiful panel pictures in full color." Editions of certain favorite pictures ran into hundreds of thousands and could
be found on the walls of many homes throughout the country.

Following Babbitt's success with the picture offer, he steadily increased
the use of premiums, especially after the Civil War. The program had something for everyone. In exchange for twenty-five wrappers, people could get
a harmonica, handkerchiefs, and Roger's Plate silver-plated coffee spoons;
for fifty wrappers, a photo frame, buckhorn handle pocketknife, and
schoolbag; and for six hundred wrappers, a lady's watch.[78] It worked. To
meet demand, Babbitt expanded the production facilities to produce fifty
million pounds of soap every month by the turn of the century. About Babbitt's accomplishments, the *Soap Gazette and Perfumer* observed that the
soapmaker's patents on soap and manufacturing equipment "display an
originality which found full sweep in the marketing of his product."[79]

This singular effort to turn relatively generic bulk goods into far more
popular and identifiable products served as a model for other soapmakers.
A manufacturer put a wrapper around a consumer-sized commodity, used
advertising to create a particular perception of the company or personality
for the brand, and turned the goods into something desirable. The success of
selling standardized, small packaged goods also depended on a "name." Yet
it was something more than a name; it established identification of a "brand
name." This identity differentiated the product from others in the market
and enabled buyers to appraise the value of the merchandise before buying.

Although some soapmakers made ambitious attempts to advertise their
brand-name products extensively, other producers prospered without
advertising as people understand it today. They apparently had yet to be

convinced that advertising was necessary. The traditional way to do business was to surround oneself with a circle of customers and to cultivate personal relationships with them; superior quality of goods and word of mouth would do the rest. If wider markets were needed, manufacturers would send respectable traveling peddlers out on the road and pay them commission. Although a few peddlers or general stores inserted paragraphs in newspapers or posted notices to announce the arrival of new merchandise and to list merchants' products, generally advertising was aimed only at local readers. Manufacturers of a few such soaps attempted to distribute them beyond their local trading areas, relying on wholesale merchants who would take their consignments of soap and candles and sell them to small retailers in their service areas.

By the mid–nineteenth century, the economy was booming. A network of waterways, roads, and railroads opened new markets and reduced transportation costs dramatically. For example, between 1820 and 1860, the cost of shipping a ton of goods dropped from twenty cents to a penny, and the goods arrived five to ten times faster.[80] In particular, Colgate, Procter & Gamble, and Babbitt flourished during the pre–Civil War period, when the railroad was transporting goods far from their place of manufacture.

The Civil War subsequently fueled the rise of a consumer economy. Prior to the war American families living on farms formed tightly knit economic units. Husbands, wives, and children lived and worked together. The women performed such important functions as preserving foods, spinning, sewing, making clothes, and processing soap. The men worked in the fields, managed the family's money, and made most of the purchases. And the children pitched in wherever they were needed—in the fields, the barnyards, and the home. With men gone to war, many women did "men's" work in the fields and factories. Now, instead of the men, it was often the women, with their wartime earnings, who shopped the stores and purchased goods from peddlers. With less time for household tasks, women bought the clothing, canned goods, bakery items, and soap that they previously would have made themselves. In the process women became consumers, assuming responsibility for choosing what and how much to buy. After the war this purchasing trend continued as many people left the farms to work in urban factories.[81] As a result they came to rely less on their own production and more on the purchase of affordable mass-produced goods.

Fig. 2.8. A typical country store around 1870, from *J. Walter Thompson News Bulletin* (December 1923). Courtesy of J. Walter Thompson Company.

At the same time, the soapmakers found an increasing number of retail outlets for their merchandise. General stores sprang up as communities grew and the demand for goods increased. Usually located at the crossroads of a small rural town, the general store had a near monopoly on manufactured goods. The small, windowless stores crammed everything under one roof: food, clothing, hardware, kitchenware, medicines, saddles, and so on. The shopkeeper portioned out bulk food from open containers and cut the house soap from huge slabs, selling the goods by weight. In the urban areas, city dwellers might visit specialty stores to obtain basic foods, clothing, and other items. Here shoppers typically found goods placed behind a counter; a salesclerk searched the shelves or portioned out from containers (see Fig. 2.8). Or they might shop at large retail shops or department stores, which offered elegant surroundings, selection, and service. To facilitate sales, the age-old practice of negotiation eventually gave way to a system of uniform, fixed prices after the Civil War. Overall, marketing, technology, and the economy continued to evolve.[82]

After the Civil War, the notion of washing the body with soap became more commonplace. In response to this development, American soap manufacturers expanded into the toilet soap trade while continuing to produce coarser grades of soap used for washing and general laundry use. By the late nineteenth century, soapmakers had the means to distribute their goods coast to coast and to deliver their advertising messages through newspapers, magazines, and direct mail. The next chapter examines how advertising propagated faith in soap as essential to good health.

3

Rise of the Mass Market, 1875 to 1900

n the late nineteenth century two things were thought to cause disease. As the obsession with dust heightened, the notion that fomites (inanimate objects such as towels and bedding) spread infection became widespread. Sanitarians of the period considered the bedroom a particularly dangerous source of potential disease because of American sleeping and washing practices. In the 1889 magazine *Household*, one Dr. Cook warned that neither "the unhealthful thing called a comfortable [comforter] nor the unsightful covering called a patched quilt should be seen in a bed on this day."[1] According to the other explanation for the spread of disease, infectious organisms could multiply within the body and cause disease. Each of these views took root under the growing health movement that advocated prevention of disease. The idea that noxious atmosphere caused disease had roots in superstition, while the other idea provided a scientific basis that connected sickness and germs.

Both of these views, known as the filth theory and the germ theory, were as much a matter of popular belief as a matter of fact. Dr. Cook argued that about 40 percent of all deaths were due to the influence of impure air.[2] In 1889, *Good Housekeeping* offered even more alarming statistics, noting that "55 out of 100 white children die before they complete seven years of life . . . hardly five of that number are born with germs of an early death . . . two thirds of the remainder perish from want of life-air." But warnings of "bad" air shifted from "fact" to medical myth as new ideas gained ground among the enlightened scientific community.

In contrast, the germ theory marked a significant change in conceptions about sickness. It began when France's Louis Pasteur isolated microbes responsible for fermentation and silkworm diseases in 1864; but another decade passed before, in 1876, German scientist Robert Koch showed that a specific bacillus caused a specific disease. In particular, Koch's work with anthrax and tuberculosis established the germ theory of disease and had immediate implications for diagnosis and treatment. When Koch eventually published his findings that identified the microbe that causes TB in 1882, the famous postulates showed how a given organism could be linked to a specific illness—principles that are still used today. By the turn of the century, the work of Pasteur and Koch ushered in the science of microbiology and led to advances in immunology, sanitation, and hygiene that have done more to increase the lifespan of humans than any other scientific advance in the past one thousand years.[3] Still, notions of the filth theory lingered well into twentieth century.

This was an era when doctors continued to stigmatize bathtubs as carriers of disease, pronouncing them unhealthy when filled with warm water, and soap was almost as rare as baths.[4] In 1875, soap as people know it today barely existed, and the market for brand-name packaged soap was limited at best. There was no real, universal distinction between hand soap and laundry soap, and there would be no difference until the 1920s. Soap was soap, but it was through the advertising and the fashion system that commodities like soap could take on new meanings as new consumer rituals emerged.

THE NEW CULTURE OF CONSUMPTION

After the Civil War, rapid industrialization created new patterns of social life and changed the character of the American middle class. Historians have pointed out that one important aspect of this era was the growth of a culture of consumption.[5] Influenced by their English counterparts, urban middle-class American families embraced the sociocultural standards of the era, including rigid gender roles, extravagance, and philanthropic projects like sanitary reform to "uplift" society.

Late-nineteenth-century society was based on clear-cut boundaries between men's and women's spheres. The man often earned wages away from the home in an office or factory while the woman remained at home, cleaning, cooking, and raising children. Instead of producing their own everyday necessities, households increasingly bought clothing, canned goods, bakery items, and soap. With men toiling at work, women became consumers, assuming responsibility for choosing what and how much to buy, purchasing items like foodstuffs, clothing, and soaps outside the home. As a result, people came to rely less on their own production and more on the purchase of affordable, mass-produced goods. They simply could not match the variety, attractiveness, and particularly the prices of goods produced by American manufacturers, from clothing and furniture to food and drink.

During what is often called the Gilded Age, fashionable goods provided status and identity for individuals with social aspirations. Possession of material objects afforded upwardly mobile individuals and families with an entry into a desired world, as well as a means to differentiate themselves from other social groups. Victorian extravagance encouraged men and women not just to dress, but to overdress. Guides to etiquette and dress urged the middle class to define itself through consumption. Or, as *Decorum* aptly described the practice in 1881, it was "every woman's duty to make herself as beautiful as possible; and no less the duty of every man to make himself pleasing in appearance." Social conventions endlessly reminded people that they were on conspicuous display in a world where others naturally judged them by their outward appearance. People were thus urged to overdress and to clutter their homes with displays of ornate, overstuffed furniture and other mass-produced items. For some people, however, conspicuous consumption became less of a false face than a dramatic expression of the self in a culture increasingly oriented to display, spectatorship, and consumption.

In the process of becoming consumers, however, women increased their economic dependence because the woman traditionally spent money given by a wage-earning husband or parents. Even poor married women who earned a wage out of economic necessity still looked to their husbands for money to spend. The mass media played a major role in creating and sustaining this idealized image of the Victorian middle-class family and the woman's role in it. In particular, the culture promoted strict adherence to the traditional role assigned to women in society. Literature fostered the sentimental view of the home as a sacred place or a haven where women cultivated nurturing relationships. Moralizing tales preached against women leaving the home, accumulating possessions, and having social aspirations. Poems, songs, stories, books, and dramas invoked the hopes and joys associated with romance and wedded bliss—a woman's wealth, social standing, home, and happiness came through marriage.[6]

The promotion of domesticity also increasingly bound American women to the role of agents of cleanliness. Representative of regular columns, an 1896 editorial in the *Ladies' Home Journal*, entitled the "The Morals of the Bathtub," illuminated several key points that marked the decisive turn of American society toward the heightened importance of image making and self-performance in everyday life. First, the essay delineated that woman were responsible not only for their own personal cleanliness and neatness but also for the appearance of American men. According to the *Journal*, such habits had become an important factor in the betterment of the world's morality. "Let a man be careless of his surroundings, of his companionships, of his dress, his general appearance and of his bodily habits, and it is not long before the same carelessness extends into the realm of his morals."[7] Such assumptions drew legitimacy from dominant religious beliefs, echoing Reverend John Wesley's eighteenth-century admonition that cleanliness was a virtue. Cleanliness ensured health and order; it disciplined and built character—but it also offered greater benefits.

The idealization of cleanliness occurred within a middle class beginning to define itself through consumption. Other places in which private and public intertwined—the clothed body, the well-furnished parlor—were also accepted, indeed celebrated, as sites of commodity culture. At the same time, tidily ordered patterns of hygiene, domesticity, and manners focused on the body. Soap, too, was deemed fashionable, a sign of true identity. Even as it served a highly artificial self-presentation, the new ideal did not entirely displace earlier perceptions that cleanliness ensured health, order, discipline, and character. But when cleanliness was tied to material gain, it broadened the appeal to many more people.

The *Journal* editorial implicitly tied cleanliness to materialism, offering women a powerful rationale to place a heavy emphasis on cleanliness in the home. When confronted with a man's slovenliness, a hard habit to cure, the *Journal* reminded women that the most arduous campaign where a man's cleanliness and appearance was concerned was well worth the investment. Indeed, woman's efforts would come back "tenfold," keeping the husband, son, and brother up to the highest standard in the public world of business. According to the *Journal*, the man "who makes a point of keeping himself clean, and whose clothes look neat, no matter how moderate of cost they may be, works better, feels better, and is in every sense a better business man than his fellow-worker who is disregardful of his body and dress."[8] It followed that a man's success brought an increase in income, especially important to the middle class, which complained about the rising cost of living. At the time, they needed proportionately more money for display of the "paraphernalia of gentility," explained Joseph A. Banks in *Prosperity and Parenthood*, including servants, special clothing, more frequent washing, fine food, imported wine, tasteful decoration, and, above all, the maintenance of feminine leisure.[9] Thus, cleanliness became linked to the material success myth. In America, cleanliness combined with hard work, thrift, and diligence would lead to good fortune for the virtuous individual.

Finally, cleanliness was given an almost supercharged aura. It could turn humans into productive engines. Because men of tidy appearance worked at a distinct advantage, invigorated by a morning bath and the feeling of clean linen, they performed at their optimum levels, an important factor in the office or on the assembly line. This notion also embodied the metaphor of man as machine, a new vision for the industrial age. This fundamental premise was also evidenced in the *Journal* essay:

> A machine of metal and steel must be clean before it can do good work. So, too, the human machine. . . . Now a man rarely works better than he looks; certainly never better than he feels. And if a man feels unkempt the work he does will be of the same grade. If, on the other hand, he feels clean, he works clean. The feeling of the working inevitably communicates itself to his work.[10]

This argument drew legitimacy from the nineteenth-century idea of progress that had gained prominence with the Industrial Revolution, building on the Enlightenment's celebration of scientific and technological advances, as well as Puritan religious values espoused since the sixteenth century. Good fortune came as a reward for hard work, a clean mind, and a clean body.

Thus, the virtue of cleanliness absorbed the basic values of religion and science; it also was also more decidedly guided by a materialistic voice. In the new industrial America, cleanliness was not only healthy and moral; it was success driven.

FROM DOMESTIC TO MUNICIPAL HOUSEKEEPER

With the "haves" came the "have-nots." American's booming economy led to fortunes for some, and many palatial mansions were built after the Civil War. Modern conveniences, such as running water, indoor bathrooms, and gaslights were available only to the affluent; another generation would pass before the masses began to enjoy these luxuries. The correlate to this development was that certain sectors of the "have" society initiated philanthropic projects to "purify" or uplift America. Some groups tried to make people stop drinking, having sex, and gambling; others organized to fight grime.

Cleanliness crusaders were seriously challenged in their efforts because public services like sanitation, water, and utilities often proved inadequate for the burgeoning cities where overcrowding was standard. Even though multistory apartment buildings began to appear in New York City around 1870, middle-class families often were crammed into crowded flats and boarding houses. The less fortunate dwelt in far more primitive quarters. Epidemics, impure drinking water, and sewage problems accompanied the urban population explosion and industrialization of the period. It was no longer simply a matter of annual or seasonal hauling away of rubbish but a campaign for the daily elimination of filth. Lack of sanitation had become a serious menace to public health.

New views on urban planning and an increased understanding of infectious disease came together in a broadly focused movement for preventive sanitation then known as sanitary reform. With the success of the U.S. Sanitary Commission, formed during the Civil War, as a model, thousands of women organized to deal locally with social problems through new institutions, women's clubs.

Following the founding of the first women's clubs in 1868, the New England Women's Club of Boston and the Sorosis Society of New York, the idea gained rapid acceptance. For several decades, the women's clubs ostensibly served as organizations for self-improvement, but the thrust later shifted to civic affairs. The clubs united in 1890 as the General Federation of Women's Clubs, representing over three thousand clubs with a total membership of about 275,000 women.[11] The purpose of such women's clubs was threefold, claimed writer Martha E. D. White in 1904: "to educate its members, mentally and morally; to create public opinion; to secure better conditions of life." White also gave an explanation for the transition: "The ladies longing for power, coupled with confidence in the wisdom and beneficiaries of whatever women should do, brought the leaders of the club movement to a conception of social service."[12]

Clubwomen interested in sanitary reform set out to accomplish what the men of the city had failed to achieve: programs for clean streets and alleys. One group was particularly motivated by an enormous, foul-smelling manure pit in their exclusive Beekman Hill section of New York City. They formed the Ladies Health Protective Association in 1884 and went to court successfully to force the removal of the pit. The group also made specific recommendations to the mayor for improving the conditions of city streets. Aside from creating greater public awareness, the Ladies Health Protective League achieved few remarkable results until George Waring, appointed street commissioner in 1894, instituted the use of "white wings" (white-uniformed street cleaners).[13] New organizations modeled themselves after the Ladies Health Protective Association and helped New York and other cities understand the seriousness of their sanitation problems.[14] In Chicago, for example, a group of women established the Municipal Order League. Led by Mary McDowell, "Chicago's Garbage Lady," they promoted healthfulness and cleanliness in the city, but their first objective was street cleaning. Lugenia Hope subsequently organized Atlanta's Neighborhood Union to improve African American neighborhoods, while Charlotte Bartlett Crane organized the Women's Civic Improvement League to clean up the streets of Kalamazoo, Michigan. Thus, the popular image of the clubwoman associated with these organizations formed the basis of one of the most enduring archetypes of women in most American communities—what has been called the respectable, club-going, Christian wife.

The sanitary reform movement engaged large numbers of women in volunteer social service, but it also involved a young cadre of paid cleanliness experts or sanitarians. Although professionals and charity workers acted partly to uphold their specific interest and perspectives in bringing sanitation to American cities, they were also connected to the larger middle-class culture of which they formed a part. By the turn of the century, the sanitary reform movement developed into a large-scale effort to mold the values of the population, focusing on the family, schools, churches, and eventually the workplaces of the nation. A new wave of settlement houses, social workers, public health educators, and volunteers then carried on the struggle to heighten the sensitivity to the health implications of cleanliness, emphasizing training and education.

FROM OUTHOUSE TO IN-HOUSE

By the end of the nineteenth century, advances in plumbing technology enabled large cities to develop both water supply and sanitary disposal systems, which made keeping clean easier. As personal cleanliness rituals became more elaborate, domestic space also became specialized, with different spaces or rooms assigned to various functions.

For Americans, the indoor bathroom emerged as a status symbol for those few who could afford to install one—but it was only a room to bathe in. The toilet, or water closet, was in a separate room, if it was in the house at all. During bad weather and at night, families continued to use chamber pots in the house; otherwise, a privy in the backyard served as the main toilet. Most personal cleanliness rituals were performed in the bedroom. The *Household* advised women that "no matter how humble your room may be, there are eight things it should contain: a mirror, washstand, soap, towel, comb, hairbrush, nail brush, and toothbrush." A pitcher and basin usually accompanied these items.[15] Upon these minor details of the toilette depended, in a great degree, the health as well as the appearance of the individual.

When portable tubs eventually began appearing in fashionable American households, the ritual of bathing grew more frequent. For that occasion, domestic guides recommended using a large piece of oilcloth, which could be laid upon the floor of an ordinary dressing room or bedroom. Upon this was placed a basin or a tub of wood, zinc, or painted tin. Consequently, bathing done in a portable tub took place in the warmest room in the house and generally in front of a source of heat. In the workingman's home, this would be the kitchen; in the rich person's home, it would be the bedroom. Before hot and cold running water was supplied to homes, it had to be pumped and carried to its place of use. It was quite a backbreaking chore to carry ten to twenty gallons of water to the stove to be heated and then transfer the warmed water to the tub. Finally, the bath water had to be discarded, bucket by bucket, by tossing it out the back door.

Water heaters were introduced in the 1870s, although the early models were often explosively dangerous devices. They heated the water with gasoline, oil, or natural gas, requiring from minutes to hours to heat the water sufficiently for bathing. In some models, the water was heated before it filled the tub by being run through pipes heated by fire. Other models heated the water after it filled the tub through burners placed under the unit to warm the water. Portable folding bathtubs also came on the market. These operated the same as a folding bed; being placed on casters, so they could be closed up and stored in any room. Other popular bathing apparatus included portable shower chambers; some even made a pretty piece of furniture. When a bather pulled a cord or worked a pump with a foot pedal, the water would come down in a shower (see Fig. 3.1).

By the turn of the century, however, people could select from three types of built-in tubs with single taps for hot and cold running water. The best medium-priced tub was ellipse-shaped and made of porcelain-covered iron with a wooden rim around the top, which served as a seat. Also in the medium price range was the painted, enameled cast-iron tub with ball-and-claw feet or, less commonly, with paw feet. Solid porcelain tubs were also advertised, but their curved top edges were thought to be slippery and unsafe, unlike the wood-rimmed edges of the iron tubs. In 1892 the Standard Manufacturing (later Standard Sanitary) trade catalogue offered such a porcelain-covered iron tub, called the "Celebrated Rolled Rim Bath," that met the "approval of the most critical sanitarians"; prices ranged from

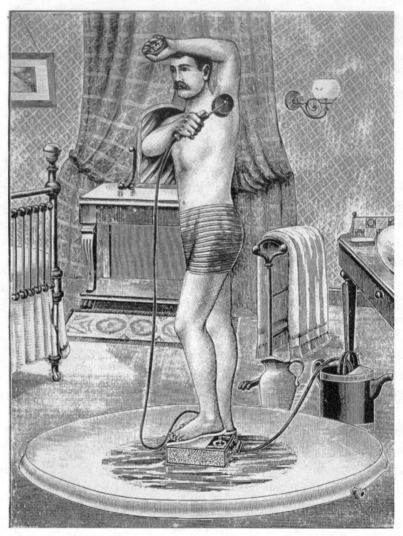

Fig. 3.1. Bathing apparatus, circa 1897.

$61 to $73. The new model offered the strength of iron, as well as the purity of the porcelain. "A bath in a china dish" headlined one 1892 ad. "Can you imagine anything in the way of a bath that would be more inviting than a china dish the size of a bath tub filled with clear, sparkling water?"[16] Standard also offered more luxurious tubs finished in ivory-white porcelain and decorated with beautiful floral embellishments, such as the "Madeline Pat-

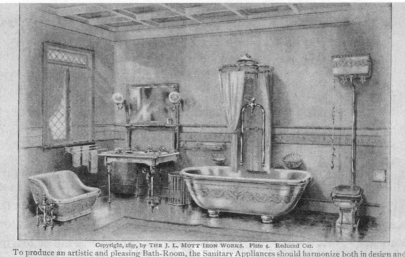

Copyright, 1897, by THE J. L. MOTT IRON WORKS. Plate 4. Reduced Cut.

To produce an artistic and pleasing Bath-Room, the Sanitary Appliances should harmonize both in design and decoration. We are prepared to furnish complete outfits in any of the prevailing designs—Rococo, Renaissance, Empire, etc. Interested parties are invited to visit our Show-Rooms. Illustrated price-lists mailed on application.

THE J. L. MOTT IRON WORKS, 84 to 90 Beekman St., New York.

311 & 313 Wabash Ave., Chicago.   332 & 334 Boylston St., Boston.   Wainwright Building, St. Louis.
Flood Building, San Francisco.   Builder's Exchange, Philadelphia.

Fig. 3.2. A deluxe bathroom plan, advertisement, Mott Plumbing, 1897.

tern" that cost $163, nearly three times the amount of their undecorated, rolled-rim models.[17]

Large manufacturers offered a variety of designs to reach both the high and low ends of the market. For example, J. L. Mott Iron Works offered a choice of nine suggested bathroom sets in its 1898 trade catalog, including many plans that consolidated the tub, sink, and toilet in one room. The plans included everything from bath, lavatory, shelf, and mirrors to water closets. Prices for the fixtures ranged from around $220 for the standard porcelain "Bath Room" to $1200 for the "Renaissance Design," fittings and installation not included. The deluxe models featured a combination bath and shower with a rubber curtain, hip bath, fixtures embossed with white and gold decorations, marble basins, and beveled plate glass mirrors (see Fig. 3.2).[18]

By urging ordinary American people to imitate the lifestyles of the elite by buying bathtubs and creating specialized places for bathing, sanitary fixture manufacturers further validated personal cleanliness for a broad range of people. The 1898 Mott trade catalog noted this trend:

Only a few years ago the Bath Room was a secondary consideration in laying out the plans for the house, and it was generally relegated to some part or space that could not be utilized for any other purpose. Today, it is almost the first thing to be considered in laying out the plans, for not only palatial residences, but even for dwellings of very modest pretensions.[19]

Still, baths were not an everyday occasion. Although plumbing manufacturers promoted indoor bathrooms as a convenience, built-in tubs, toilets, and sinks would not be within the reach of ordinary citizens until World War I.

Paradoxically, Americans responded to these changes in domestic architecture in different ways. Certainly an indoor bathroom was far more convenient than a trip outdoors to the privy. But the thought of going to the bathroom inside the home also evoked embarrassment. Nineteenth-century Americans considered it a shameful secret to be seen entering or leaving the smallest room in the house, the water closet, while their company anguished over the flushing noise of a plug being pulled, trumpeting the purpose of their absent companion. Today, the lavatory taboo still runs strong. Among Americans, it still is customary to excuse oneself to the "restroom," "lavatory," or the "facilities." Men leave for the "men's room" and women excuse themselves to the "ladies room" or "powder room"; it is considered bad manners to plainly say, "excuse me, but I have to use the toilet." Or people will turn on the faucet, so that the sound of running water covers up or hides, and even denies, one of the body's most natural functions—eliminating bodily wastes. Indeed, taboos centering on the horror of the body linger on in the twenty-first century.

When indoor toilets appeared, Philadelphia paper sellers Irvin and Clarence Scott bought sheets of tissue wrapping paper, cut them into a convenient size, and repackaged them for the home bathroom. Few people wanted to spend money for pads of "medicated paper," as it was called then, when the pages of mail-order catalogs filled the need. Even after indoor plumbing had become standard, however, people were still embarrassed to ask grocers for toilet paper. The company overcame the problem by using an almost plain wrapper, which merely gave a trade name and did not reveal what the wrapper contained. A well-brought-up shopper could then ask the shop assistant for "Scott Tissue," without mentioning that one was buying rolls of toilet paper.[20] Thus, American society continued to define hygiene and appearance as a matter of good and bad manners, the mentionable and the unmentionable. Such incongruities and paradoxes were not incidental by-products but governing axioms in the mass market for personal care products.

SOAP TRADE AND THE ERA OF THE NATIONAL MARKET

As bathrooms became more commonplace, so did the notion of washing the face, hands, and body with soap. The increased use of toilet soap was noticed by the American manufacturers, who began to cater to this trade with a greater diversity of milder soaps for bathing, shaving, and shampooing while continuing to produce coarser grades used for laundry and general household use. As markets expanded for soap products, the manufacturers increased their production, found new outlets to sell their products, and created new forms of advertising. The completion of the railroad and telegraph networks helped to create a national market, enabling soapmakers to distribute their products to a wider geographic area. Local manufacturers went regional, and some regional manufacturers went national.

At the same time, competition for consumers' expenditures increased. Not only did similar products and services compete with each other, but also new products competed with each other. The competition for consumers' attention increased as the intensity of promotional efforts grew into a self-fueling spiral, with each advertisement attempting to grab attention away from other promoters. The cumulative consequence of this spiral, of course, added to each advertiser's perceived need to forever increase promotion. Firms also divided according to whether they specialized in marketing themselves, secured the services of people who specialized in advertising, or combined their expertise with that of the specialists.[21] In this period of flux, advertisers experimented with packaging, chose appealing brand names, and altered the form and content of media. It was the soapmakers who took the lead in advertising on a large scale. In the United States, Babbitt, Procter & Gamble, Colgate, and Sapolio set the trend, but several European marketers, including Pears and Lever Brothers, also exercised an important influence on the introduction of large-scale advertising in America.[22] Thus, the protocols for promoting soap products for personal care were established between 1875 and 1900.

The Packaging Revolution

Goods of all kinds, including soap, looked pretty much alike in 1875. Grocers' shelves were practically the only medium to display an advertising message such as a product's trademark, if it had one at all. The names of most manufacturers were virtually unknown to the people who bought their products. Common household soap was sold in generic slabs with no identifying marks; the storekeeper would cut off a chunk, weigh it, and wrap it up for the customer. According to business historian Richard Tedlow, brands were few. "This was an era of commodities—of crackers out of barrels, of coffee out of sacks, of flour from the gristmill."[23] If customers liked a product and wanted to find it, they welcomed any form of distinguishing mark. Manufacturers who recognized this consumer desire began to identify their products with labels, wrappers, and boxes, so customers could recognize the manufacturer's trademark and remember its quality.

Along with patent medicine manufacturers, early soapmakers pioneered the merchandising and packaging of brand-name goods. In particular, the makers of expensive, imported toilet soap used elegant shapes and wrappers, usually in decorative boxes to distinguish their brands from others on the market. Toilet soap companies had found that more creative names helped sell their products. Cashmere Bouquet, White Rose, and Golden Hyacinth sold delicate, floral bouquets for women, while Jockey Club suggested a stronger scent for men. To make sure buyers picked the right toilet soap from the store shelves, the manufacturers experimented with elaborate packaging, often featuring decorative labels with their own name. Names like Bayley, Low, and Yardley from England; Coudray and Lubin from France; and Colgate from America became well known to affluent ladies.

Like toilet soapmakers, manufacturers of common soap began to package their goods for sale directly to the consumer. Following Babbitt's strategy of marketing a household soap in small, consumer-sized packages with identifying wrappers, companies like Procter & Gamble began to offer several of their commercial soaps in one-, two-, and three-pound bars. Manufacturers also recognized that they could charge a higher price for goods with a memorable brand name and attractive packaging; in turn, they urged consumers to accept no substitutes. The brand name had to be one that people could remember, felt comfortable with, and believed to represent an established firm as well as a quality product. If manufacturers could inspire confidence, this gave customers a reason to choose their product instead of a competing brand. Thus, many early manufacturers packaged their soap, put their name on the package, and used their portraits as trademarks and advertising motifs to inspire confidence in their goods. Colgate, Procter & Gamble, Babbitt, Dobbins, Woodbury, and Larkin, among others, used this technique

Manufacturers who based their advertising upon their name, reputation, and known integrity exhibited a superior confidence in their products. Almost like a guarantee of advertised products, this was an attempt to show the confidence and pride of the manufacturer in the manufactured article and thereby induce the acceptance of the consuming public. "Again it is because *people* remember *people* much more easily than they remember *things*," an industry executive exulted. "It *humanizes* what is inanimate."[24]

Other marketers believed that the brand name should suggest something desirable about the product and its performance. These strategies may be seen in brand names of soaps like Cuticura, La Perle Obesity Soap, and Dobbins Electric Soap. Powerful suggestions and an aura of mystery also proved to be effective promotional devices. An outstanding example was Cuticura Soap, which conspicuously suggested the mysterious, curative qualities of the ointment of the same name, touted to cure ailments from pimples to scrofula. As early as 1880, Cuticura became a national advertiser and eventually went international in 1896; the company's small ads quickly became a familiar sight in newspapers and periodicals.[25]

When La Perle Obesity Soap Company advertised in the personal columns of the New York *Herald* newspaper, it made even greater curative claims, promising weight reduction and "A Perfectly Formed Woman To Order." The "absolutely harmless" soap claimed to take tens of pounds of fat off any part of the body "without the slightest harm to the tenderest skin or most delicate constitution."[26] Other soapmakers also capitalized on a current fashion. For example, Dobbins Electric Soap used the electrical motif as Americans celebrated the wonders of science and technology. The name Electric Soap evoked an odd mixture of a powerful, magnetically charged cleansing agent with magical powers. Yet Dobbins made no medical claims based on alleged or real applications of energy, as did some practicing electroquackery.[27]

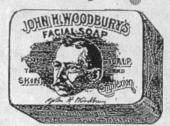
Fig. 3.3. Woodbury's Facial Soap, advertisement, *Nickell* magazine, 1899.

The challenge, however, was to convince buyers that they could not pass up the advantages of nationally advertised brand-name products, which usually cost more than the generic ones. To distinguish one product from another, marketers advertised both a specific brand name and a graphic image or symbol for visual identification, eventually called a "trademark," that identified the source of goods in trade. Advertising helped manufacturers sell an enormous amount of products both at a lower cost and at a profit.

For example, the druggist Dr. John H. Woodbury decided never to put out an ad for Woodbury's Facial Soap unless it included his face in the advertisement (see Fig. 3.3). The advertising and the packaging promoted the soap as a cure for skin diseases; it also was part of a family of specially formulated remedies for the skin, hair, and scalp. Advertising further invested the soap with a sacred status. Ads featured sensational copy, dramatic before-and-after pictures, testimonials, and promises of magical transformations similar to those used to sell cure-all patent medicines. Thus, Woodbury's trademark face came to be associated with a set of assumptions about curative powers that conditioned consumers to want the products.

As the use of brand names and commercial trademarks spread, so did the practice of imitation. The U.S. Constitution protected the rights of ownership in copyrights and patents but did not grant exclusive rights to some marks placed on products until 1870, when the nation's first federal trademark law was enacted. The protections of the new trademark laws encouraged manufacturers to rely more heavily on well-advertised commercial symbols. All things being equal, brands from well-known companies proved more valuable than those names from unknown companies. Branding also protected manufacturers from price competition to some degree as consumers came to accept no substitutes for particular brand-name goods rather than settle for the least expensive product available.

ADVERTISING AND MASS PRODUCTION

Despite advances in the trade, selling soap during this period still presented three marketing problems. As business historian Pam Laird aptly remarks:

FREE PREMIUMS!!

For the Trade Marks from the Wrappers and Packages of

B. T. Babbitt's Best Soap or 1776 Soap Powder.

Only Premiums mentioned in the following List will be sent by Mail.

No.	Name of Premium.	Trade Marks Req.
343	Baby's Rattle, (Rubber)	25
379	Harmonica,	25
427	Silver Plated Tea Spoon,(Roger's Plate)	25
448	Child's Leather Purse,	25
483	Lady's Handkerchiefs, Two for	25
486	Lady's Fancy Handkerchief,	25
488	Towel, (Red Border)	25
498	Napkins, Red or Blue B'der or all White,2 for	25
521	Aluminum Tea or Coffee Strainer,	25
522	" Pin or Ash Receiver,	25
529	Stamped Doylies, (12 in.) Three for	25
505	Kindergarten Doylies, Twelve for	25
454	Fringed Table Doylies, Two for	25
534	Silver Plated Coffee Spoon, (Roger's Plate)	25
550	Aluminum Memorandum Book,	25
551	" Whist or Euchre Counter,	25
436	Collar Button Set,	25
553	Paper Dolls, (to cut out) 6 different kinds for	25
519	Euchre Tally Cards, Fifty for	25
364	Harmonica,	50
413	Buckhorn Handle Pocket Knife, Two Blades	50
473	Writing Paper, (in Box,)	50
517	Kitchen Knife and Fork,	50
520	Aluminum Photo Frame,	50
523	Salt and Pepper Shakers,	50
524	Silver Thimble,	50
525	Case Pins and Needles,	50
543	Game of Card Dominoes,	50
555	Baby's Silver Bracelet,	50
526	Boy's School Bag,	
552	Pair of Uncle Sam Suspenders,	
416	Bone Handle Pocket Knife, (Two Blades)	60
541	Baby's Ring, (Solid Gold) Sizes 1, 2 and 3	75
428	Silver Plated Table Spoon, (Roger's Plate)	75
429	" " Knife,	75
430	" " Fork,	75
433	" " Butter Knife,	75
434	" " Sugar Shell,	75
544	Playing Cards, (Gilt Edge)	75
450	Lady's Pocket Book,	75
471	Writing Paper, (in Box),	75
481	Button Hole Scissors,	75
443	Link Cuff Buttons,	75

Trade Marks from the Wrappers of B. T. Babbitt's Best Soap or the Packages of B. T. Babbitt's 1776 Soap Powder are of equal value, and will be taken in mixed lots in the selection of Premiums.

No.	Name of Premium.	Trade Marks Req.
491	Sterling Silver Handle Nail File,	75
492	" " " Button Hook,	75
493	" " " Shoe Horn,	75
494	" " " Paper Cutter,	75
495	" " " Tooth Brush,	75
496	" " " Hair Curler,	75
497	" " " Cuticle Knife,	75
499	Sewing Scissors, (5½ in.)	75
504	Creponette Dresser Scarf, (66x25 in.)	75
415	Bone Handle Pocket Knife, Three Blades,	100
545	Fortune Telling Cards, (Ye Old Witches),	100
451	Lady's Pocket Book,	100
490	Pocket Match Safe,	100
446	Link Cuff Buttons,	100
556	Gold Plated Watch Chain,	125
546	Playing Cards, (Fancy Back Priscilla),	125
527	Embroidered Felt School Bag,	125
547	Playing Cards, (Fancy Back Minuet),	125
528	Lawn Bureau Scarf and Three Doylies,	125
548	Playing Cards, (Fancy Back Good Night),	125
440	Link Cuff Buttons,	125
414	Buckhorn Handle Pocket Knife, Four Blades	125
431	Silver Plated Cold Meat Fork, (Roger's)	150
456	Lady's Pocket Book,	150
540	Solid Gold Ring, (3 Pearls) Sizes 2,3,4,5 & 6	150
531	Silver Plated Gravy Ladle (Roger's Plate)	150
535	Solid Gold Scarf Pin,	175
530	Fountain Pen, (14kt. Nib)	175
432	Silver Plated Berry Spoon, (Roger's Plate),	225
459	Lady's Pocket Book,	225
539	Solid Gold Ring,(3 Emeralds)Sizes 5,6,7 & 8	325
537	" " (2 Rubies)Sizes 5,6,7,8 & 9	325
538	" " (12 Torquois)Sizes 5,6,7,8 & 9	350
536	" " (12 Pearls) Sizes 5,6,7,8 & 9	350
	* See Note how to ascertain the size of ring	
503	Linen Table Cloth, (Red Border),	350
417	Lady's Gun Metal Watch,	600
418	Boy's Nickel Watch,	600
421	Gentleman's Gun Metal Watch,	650
419	Lady's Silver Watch,	700
549	" Belt Watch,	800
554	Gentleman's Raised Metal Watch,	800

Fig. 3.4. B. T. Babbitt, newspaper advertisement, no date.

First they had to convince buyers to consume more soap to absorb their collective productivity. An additional factor that exacerbated competition between soapmakers resulted from their decisions to market their products in small, consumer-sized packages with identifying wrappers. Second, they had to convince buyers to cast off long-standing traditions of either making their own soap or buying it in blocks from their generic cakes. Third, they sought to foster brand loyalty—that is, specific demand—for products with only minor differentials.[28]

Whether old or new, products jammed the marketplace, and advertisers sought new ways to reach potential consumers. The emergence of three trends particularly reflected this effort: (1) premium promotional programs, (2) collectible strategies, and (3) magazines as advertising vehicles.

Something for Nothing

To encourage consumers to abandon generic soap, manufacturers had invented the gimmick of trading the soaps' wrapping for other commodities. The soap packaging itself became a commodity to barter for other goods, which were, in turn, promoted as premiums. The promotional programs of B. T. Babbitt demonstrated that it pays to give something away. As early as the 1850s, the company convinced the public that its premiums had genuine merit, giving away such items as a lithograph, finger ring, scarf pin, bound novel, bronze clock, soup ladle, and salt cellar "with an iconoclastic zeal suggestive of the enthusiasm of a convert from idolatry" (see Fig. 3.4).[29] Soon the entire soap industry had switched to Babbitt's premium approach, and all of the major soap companies, including Babbitt, Procter & Gamble, Larkin, and Pears, developed variations on this practice at one time or another. At first soapmakers offered chromolithograph prints (chromos) as premiums, and later everything from jewelry to furniture.

In order to compete with the Babbitt Company and other soap manufacturers, John Durant Larkin began including larger and more interesting gift premiums than the competition. Larkin set up shop in Buffalo, New York, as J. D. Larkin, Manufacturer of Staple and Fancy Soaps. Advertising, however, did not dominate the company's marketing efforts to sell its products. Its first product, Sweet Home, was sold through street vendors; it was followed shortly by Oatmeal Toilet Soap. The firm shrewdly recognized that the great expansion of mail-order houses such as Montgomery Ward and Sears, Roebuck & Co. had demonstrated the possibilities for sales through direct marketing on a national scale. But it was the marketing genius of Larkin's partner, Elbert Hubbard, who directed advertising and promotions from 1882 to 1893, that took the strategy of a mail-order operation offering premiums for soap wrappers well past its initial origins.

Over the years, the Larkin Company gave away a wide variety of articles. The gift premiums began modestly, with small souvenir picture cards with purchases of Sweet Home, a best-selling product. From there, Larkin and Hubbard experimented with promotional products such as a free handkerchief with Pure White Toilet Soap, and a bath towel with the purchase of Ocean Bath Soap.[30] The success of this strategy led to grander schemes in the 1890s. Larkin astutely observed that consumers tend to associate the

Fig. 3.5. One of Larkin's most popular giveaways, the Chautauqua desk.

quality of a premium with the quality of the company providing it, so Larkin leaned toward more expensive gifts for consumers.[31]

Larkin's master plan was to market directly from the factory to consumers; the money he saved on commission allowed him to provide better premiums. He offered unusually substantial inducements—piano lamps, Morris chairs, and oak dining chairs—for the wrappers and a small amount of cash, a combination that today is called a self-liquidating premium.[32] In 1893, Larkin began sending a semiannual catalog to the company's one and a half million customers. In exchange for a specified number of wrappers and cash, it offered twenty-seven premiums, including silk handkerchiefs, silver-plated butter dishes, and a solid-gold pocket watch. One of the most popular giveaways was the Chautauqua Desk. For a ten-dollar order of soap, the customer received not only the soap, but also the desk, a ten-dollar premium (see Fig. 3.5). If an individual did not feel inclined to invest that sum, there was the "Larkin Club-Of-Ten" option. A group of ten families arranged to buy one case of Larkin Soaps each month for ten dollars; they then divided the soaps and cost equally. In ten months, each of the ten, in turn, would own one Larkin premium.[33]

To meet the increasing customer demand, Larkin found it necessary to manufacture its own goods for the most popular premiums. The company set up furniture and pottery factories in Buffalo and negotiated contracts with other firms to produce glassware, silverware, and men's apparel for its expanding line of premiums. The product line, too, continually expanded. By the turn of the century, Larkin had added household products ranging from cleaning products to spices. The company sales rapidly increased from nearly $500,000 in 1893, to over $13 million by 1904.[34]

Advertisements As Collectibles

Advertisers and printers even devised ways to encourage popular demand for the advertisements themselves by making them collectibles. Observers referred to them as souvenirs in a "craze" that was "absolute " in its intensity.[35] After the Civil War, chromolithographs quickly became the dominant printing medium to achieve convincingly real images. Chromos appeared in such forms as greeting cards, bookmarks, paper dolls, and linings for suitcases and trunks. But it was the advertising industry's application of

Fig. 3.6. Babbitt's Best Soap, trade card.

striking designs, bright colors, and innovative forms that popularized chromos. Printers also ran large quantities of vibrant trade cards, calendars, and posters. Often picture calendars and posters looked appealing enough to put on the kitchen wall or to frame for the parlor; images of the home with women and children proved especially popular (see Fig. 3.6). Other advertisers also distributed storybooks, paper dolls, and games with their advertising message (see Fig. 3.7).

Fig. 3.7. Banner Lye distributed a game with its advertising message, circa 1860–1899. Courtesy of the Winterthur Library, Joseph Downs Collection of Manuscripts and Printed Ephemera, no. 89 × 28.

Although advertisers paid printers to create unique images, many used "overprints" as a cost expedient. To save an advertiser money, for example, printers often designed trade cards with a basic generic image and a blank area, which they printed in large numbers; then, they overprinted the name and location of the company. As a group these generic image or overprints provided a contrast to specifically commissioned advertisements that carried messages promoting product features. Some companies induced trade card collecting by ordering sets with themes: flowers, exotic peoples, actresses, game birds, tropical birds, city newspaper editions, military heroes, Native Americans, and sports champions, among others. In many

Fig. 3.8. Three of a set of six trade cards for Elite Toilet Soap distributed by the Larkin Company.

cases, manufacturers distributed vibrant posters to local retailers to show all of the cards in a given set. For instance, Colgate commissioned a set of trade cards featuring floral bouquets to promote its scented toilet soaps.

Other trade card themes pertained little or not at all to their product, with scenes from foreign lands or pictures of animals. Larkin Soap, for example, distributed a set of six trade cards for Elite Toilet Soap featuring animated frogs who played the banjo, fished, and enjoyed other everyday activities (see Fig. 3.8). The back of the cards, however, made no mention of product features or claimed that the soap might foster loveliness. Instead, the Elite cards carried two other specific messages encouraging brand loyalty: (1) for the soap customer, a fine Japanese silk handkerchief in every box of Elite Toilet Soap; and (2) for the card collector, an opportunity to collect all six designs in the set, Larkin sent the full set on receipt of a three-cent stamp.

Together, these poster and card sets illustrate how advertisers encouraged brand loyalty and frequent use. Large numbers of scrapbooks survived, demonstrating the success of the collectible strategy, with vibrant advertising cards often preserved next to gift cards and other nonadvertising items.[36] The popularity of chromos declined around the turn of the century, however, as advertisers turned to popular illustrated magazines and expanded their use of photography.

Magazines As Advertising Vehicles

A new generation of magazines appeared as advertising vehicles in the 1880s and 1890s. Their styles ranged from the women's magazine *Godey's Lady's Book* to the reformist *McClure's* magazine and the impassioned *Munsey* magazines. Although they varied in content, these magazines had one thing in common: they depended on a new class of subscribers, the middle-class readers who were ready to buy consumer goods advertised in an appropriate fashion.

During the 1880s and 1890s, the number of women's magazines increased, reaching middle-class women, predominantly homemakers. The magazines offered low subscription prices to gain large circulation because advertising rates were circulation-based. Yet it was Boston advertising solicitor Cyrus H. Curtis who truly expanded the magazine as an advertising vehicle. Curtis began with the weekly four-page the *Tribune and Farmer* and invited his wife to edit a women's column. The column stirred so much interest that Curtis turned the page into the *Ladies' Home Journal* in 1883. The *Journal* offered the right mix of abundant reading on decorating and needlework patterns, as well as fiction and romance. Curtis accepted only high-grade advertising and reset many ads for a more pleasing appearance. He also invented the modern advice column. Young women could write to editor Edward Bok or to Bruce and Beatrice Gould for commonsense answers on courtship, marriage, child rearing, and divorce. At twenty-five cents an issue, the periodical reached a broad audience in terms not just of content but also of price; fashion books typically cost $2 or $3.[37]

The *Journal* created a model for the successful women's magazines of the time: *Delineator* (1872), originally just a compendium of sewing patterns; *Good Housekeeping* (1885); *The Woman's Home Companion* (1897); *Pictorial Review* (1899); and *McCall's* (1897). Referred to as the "Big Six," they focused on homemaking, entertainment, fiction, and social reform.[38] Another influential magazine emerged in 1897, when Curtis purchased the failing *Saturday Evening Post* and revamped it into one of the most widely read magazines ever produced. The *Post*, the first to break the one-million circulation mark, published the work of such writers as Ring Lardner, F. Scott Fitzgerald, and Sinclair Lewis, along with Norman Rockwell's wholesome small-town scenes.[39]

At the same time, the first illustrated ads appeared as the American art world became fascinated with the brilliant lithographed art posters from France and England with their bold, flat colors. The introduction of photo-engraving in 1890, however, permitted good color reproduction with gradation of light and dark tones, called halftones, creating the illusion of shading as in a photograph or oil painting. Not only did this process produce pictures that looked like paintings instead of pen- and ink-sketches drawn by hand, but the pictures were much cheaper to make. This work set the stage for the illustrators who would later dominate advertisements well into the twentieth century. Their artwork appeared on magazine covers and literary posters and in magazine articles and upscale advertisements. Accompanying the expansion of magazines as advertising vehicles was the emergence of the first national advertisers.

THE FIRST NATIONAL ADVERTISERS

Soap became one of the first nationally advertised products in America, along with cereals, baking ingredients, and foodstuffs.[40] American soap-makers B. T. Babbitt and Procter & Gamble along with British-based Pears' Soap emerged among the more enterprising large-scale advertisers in the United States. By 1900 Babbitt was spending $400,000 for a single year of advertising; five years later Procter & Gamble was spending the same amount, a considerable figure for the time.[41]

The success of soapmakers like Babbitt, Procter & Gamble, and Pears demonstrated a classic, threefold formula for success: (1) identify a gap in the market, (2) develop a high-quality product to fill it, and (3) convince as many people as possible to buy that product by the extensive use of promotion and advertising. Although soap manufacturers drew upon conventions of white, middle-class life and beauty, they also cast a wide net for consumers. Before the advent of market research, advertisers had no way of knowing who actually purchased their soaps, so their ads targeted not only native-born, affluent white women, but other women aspiring to middle-class standards.

Fig. 3.9. The first cake of Ivory was sold in 1879; special commemorative wrapper, 1979.

The Soap That Floats

By 1875, the Procter & Gamble Company was already firmly established in Cincinnati, Ohio, supplying soap and candles to the armies of the West. Soapmaking produced 25 percent of the company's sales; kitchen lard and candles made up the rest. Advertising was still limited, but the company was on the threshold of large-scale commercial success. The two founders' sons, Harley Procter and James N. Gamble, had come back from college with knowledge of chemistry that changed the course of the business.

At the time, soapmakers typically made commercial soap from animal fats, but this proved too perishable to sell outside of regional markets. To solve this problem, James Gamble hired the firm's first full-time chemist, and the two of them set out to duplicate the qualities of the expensive, white "castile" soap made from pure olive oil and imported in small quantities from England. Using materials available in Cincinnati, they perfected a white, perfumed soap made from vegetable fats that was mild enough for the laundry or the nursery. They named it P & G White Soap, designed a special wrapper for each individual bar, and put the product on sale. By mistake, a plant worker apparently left a batch of soap inside the stirring

Fig. 3.10. The first Ivory Soap ad appeared in a religious weekly called the *Independent*, in 1882.

THE "IVORY" is a Laundry Soap, with all the fine qualities of a choice Toilet Soap, and is 99 44-100 **per cent. pure.**

Ladies will find this Soap especially adapted for washing laces, infants' clothing, silk hose, cleaning gloves and all articles of fine texture and delicate color, and for the varied uses about the house that daily arise, requiring the use of soap that is above the ordinary in quality.

For the Bath, Toilet, or Nursery it is preferred to most of the Soaps sold for toilet use, being purer and much more pleasant and effective and possessing all the desirable properties of the finest unadultered White Castile Soap. The Ivory Soap will **" float."**

The cakes are so shaped that they may be used entire for general purposes or divided with a **stout** thread (as illustrated) into two perfectly formed cakes, of convenient size for toilet use.

The price, compared to the quality and the size of the cakes, makes it the cheapest Soap for everybody for every want. TRY IT.

SOLD EVERYWHERE.

machine too long, and the mixture hardened with a pocket of air inside. The resulting soap had a curious property: it floated in water. Customers apparently liked the "soap that floats," so Harley Procter adjusted the manufacturing process to produce nothing but floating bars.

While the peculiar floating property came from an accident, the name Ivory came from divine inspiration. Harley Procter received a heavenly suggestion in church one Sunday morning as the congregation read the following psalm: "All thy garments smell of myrrh, and aloes, and cassia, out of the ivory palaces whereby they have made thee glad." In 1879, Procter & Gamble changed the name of P & G White Soap to Ivory, identifying the soap with purity, and then set out to market their product nationally (see Fig. 3.9).

With this in mind, Procter & Gamble shaped Ivory Soap into a total product concept, a multipurpose soap mild enough for a baby's skin. By emphasizing the purity of the soap, Procter & Gamble had found another way of saying that its soap was exceptional. The castile soap imported from England served as a benchmark of purity, since the product consisted of nothing but fatty acids and alkali. When the report on random samples of their simple Ivory Soap came back, it showed the impurities came to .56 percent uncombined alkali, carbonates, and mineral matter. Subtracting the amount of this unnecessary substance from 100 percent produced "99 and 44/100 pure," one of the most famous trade lines in advertising history, still as recognizable today as it was a hundred years ago. Moreover, the slogan quietly but powerfully stated that the product was of extremely high quality. It also assured consumers that they could always depend on getting exactly what they expected Ivory to be—a pure, uniform product. Procter & Gamble managed to sustain this image through decades of advertising.

To Procter & Gamble, the most important component for success was continuous advertising. But the company also faced a problem that many other manufacturers had previously encountered. There really were very few places where one could place advertising for a national audience at the time, so it started with a six-inch ad in a religious weekly, the December 21, 1882 issue of the *Independent* (see Fig. 3.10). From there, as more and more magazines appeared on the scene, Ivory appeared in country weeklies, farm journals, and ultimately the new popular magazines such as *Ladies' Home Journal*, *Good Housekeeping*, and *Harper's Weekly* that enabled the soapmaker to sell its products nationwide.

The limited number of magazines and newspapers spurred Harley Procter to search for other ways to promote the soap products. Procter thus poured the company profits into preprinted magazine inserts that stood out among the black-and-white pages, and outdoor poster displays. The firm even offered free soap samples before purchase; when this inducement was not enough, it offered consumers extra bars free when they purchased a large quantity of soap. Enterprising Procter also knew how to get customers involved in a promotion. In 1892, for example, Procter offered prizes for the twelve best verses submitted praising Ivory Soap. The response was overwhelming. One competition alone attracted nearly twenty-four thousand entries, and the best verses appeared in monthly magazine ads over the next year and a half.

Procter & Gamble believed that keeping the Ivory name in front would sell the product, that is, the reputability of the manufacturer. "Keeping" meant continually, endlessly, but not monotonously. For decades P & G never repeated a single ad after it was run; therefore, the pressures on its agency to find new ways to say the same thing were monumental. In 1891, the catchphrase "It floats" was added to the Ivory slogan; the line eventually became so identified with the product that it was registered as a trademark with the U.S. Patent Office.

The Ivory advertisements always contained an interesting idea and an attractive illustration. The Ivory ads that covered the country all included a friendly appeal, an image that was Ivory's alone, and above all else, a selling idea. For instance, one 1894 Ivory ad claimed that a cake "will do more work than a cake of ordinary, poorly made soap and by its harmlessness will save five times the difference in price." Later ads urged readers to purchase Ivory Soap a dozen bars at a time and to keep a cake of the soap that floats handy in every room, since it could be used for different purposes; it was good in the bath and superior for general household use, laundering linens, and washing fine fabrics. To wash laces and other delicate things, for example, ads instructed housewives to pare the soap into "fine shavings," since the flakes would quickly dissolve in water and fill the sink with suds.[42]

Procter & Gamble engaged in many other activities to enhance Ivory's product concept and increase sales. It was early established that pictures of little children could sell anything. To emphasize the Ivory brand's mildness (safe enough to use on a baby's skin) and suitability for washing fine products, Harley Procter introduced the Ivory Baby and gave grocery stores a life-size

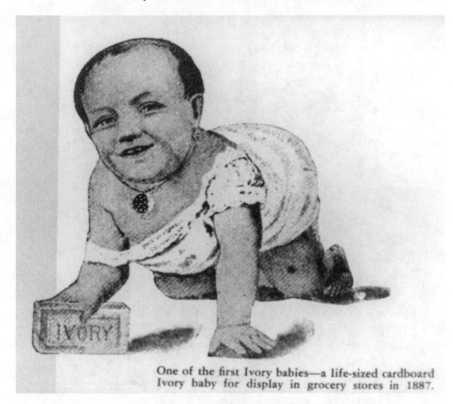

One of the first Ivory babies—a life-sized cardboard Ivory baby for display in grocery stores in 1887.

Fig. 3.11. One of the first Ivory babies, a life-sized cardboard display for grocery stores. From *Ivory 75*, Procter & Gamble, company publication, 1954. Courtesy of Hagley Museum and Library.

cardboard cutout to display. Interestingly, the first Ivory Baby appeared with a rather startling head of a forty-year-old man apparently pasted on a six-month-old body (see Fig. 3.11). Nineteenth-century Americans saw the child as an image of their own making, that is, a child grew from infant to "miniature adult."[43] A more credible portrayal of children came later, when the spread of image-making technologies changed how Americans perceived portraits of children. When Maude Humphrey, mother of actor Humphrey Bogart, painted a charming portrait of a young girl hanging the "family" wash out to dry—in this case, doll's clothes—for an early Ivory premium offer in 1896, it idealized a childhood of charm, beauty, and innocence (see Fig. 3.12). Procter asked retailers to display the featured picture as an inducement for customers to buy Ivory and thereby acquire their own copy of the

Fig. 3.12. An early Ivory premium offer, 1896.

print, without promotional lettering on the front and without extensive advertising on the reverse, in exchange for the soap wrappers.

Together the Ivory ads and sales promotions demonstrated to businesspeople a simple principle: Remind them. Advertising designed to keep the
name of the product in readers' minds had a positive effect; it increased

their familiarity with the brand, even though nothing new may have been said about the brand.[44] As a result, Procter & Gamble ranked as a leader in the soap industry "well up toward the top of the list, if not at the top."[45]

More important, Harley Procter had introduced an advertising strategy for Ivory Soap that continues virtually unchanged into its second century. The success of Ivory Soap was based on four factors: (1) Procter & Gamble had given the floating white soap a specific, identifiable brand name, Ivory, to symbolize purity; (2) the soap could be used for multiple purposes, yet it was safe for a baby's skin; (3) Ivory was identifiable by color and the ability to float; and, (4) Procter & Gamble told people about it through advertising. Instead of relying on local grocers to advertise that Ivory Soap was available in their stores, Procter & Gamble set out to convince the individual buyer that what she wanted was specifically Ivory Soap. The soap ads also described why the product was better than any other and how it could be used to benefit the purchaser. Although this appears obvious today, it was a novel concept at the time.

Other American soap manufacturers also added milder soaps to their product lines for washing the hands, face, and body. Among them was Enoch Morgan and Sons, who made the popular Sapolio soap for heavy cleaning, later adding "Hand Sapolio" to an already extensive line of soaps. The soapmaker initially positioned it as a heavy-duty handwasher for workers in machine shops, mines, mills, and foundries. Early advertisements claimed it instantly removed "Paint, Tar, Ink, Grease, and all stains; it also could be used for household cleaning purposes." To reach a wider audience and to compete with milder soaps like Ivory, Enoch Morgan and Sons wrapped each cake of "Hand Sappolio" in foil with a red band and shifted the selling pitch from a heavy handwasher to a beauty aid in the 1890s, calling it the "Dainty Woman's Friend." By using the soap, she "will gain, or retain a natural beauty that no cosmetics can produce."[46] Steady advertising in rural weekly newspapers, on the sides of streetcars, and in magazines, with slogans like "Be Clean" and "Sapolio Scours the World," made Sapolio a household word by the turn of the century.[47] The introduction of milder soaps such as Ivory and Hand Sapolio certainly pointed to the growing importance of washing the face, hands, and body, promising not only to cleanse but also to beautify.

Fig. 3.13. Pears' Soap, advertisement, *Godey's Lady's Book*, 1889.

Soap and Sentiment

As with Ivory Soap, catch slogans and a flood of advertising made Pears' Transparent Soap one of the most recognized brands of the day. The success of the Pears brand provides another early example of how people might buy a product not for the product itself, but for the particular image, one that might be tasteful, restrained, and sentimental.

Pears' Transparent Soap was the undertaking of Andrew Pears, who had worked in London since 1789 as a barber. Pears also used the shop for the manufacture and sale of cosmetics, dentrifices, and other beauty aids. An astute businessperson, he recognized the potential for a purer, gentler soap than the harsh ones then used in Britain, a cleansing agent that would treat kindly the delicate alabaster complexions of gentility. After much trial and error, Pears perfected a manufacturing process that removed impurities and refined the base soap before adding the delicate perfume of English garden flowers. Not only was the product high quality, it also possessed the novelty of being a transparent amber; the element that gave Pears' Soap a distinct image. Because of the high price of the bar, Pears enjoyed an exclusive following and advertised very little.

In 1865, Thomas A. Barratt, another Briton, bought a partnership in the prosperous Pears Soap Company and expanded advertising expenditures far beyond those of any previous manufacturers in England. Barratt lavishly used posters and newspaper advertisements containing glowing testimonials to Pears' Soap from prominent skin specialists and chemists, and from Lillie Langtree, the renowned actress and beauty. Barratt also devised a series of audacious schemes that earned valuable publicity for the soap, and others that also sparked controversy. Most indicative of Barratt's creativity was the importation of a quarter of a million French ten-centime pieces (accepted in lieu of a penny in Britain) that had the name Pears' Soap stamped on them; he then put them into circulation. The coins appeared to work as currency until an act of Parliament declared them illegal tender.[48]

After Barratt became sole owner of the Pears' Soap business, he began promoting the product in the United States, following the same extravagant practices. Barratt's publicity and advertising strategies had a great impact in America as well as England. First, Barratt persuaded the enormously influential Reverend Henry Ward Beecher to equate cleanliness with godliness, and Pears' Soap in particular; he then displayed this testimonial on the entire front page of the *New York Herald* newspaper and in issues of popular magazines in 1889 (see Fig. 3.13):

Henry Ward Beecher's Testimony

His opinion of Pear's Soap

> If cleanliness is next to godliness, Soap must be considered as a means of grace, and a clergyman who recommends moral things, should be willing to recommend soap. I am told that my commendation of PEARS' SOAP has opened for it a large sale in the United States. I am willing to stand by every word in favor of it that I ever uttered. A man must be fastidious indeed who is not satisfied with it.
>
> [Signed] Henry Ward Beecher[49]

As another means of gaining publicity, Barratt honored the arrival of newborn infants commemorated in the *New York Times*, sending the family a complimentary cake of soap and pictorial advertising leaflets.[50]

In order to promote Pears' Soap to a diverse audience in America, Barratt popularized soft-sell art in American advertising using conventions common in England, catchy slogans like "Matchless for the Complexion," and reproductions of full-color oil paintings. Although slogans had been used before, they did not catch the public's fancy the way Barratt's questions did. In one ad, a mother asked a child, "How do you spell Pears' Soap, my dear?" The child replied, "Why Ma, P-E-A-R-S, of course." Another series of full-page ads appeared with this famous caption: "Good morning, have you used Pears' Soap?" One amusing ad portrayed a Christmas scene with a cheerful child querying a surprised Santa Claus. Children, adults, and even political cartoonists and writers of the day so enjoyed the phrase "Have You Used Pears' Soap?" that they reportedly teased their acquaintances and friends with the query for years.[51] The slogans were simple and unchanging; only the pictures themselves changed

Pears' Soap advertising exemplified the trend toward color in full-page magazine ads. Barratt had combined original genre paintings or scenes of everyday life with the all-important product name, identifying trademark, and slogan. Unashamedly sentimental, the Pears ad campaign catered to the tastes of the day. Images of charming children, fashionable women, cute animals, and fragrant flowers proved popular, especially when aimed, as Pears' Soap

Fig. 3.14. The famous "Bubbles" Pears' Soap advertisement, *Harpers* magazine, 1888.

mostly was, at female buyers. The Pears' Soap iconography portrayed the home as a haven, an assemblage of domestic artifacts as display of respectable status, and idealized images of children as props of fashionable performance.

Perhaps the most celebrated Pears advertisement featured the use of a painting by Sir John Everett Millais, called "Bubbles." The curly-headed little model was the artist's grandson, who first made an appearance at a London gallery in the 1886 painting titled "A Child's World." The *Illustrated London News* then bought the picture for reproduction; and after its use, Barratt purchased the painting for twenty-two hundred pounds. Through this transaction the Pears Company gained an exclusive copyright on the image, but the agreement also required that the firm obtain the artist's permission before the painting could be modified for use as an advertisement by the addition of a bar of soap and type. Although Millais initially considered the matter a commercial exploitation of an artist's work, he did eventually agree to the idea after seeing the high quality of the proofs. As the number of individual reproductions ran into the millions, however, Millais felt obliged to defend himself against a hostile world until he died in 1896.[52] Certainly a success, even today, "Bubbles" remains one of the most instantly recognizable advertising symbols ever devised, reflecting Americans' fascination with childhood and youth (see Fig. 3.14). Many of the prints, which Pears' Soap later made available to the public, were framed and hung in living rooms around the world.[53]

Indeed, the purchase of Pears' Soap created an iconic connection in a sense with the brand and among the purchasers. The net effect of Pears' Soap advertising had been to exude an aura of quality. People who came across an ad for Pears' Soap, and then bought the product as a result, probably did share some similar attitudes. Using Pears' Soap declared that the users had a sense of gentility. Or that they thought they had made it. Or at the least that they wanted people to think they had made it. The purchase of Pears' Soap did indeed validate the perception of belonging to an interpretive community, the soap became an icon of a genteel culture—tasteful, restrained, and envied for its social status.[54]

Barratt had capitalized on two points. First, Pears' Transparent Soap was an immediately recognizable product, possessing the novelty of being transparent amber. The see-through quality of the soap also implied the absence of impurities, reinforcing the notion that the soap was safe and healthy for

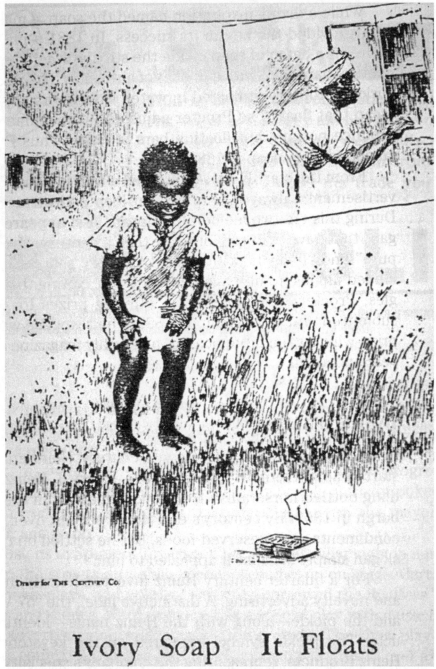

Fig. 3.15. Ivory Soap's memorable slogan first appeared in this 1891 ad.

even the finest complexions. Second, Barratt created an iconic connection between the brand name and the genteel culture represented by "Bubbles" with tasteful and restrained advertising. What people chose to put on the walls of their homes helped them create an environment in which they felt comfortable and which they believed reflected their tastes and values. Thus, the millions of Pears' Soap prints in the nineteenth-century homes validated that family values were the most important American values.

BRIGHTENING THE "DARK CORNERS OF THE EARTH"

Despite advances in soap advertising like Pears, there was at least one major failing: racist representations proliferated in soap ads during the latter half of the nineteenth century, a period of rising social tension as many whites feared losing their status. Evolutionary science fitted African American bodies into new visual classifications of inferiority; literature of advice reinforced the virtue of white, middle-class ideals, and advertising caricatured blacks as suitable only for menial labor. For white Americans, sustaining a visual distinction between white and black maintained an artifice of supremacy.

In any case, the people of color portrayed in ads with racial overtones can be categorized into two sets of stereotypes that demonstrated what the products could do for consumers. One set of character types appeared incompetent and unattractive; the other group was competent enough to select the better product and therefore prosper. In so doing, advertisements, package illustrations, and trademarks perpetuated grotesque racial caricatures and stereotypes. For example, such images attempted to starkly define African Americans as the opposite of the prevailing American beauty ideal. Kinky hair, dirty or ragged clothing, apish features, and shiny black faces dehumanized the group while denying them social and political equality. African Americans were frequently stereotyped as childlike and ignorant, reinforced by images of the elderly "Uncle Tom," the lazy "Sambo," the plantation "Mammy," and the child or "pickaninny" (see Fig. 3.15). Other advertisements also stereotyped Asian Americans, Native Americans, and the foreign born. The ads took a specific trait and incorpo-

Fig. 3.16. Illustration from Bogue Soap, trade card, no date.

rated it into a racial or ethnic character. Both the illustration and the wording of the text expressed ethnic differences. For instance, a trade card for Bogue Soap pictured an unattractive Asian American with long braids and slanted eyes with the following caption: "Lookee . . . No Boilee! Washee Washee. Wellee Quickee" (see Fig. 3.16). Appearance not only indexed the moral and social status of an entire population, but also equated clean, white skin with social superiority.

Other soap purveyors used before-and-after formats throughout the nineteenth century, offering images of personality or lifestyle transformations from using the advertised product. These accounts were narrated by means of pictures and minimal text. Tales about soaps that magically turned red, brown, and even black skin into white complexions also appeared repeatedly. The setting for this story varied from the plantation to the city to the frontier; but in each ad, the soap-using characters were magically transformed because their dark complexion had turned lily white. For instance, one children's storybook featured six panels with charming illustrations; the tale told children how a "little red skinned Indian," when rubbed with Bell's Buffalo Soap, not only turned white, but "it gave him fuller scope than he had ever known before."[55] Along the same lines, a four-panel trade card, titled "A Tale of the Larkin Soaps," recounted a similar before-and-after tale, but aimed at an older audience. As the verse went, three "white Caucasian maids" turned their backs on three "Turks whose skin was brown," but with rare courage they went to work upon each Turk with Sweet Home Soap:

> And scrubbed and scrubbed and scrubbed:
> Their features bright
> Grew milky white
> And light as sunny day—
> Instead of mad and being sad
> The Turks and maids were both so glad,
> That to this talk we need but add—
> They married right away![56]

By promoting what the advertised soap could do for Native Americans, African Americans, and the foreign born, the admakers thus exaggerated the benefits of passing for white and what failure to use the product implied about one's character.

Notions of Anglo-American cleanliness in the nineteenth century were also asserted in relation to people of color around the world. Nineteenth-century travelers, missionaries, anthropologists, and scientists habitually viewed cleanliness as a function of race. Even though various cultures perceived cleanliness differently, Americans persistently proclaimed the superiority of white, middle-class rituals of cleanliness. Many Americans found dirtiness in the foreign born, especially as they asserted that they considered darker gradations of skin inferior to their pure, lily-white ideal. "The Dutch are the cleanest people in the world, and the latest published statistics show that Holland, in proportion to its population, is the most moral nation on the globe," claimed the *Ladies' Home Journal* in 1896. Once seen as a virtue with spiritual, moral, and material rewards, cleanliness came also to be an indicator that some European-Americans, white people, were more civilized than others.

Fig. 3.17. Sapolio, advertisement, *Ladies' Home Journal*, July 1899.

During the 1890s, soap took on new magical powers. It emerged as a powerful symbol of purification, civilization, and progress that reached beyond the iconic. The assumptions behind it implied an ability to transform not only individuals, but also entire populations from uncivilized to civilized enlightened people. In particular, advertisements for Sapolio, Babbitt, and Pears' soaps asserted Anglo-Saxon virtues, offering cleanliness as a talisman, as well as a justification for American expansion,

For example, one 1899 Sapolio ad ran this bold headline: "The strong right arm that holds for peace shall with our nation's emblem go to darker lands beyond the seas, and light them with Sapolio." The text, or body copy, goes on to explain the power of the brand:

> An American product that has won the patronage of the civilized world. The use of Sapolio was portrayed as a distinguishing mark of enlightened people. Darkness, dirt and disease are driven before it. No nation is stronger than its homes. Sapolio makes bright, clean, and happy homes, and a powerful, progressive, peaceful nation is the result. Sapolio must clean, the flag must civilize.[57]

Indeed, this advertisement and others not only promoted cleanliness as a marker of civilization, but the rhetoric to lighten the lands overseas by driving out darkness, dirt, and disease further reinforced the assimilationist message (see Fig. 3.17).

Similarly, B. T. Babbitt's Best Soap placed the Babbitt factory at the core of civilization. In the 1880s and 1890s, the dominating image of countless trade and show cards was Babbitt's factory with its belching smokestacks; it contrasted sharply with five vignettes of non-Western peoples who eagerly received crates of Babbitt's Soap (see Fig. 3.18). The slogans "Soap for all nations" and "Cleanliness is the scale of civilization" boosted Babbitt's contributions to progress as provider of soap's civilizing touch. Of course, the nineteenth-century ethnocentric implication that exotic peoples could not be civilized until they received the goods of Western production, in this case Babbitt's Soap, was not limited to the soapmakers. Certainly, the Babbitt campaign was a concrete example of the myth of technology as savior and protector, a belief that technology by definition is beneficial, that nearly all problems are solvable with new inventions. Overall, the scene suggested an ecstatic confidence in the future of the United States domi-

Fig. 3.18. B. T. Babbitt's Best Soap, trade card.

nated by white European Americans made possible by the technology of the factory and perfected in a remote land. With such a combination of technology and American expansion, the horizon for the Anglo-Saxon entrepreneurs appeared limitless and infinitely promising.

One of the most explicit of these ads appeared in 1899, in a period of deepening anti-imperialism. At this time, *McClure's Magazine* featured an illustrated tribute to Admiral George Dewey on the cover and articles about him by Governor Theodore Roosevelt among others. On the inside cover of the same issue, however, a full-page ad showed Dewey washing his hands with Pears' Soap, surrounded by images that symbolized progress (see Fig. 3.19). The text of the ad drew from a poem titled "The White Man's Burden" by Rudyard Kipling, the famous English poet.

> The first step towards lightening The White Man's Burden is through teaching the virtues of cleanliness. Pears' Soap is a potent factor in brightening the dark corners of the earth as civilization advances, while amongst the cultured of all nations it holds the highest place—it is the ideal toilet soap.[58]

Fig. 3.19. Pears' Soap, advertisement, *McClure's* magazine, October 1899.

Typical of the period, the phrase "virtues of cleanliness" referred to the idea that a good many Americans as well as people in England believed that appearance and character were commensurate. "Brightening the dark corners of the earth" could be interpreted not only as cleansing or purifying, but as literally "lightening" the region by white settlement, industry, and commerce, justified as progress. Hence, cleanliness expressed Anglo-Saxon virtues and civilization, and it justified white supremacy in a period of American expansion. Thus, advertising conventions reinforced this racial and national taxonomy. Soap had become the icon for white supremacy and capitalistic hegemony.

The Pears' Soap ad may not have sparked controversy, but Kipling's poem did. One stanza of Kipling's verses may be interpreted by some as an appeal to the United States to join Great Britain in controlling the tropics, in particular, India, the Philippines, and Cuba:

> Take up the White Man's burden—
> Send forth the best ye breed—
> Go, bind your sons to exile,
> To serve your captive's need;
> To wait in heavy harness,
> On fluttered folk and wild—
> Your new-caught sullen peoples
> Half devil and half child.

Subsequently, a flood of anti-imperialist editorials, essays, and poems appeared in major newspapers, influential magazines, and the black press in 1899, the same year that the Pears' ad appeared. Critics claimed that the motive was not the civilizing and Christianizing of all but for financial profit. For example, David Starr Jordan, vice president of the Anti-Imperialist League, argued that the "control of the tropics" thinly disguised the old spirit of slavery. "The white man's burden, in the British sense, is to force the black man to support himself and the white man, too."[59] Similar editorials appeared in the black press. The *Washington Bee*, for instance, emphasized that "the self-appointed mission to humanize other races will not be successful unless the operators depart from their unchristian moorings," and act justly and fairly toward "colored people."[60]

Ironically, the same critique that the motive was not moral uplift, but profit for individual enterprise, can be also made of the extensive advertising practices of the soap industry. Popularizing this "conviction of authorities" may have been in the spirit of moral uplift; but it also tied in with the spirit of American enterprise, the profit motive. Thus industry was part of a larger attempt by the state, civic groups, and churches to transform Americans into their vision of clean and proper-looking bodies. By the dawn of the twentieth century, this cultural discourse promoted a powerful message. Cleanliness was equated with success and the American way of life, reinforcing a mix of private and public values, and pointing in the direction of moral uplift. Americans had not come clean enough.

The rise of the mass market coincided with the rise of advertising to sell soap. Since the racism of the period was embedded in Western culture, it became enmeshed in the mass marketing that arose in the late nineteenth century. It would not disappear any time soon. Meanwhile the businesses that disseminated their products along with racist assumptions also began to move into philanthropic arenas. Soap manufacturers clearly had an interest in the health revolution they had, in part, informed. Thus, it is important to investigate the connection between soap businesses and institutions like settlement houses, public health education, Americanization, and industrial programs, as well as the ongoing evolution of the bathroom. The next chapter explores how these notions became commonplace: how soap manufacturers developed an ever-increasing variety of products to sell, how they further developed the means to distribute their goods coast to coast, and how they employed more scientific arguments to promote their products through newspapers, magazines, and direct mail.

4

Soap, Sex, and Science, 1900 to 1920

Order, efficiency, and scientific principles became the watch-words of the Progressive Era (1901 to 1916). Through collective efforts individuals, citizen groups, government agencies, and industries revamped, reformed, or otherwise sought to improve virtually every aspect of American society. Municipal govern-ments and the nation's banking system were streamlined; housing and health care standards were raised; public educa-tion was expanded; and the federal government addressed the child labor issue. But through a pervasive field of laws, taboos, and censorship, sanitarians relying on institutions instructed a nation bent on progress that filth bred chaos and barbarism, while cleanliness ensured order and advancement.

Soapmakers encouraged the sanitary reform movement as well. Ad campaigns like "Spotless Town" popularized cleanli-ness, as well as making Sapolio Soap a household word. In 1900, a series of lighthearted streetcar ads for Sapolio began to appear about Spotless Town, a quaint, cobblestoned Dutch vil-lage whose inhabitants praised the qualities of Sapolio. The ads introduced new characters, eventually totaling twelve in all, as

When Dr. Brown prescribes a bath,
He's quite a staunch Sapoliopa'h.
The vial that he's dipping in
Is violent upon the skin;
But he will quickly cleanse it, though,
By using HAND SAPOLIO.

The Cook, of course, you understand,
She holds the grater in her hand.
Which is the greater you demand?
Why that upon the other hand—
The right hand's never left, you know,
It holds her HAND SAPOLIO.

Though bones are hardly fit to eat,
They're quite a bonus with the meat,
And help to make the market pay—
It really is the only weigh.
It makes a profit clean as snow,
And fair as HAND SAPOLIO.

This Cop who coppers all the street,
And from his beat beats off the beat,
Now rests from his arrests, till "Pieece"
In strident tones disturbs his peace.
His precinct he cleans up, you know,
With pluck and HAND SAPOLIO.

Fig. 4.1. Hand Sapolio, one page from *Ye Booke of Spotless Town*, 1909.

the series progressed (see Fig. 4.1). The ads gained such public favor that many people actually looked forward to each chapter, as they met the doctor, the cook, the butcher, and so on. Allusions to Spotless Town soon became a familiar sight in newspapers, on the streets, in public speeches, and even on stage. Cartoons, toys, books, plays, and political speeches borrowed Spotless Town phrases and scenes. Advertising manager Artemas

Ward even created a special play with music based on these advertisements and supplied the scenery. The show played all over the country to raise money for charity, and as a result, over a thousand proud towns featured Sapolio in their local clean-up campaigns.[1]

"Successful soap manufacturers owe it to the progress of the world to point out to the public how everybody can become more successful, more healthy, happy and contented," proclaimed George Schmidt in the trade magazine *Soap Gazette and Perfumer* in 1908.[2] In a regular column called "The World's Progress and Soap," the Chicago soap manufacturer wrote passionately about cleanliness over a twenty-year period, from 1900 to 1920. In a short time, sales of soap rose sharply, as the product became an affordable necessity for Americans across the economic spectrum. To all appearances, the soap industry had embraced Progressive notions and set out to remake the lives of Americans, delivering the message that there was health and wealth in cleanliness.

Such a large-scale effort to bolster the virtue of cleanliness was inherently linked with the progress of the nation and of the world. Still, these messages of moral uplift did not fully explain how the American culture of cleanliness came to be established. The underlying motive of this self-appointed mission of the soap trade went beyond moral uplift; it also concerned increasing profits to individual enterprise. Indeed, cleanliness had become big business. Important to the country's standard of living, health, and social welfare, soap was also a source of big profits. Certainly popularizing cleanliness may have been in the spirit of moral uplift and the Progressive Era; but it also tied in with the spirit of American enterprise, the profit motive.

THE GREAT UNWASHED

In the eyes of upper- and middle-class Americans, the "great unwashed" were immigrants from Southern Europe, who had recently arrived in the country's cities, and, later, blacks from the rural South. The burden of cleanliness primarily fell on wives and mothers, but the practice of cleanliness meant more than keeping home and clothing clean. It also included personal hygiene and bathing. This posed special problems, because many immigrants considered the practice useless and only occasionally bathed during the summer months in local rivers or streams. Even people who recognized the importance of taking frequent baths usually bathed only on Saturday evenings or before holidays—hence the phrase the "Saturday night special."[3] They also lacked plumbing and privacy as they waited their turn for a hot shower at a public bath or a large washtub at home, until improved and affordable housing included bathtubs and toilets.

Yet the scientific germ theory had begun to make significant inroads into American thought. As late as World War I, most Americans considered sewer gas to be a source of disease, and fears about sewers heightened the ardor for cleanliness.[4] Nevertheless, germ theory not only provided leading sanitarians with yet another rationale for cleaning up towns and cities, but also provided marketers with another argument to work into their sales pitches. Sanitary reformers, druggists, complexion specialists, advertisers, and columnists in magazines and newspapers all offered advice. As a result, the proliferation of soap products and the discourse about hygiene definitely recast nineteenth-century attitudes toward personal cleanliness.

"Settling" among the Less Fortunate

Settlement workers, who included aspiring students and teachers, also powerfully internalized regimens of cleanliness and discipline. The national settlement movement, which began in the 1890s, was dominated by the work of Jane Addams; no formal organization was established until the National Federation of Settlements formed in 1911. By that time, around four hundred settlements had become pivotal institutions in both social reform and politics. This reform movement had an upper-middle-class character that embodied not only progressive sentiments of female emancipation, but also a sense of moral superiority. Drawing on the talents of college-trained women, the settlement houses were elite, selective outposts, like many of the women's clubs and voluntary societies.[5]

By "settling" among the less fortunate, educated female settlement workers could transmit middle-class values and practices to the urban poor and newly arrived immigrants. The women and children who participated in the settlement programs learned the right way of living—that is, the virtues of thrift, cleanliness, orderliness, refinement, manners, culture, responsibility, and citizenship. In all aspects of their work, the settlement workers stressed cleanliness relentlessly, attacking aspects of American life that they viewed as unhygienic. Settlement residents imparted the basic lessons of domestic science, or household affairs, while visiting nurses taught health and hygiene. Residents also extended their housekeeping practices as a model into the community, by inspecting water supplies, monitoring garbage disposal and sanitary conditions, reporting violations, and insisting on improved municipal services.

Although such demonstrations of domestic practices formed the basis of settlement activities, inadequate facilities made clean clothes and regular baths unobtainable for many working-class housewives. For example, settlements like the Neighborhood House in Gary, Indiana, provided the conveniences of showers, baths, and laundry facilities that its neighboring houses lacked. The resident workers at the Hull House in Chicago took a more activist approach, agitating for the extension of basic city services to the slums.[6]

Such preoccupation with the overwhelming problems of city life was common among the settlement workers of this era. After college, many of these urban pioneers found themselves suffocated by the sociocultural expectations of their position. In the settlement context, however, these women could preserve a collegial spirit while attempting to solve social problems. Although few settlement workers made a lifetime career of it, others equally capable of making social contributions were eager to replace them. In any case, these settlements or residencies introduced many middle- and upper-class women to members and lifestyles of other social classes, provided them with remarkable female role models, and involved them in a network of knowledgeable, experienced social reformers. As experts in social welfare and spokeswomen for the "other half," many of these women became lobbyists or ended up in government, working for improved services and laws to benefit women and children. Settlement workers, who recognized their own limitations in meeting the social needs of their poorer neighbors, also encouraged public schools and businesses to use their influence to turn cleanliness into a cultural value.

In the 1910s, the focus of public health campaigns shifted attention from public cleanliness to personal hygiene. Schools, organized groups, boards of health, and businesses promoted cleanliness in both schools and the workplace through advertising. Consequently, schools and health officials conducted the crusade against diseases like tuberculosis and hookworm with a focus on personal hygiene. Proponents stressed that children had power over their health despite the hazards of untreated sewage, stagnant water, and unsanitary practices. Cleanliness standards rose quickly as the result of explicit warnings from home economists, health practitioners, and manufacturers of sanitary and cleaning products, who distributed booklets and ran lurid ads describing infectious germs.

For instance, Metropolitan Insurance joined the corps of activists with a successful advertising campaign. "Cleanliness" and "health" formed the foundation for the firm's "Health Campaign" aimed at the large numbers of immigrants who invested in insurance policies. Metropolitan then sent its agents out to befriend these families, encouraging "long life" and "great living," and handing out pamphlets that explained the causes of tuberculosis and ways to avoid the disease. In the last panel of one of the booklets, families were told that a "bath a day keeps sickness away." Metropolitan also put disposable drinking cups on several railroad lines and as a promotion gave away thousands of flyswatters imprinted with a powerful message: "Clean Homes, Pure Food, Clean Milk, No Flies and No Mosquitoes."[7]

In school and home, however, child training remained largely in the hands of women, who instructed their youngsters in moral fundamentals, disciplined them, and built character. When a massive number of southern and eastern Europeans immigrated to America, educating a new generation of Americans for citizenship in an industrialized America became as important as teaching reading, writing, and arithmetic. Learning English was only the beginning of an immigrant child's education. With an increased focus on character, textbooks emphasized such values as obedience, thrift, patriotism, piety, honesty, and cleanliness. The lessons also gave students explicit instructions on such personal cleanliness rituals as washing their hands and cleaning their nails. Indeed, school and health reformers went to great lengths to socialize and integrate the millions of poor immigrant children into American society.

Inspired by settlement work, many public schools evolved into neighborhood centers. They introduced courses in domestic science and the trades, gave free medical examinations, built public baths, and offered evening classes in English and citizenship. When children were in school, their mothers sometimes attended classes on child care and housekeeping or received home visits. Such school programs were fueled by ideas of a new breed of health educators.

Sally Lucas Jean, a school nurse trained in education, was one such woman. In 1918, Lucas formed the Child Health Organization (CHO) and used techniques similar to those used earlier by the National Tuberculosis Association. In this program, educators focused on teaching health habits through active participation, hoping to change schoolchildren's behavior and create in them a new hygiene consciousness. Bathing regularly, washing hands before meals, and brushing teeth daily were among the health chores that, when completed, earned children a promotion from "page" to "knight." The CHO staff also organized youngsters into toothbrush brigades, introduced them to a health clown named CHO-CHO, told them soap-and-water tales, and urged them to draw posters and to compose health slogans. Children also brought home these instructions in cleanliness. By bringing such activities into the classroom, the CHO educators effectively changed the behavior of many children and also influenced their parents.[8]

Ultimately, the settlement and sanitary reform movements cannot be said to have been male dominated, as were other traditional public boards in the community of the period. In fact, the movements sought to reform and organize gender, not merely use it. This gender reform meant that some women were given an opportunity to acquire a relatively powerful identity as rescuer, reformer, and even expert. Nevertheless, the vision of American womanhood promoted by the movement stressed health, women's work and role, and good social values, a view clearly reinforcing women's ascribed sphere of home and family. Paradoxically, certain middle-class women built significant careers around the sanitary reform and the settlement movements. These women doctors, social workers, and club members traveled extensively among all social classes protected by their profession. Perhaps they did not realize that their unprecedented freedom was built on a prior traditional assumption: a woman's place was in the home, which accounted for the development of the domestic woman as the primary agent of cleanliness and guardian of the home. Thus, bodily health, cleanliness, and order continued as women's moral imperative, with these values associated with genteel living and respectability.

Americanizing Agencies

Lessons on personal hygiene were also taught in the workplace as part of a general effort to promote a more efficient and disciplined workforce as the United States became more industrial, urban, and ethnically diverse. Both physical and moral cleanliness had emerged as important attributes for workers in modern society. A clean home reduced the likelihood of illness and absenteeism, and a clean mind provided a foundation for the construction of good work habits. Emulating the settlement programs, employers began to experiment with English instruction and citizenship in the early twentieth century, since immigrants spent most of their waking hours in the workplace. The World War I era further encouraged employers to create English-speaking citizens who would be loyal to both their country and their company. After the war, programs thus multiplied for socializing and acculturating newcomers in an attempt to "remake" the working class. Many manufacturers embraced Progressive Era notions, believing they served their need to create a healthy, disciplined work force and showed immigrants how to fulfill their desire to be proper American citizens. Companies like Ford, Kohler, and International Harvester adopted practices from settlement programs to achieve their ends.

One of the most ambitious of these programs was launched by Henry Ford. The automaker pioneered a number of practices, including providing his employees with unusually high wages (five dollars a day), a shorter workday, incentive pay, and an elaborate employee welfare program. Ford recognized the need to form a "labor force" and ensure good health, particularly as the United States became more ethnically diverse. According to James R. Barrette, Ford had accepted prevailing Progressive Era notions that the environment shaped one's behavior and attitudes; thus, the automaker set out "to remake the lives of immigrant workers and win them over to thrift, efficiency, and company loyalty."[9] Starting in 1914, the Ford automobile plant in Highland Park, Michigan, instituted a program that linked its hiring, firing, and promotion practices to education. Besides English, the workers learned how to eat, what to wear, and when to bathe. Company caseworkers not only investigated employee records but also examined workers' homes, looking for signs of uncleanness, debauchery, and neglected children.

The International Harvester Company, based in the Midwest, also adopted these practices. The company emphasized English classes for workers that would also supposedly promote habits of discipline, safety, and sanitation. Walter Kohler of Kohler Manufacturing Company, a producer of plumbing fixtures based in Sheboygan, Wisconsin, also inculcated high standards of clean living in immigrant workers. In 1918, Kohler built the American Club to give immigrant workers a "hygienic place to live."[10] It included dormitory rooms, a pub, a bowling alley, and a dining hall, and offered lessons in English and American citizenship.[11]

As in the sanitary reform and settlement movements, women fundamentally shaped the Americanization programs. The professions of teaching, settlement house work, and public health brought those women into close contact with immigrant families. Women also assumed major roles in the corporate and government organizations that provided the Americanization movement with its structure, ideas, and legitimacy. Thousands of women taught English, civics, and hygiene in schools, settlement houses, and factories; and as the Americanizers began to address the immigrant mother's role in the home, they urged her to maintain the new American standards of diet, hygiene, and child care in producing a second generation of "true Americans."[12] Keeping clean was not only healthy; it was patriotic, success-driven, and very American.

The cultural discourse promoted a powerful message. Cleanliness was equated with success and the American way of life, reinforcing a mix of private and public values, both pointing in the direction of moral uplift. But the progress toward universal personal cleanliness was still restricted by the lack of affordable cleanliness technologies. Not until World War I did reliable heating devices, good plumbing, and built-in tubs and sinks put convenient bathing within reach of ordinary citizens.

THE MODERN BATHROOM

Having a "modern" indoor bathroom separated the middle class from the lower classes in the early twentieth century. As personal cleanliness rituals became more complex, so did the interiors of bathrooms, from wall coverings to fixtures to accessories. Advice about the well-appointed bathroom

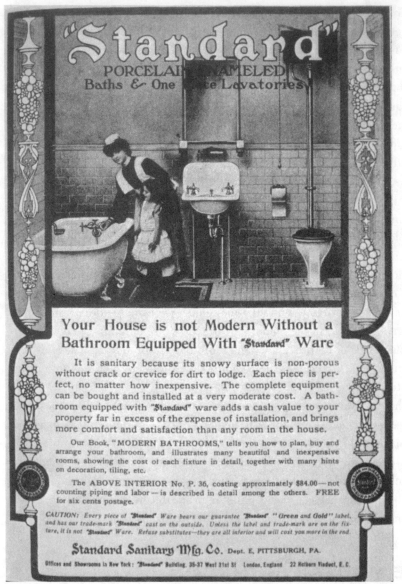

Fig. 4.2. The Standard Company promotes the modern bathroom, *McClure's* magazine, 1905.

proliferated, providing evidence of the growing importance of the bathroom to middle-class Americans. As Mary Wood Allen proclaimed in the 1905 book *What a Young Woman Ought to Know*, "Bathing appliances are marks of civilization, and the bathroom is becoming a necessity."[13]

Women's pages in newspapers, columns in popular magazines, Sunday magazine inserts, advertisements, and elaborate point-of-sale presentations offered outlets for promoting the latest bathroom fixtures, tiles, and wall coverings. In particular, home-decorating advice spurred demand by showing consumers the possibilities of bathroom interiors and urging them to install a complete line of facilities. As bathroom interiors became more important, experts urged women to put decorating money earmarked for the bathroom into nonabsorbent wall surfaces like tiles, rather than any other coverings, since they were practical and sanitary. By this time, glazed ceramic tiles were available in white, buff, and gray, as well as the more expensive tints of roseate sunsets, pearl, and gold. If the expense of fully tiled walls was too great, partially tiling the walls was a viable compromise; paint was the other recommended wall treatment. Wallpaper was to be avoided in the bathroom unless varnished since it was too absorbent; wood paneling was also not recommended because it could harbor the prolific "water bug," or roach.[14] Homeowners also had an increasing array of plumbing fixtures to chose from, but all were uniformly white.

By World War I, the production of bathroom fixtures had become a big business. Names like Mott Iron Works, Standard Sanitary Manufacturing (later American Standard), Crane, and Kohler had become household words synonymous with bathtubs, sinks, toilets, and other bathroom fixtures (see Fig. 4.2). The growing importance of bathroom interiors was evident in the trade catalogs of two national manufacturers over two decades, Standard and Kohler. A Pittsburgh supplier of bathroom fixtures, Standard issued the first edition in a series of catalogs. The 1906 catalog contained almost twice as many pages as the previous edition, filled with illustrated plans for bathroom, kitchen, and laundry interiors. Fixtures for a complete bathroom, including bath, lavatory, and toilet, could be had for $69.75.[15] But this sales pitch maintained that a bathroom was not complete without some style of shower, retailing for $25 to $500. To sell more luxurious fixtures, Standard also began to promote the bath-a-day habit. "Beauty depends more upon health than anything else, and one of the best methods of gaining and retaining perfect health is to bathe, and bathe often, once a day always, but twice is much better."[16]

At the same time, bathtubs evolved from modest portable affairs to built-in models, forming a permanent part of the bathroom interior. Kohler

Fig. 4.3. Kohler Company's innovative built-in bathtub, *Saturday Evening Post*, July 5, 1915.

introduced the one-piece, built-in bath in 1911; its production was considered almost revolutionary in the industry at the time. Previously, built-in baths were cast in two separate sections, the tub proper and the apron, or exposed side, which were fitted together by the plumber when installed. The one-piece tub eliminated all crevices, joints, and seams, but its strongest selling point was that the design was more sanitary and attractive. Advertisements told the story of Kohler's innovation and touted the distinctive features of its one-piece enameled bathtubs, lavatories, and sinks, emphasizing the "hygienic value" of the design and that the smooth, white surface was "easily and quickly cleaned" (see Fig. 4.3).[17] By World War I, the Kohler Company filled a 214-page catalog with descriptions and illustrations of its plumbing products, offering five models of roll-rim tubs, built-in baths, enameled iron toilets, lavatories, and other fixtures. More important, the built-in tub design opened the door to the evolution of the bathtub as Americans know it today.

Having successfully promoted bathroom equipment as a tie-in to building new houses, the plumbingware industry found a new market in improving old houses, encouraging consumers to modernize their bathroom facilities. There was plenty of new housing construction to occupy the plumbing supply trade until 1917, but many people found it beyond their means to build a new home with modern facilities after World War I. In 1918, *Printers' Ink* observed that there was still plenty of business in repair work. "When a man builds he buys bathrooms things, the house and fixtures grow old together, but it rarely went so far as to include the purchase of completely new fixtures, unless a house was being completely remodeled or modernized."[18] Thus, the slowdown in building encouraged some plumbingware firms to identify previously "unrecognized" needs and to show Americans how to fulfill their desires.

Thomas Maddock Sons Company of Trenton, New Jersey, was one such firm. Maddock reasoned that there were over six million private homes in America in which the bathroom fixtures were antiquated, ugly, and simply unhygienic. Why shouldn't the company turn its selling efforts toward modernizing those homes? Using the slogan "New bathrooms for old," Maddock launched a campaign to counteract a widespread impression that modern bathroom fixtures were very expensive by explaining that modernizing cost much less than most people realized. A handsome illustrated booklet, entitled "Bathroom Individuality," gave costs for seven complete bathrooms.[19] Maddock also ran a series of local newspaper ads that appeared with the imprint of the local plumbing jobber, aiming at both the homeowner and the hotelier. For homeowners, one ad depicted a housewife down on her knees scrubbing beside an old-fashioned tub with this telling headline: "How long are you going to keep your wife at this—trying to keep the bathroom clean." Another depicted a housewife showing a visitor her new bathroom with an air of pride: "You remember how it used to look." Other copy emphasized that a good bathroom helped to rent a house quicker. In the same vein, an ad targeted to hoteliers made an economic appeal, warning that competitors may be getting their lost business with new bathroom facilities.[20] The message was simple: It paid to modernize the bathroom.

THE SOAP TRADE AND MASS SELLING

The development of chain stores emerged as the next step in the mass retailing of brand-name, packaged soaps. Previously, the typical shopkeeper handled everything from purchasing and selling to displaying and advertising a wide variety of products. General merchandisers and food retailers, followed by drugstores, then began to apply the same economies of scale that had been used in manufacturing to sell their goods. That is, a centrally managed operation placed large orders at low prices, established low profit margins, and made money through volume sales; part of the savings were passed along to the customer. For example, the well-known Cream of Wheat cereal sold for twelve cents in the economy stores as opposed to fourteen cents in the traditional stores; similar low prices appeared on other well-known brands.[21]

In time, centrally managed chain stores like the Great Atlantic and Pacific Tea Company (A&P), Woolworth, J. C. Penney, and Rexall replaced many small shopkeepers who simply could not match the chains' variety and prices. Consumers could walk into the stores, view displays of packaged goods, and compare prices as more stores posted uniform, fixed prices. Still, urban groceries generally remained comparatively small and carried only a narrow selection of goods compared to the thousands of items that fill today's supermarket (see Fig. 4.4). In 1911, for example, a typical A&P grocery store in New York City carried only about twenty-five different product categories such as tea, butter, baking powder, and cornstarch.[22] Although most soap manufacturers expanded their product distribution through the new grocery and drugstore chains, the Larkin Company continued to pioneer new direct marketing strategies, opening new opportunities for women in business.

Fig. 4.4. A typical grocery store with branded, packaged goods. Clerks obtained what customers requested from the shelves and often made suggestions what to buy. Courtesy of Pictorial Collection, Hagley Museum and Library, no. 82.307.2, S81-19.

The Larkin Idea

The Larkin Company did not depend on advertising; rather, the firm capitalized on patterns of women's social life—their customs of visiting, conversations, and religious observances—so much of its trade was local and word-of-mouth. The company recruited housewives and even neighborhood boys and girls to market its products door-to-door, much like Avon later did. Women seized their chances, becoming entrepreneurs, distributors, and promoters. "Larkin Secretaries," as they were called, organized "Larkin Clubs" in their neighborhoods. The "Larkin Idea," as the company called the plan, was that each month each of the ten members of the club would pledge to order one dollar's worth of Larkin goods. That month, one member selected at random would receive the ten-dollar premium; the next month the premium would go to another member.[23]

As Larkin's business grew, so did the product line, promotional materials, and employee benefits. By 1905, the company catalog boasted 116 products, including soaps, toiletries, shampoo, jellies, coffees and teas, extracts, cocoa,

Fig. 4.5. One could furnish an entire home running Larkin Clubs, from the *Larkin Plan*, catalog no. 79, 1918.

spices, soups, and perfumes. Thirteen years later, it advertised 600 products and offered 1600 premiums. Only the Montgomery Ward and Sears, Roebuck catalogs offered a greater variety of products.[24] In addition to the catalogs, the promotional magazine the "Larkin Idea" also informed the club secretaries of new products and marketing strategies. Other promotional materials encouraged women to set up "Larkin Pantries" and decorate their home with the "Larkin Look."[25] By 1918, a home could be completely stocked and furnished with Larkin goods. Furniture, china, silverware, rugs, lamps, clocks, school supplies, bibles, apparel, and even wallpaper and paint could be obtained as premiums from Larkin orders (see Fig. 4.5).

Once the Larkin secretaries had accepted the premium benefits, the company expanded the range of employee benefits to other realms of social life. There was a Larkin Drum Corps, a Larkin Women's Council, baseball teams, pool and reading rooms, employee savings plans, and even a Larkin country club located on the shores of Lake Erie near Buffalo, New York.[26] Together, the premium and employee benefits programs served to foster loyalty to the company, rewarded performance, and created a sense of community. In the late 1930s, the company hit hard times and has since closed; but Larkin products, especially the furniture, are highly collectible today.

Although Larkin's trade did not depend on advertising, large-scale campaigns helped other soapmakers like Procter & Gamble, Lever Brothers, and Colgate to turn their essentially undifferentiated products into desirable products and their trademarks into icons. Brand names like Ivory, Lifebuoy, and Palmolive are still well known today.

Picture Magic

By 1910 magazines were filled with colorful pictures. Ad makers reproduced original paintings, delicate pen-and-ink drawings, and sketches of full-page advertisements that quickly became important sources of product image building. These ads sought to combine style, design, and tone to create an instantaneous impression called "picture magic."[27]

In this era, there was no distinction between gallery and commercial artists, and the artists shuttled back and forth between the two. During this period, almost all advertising art was done by contract, directly between the agency or magazine and the artist. Getting a "name"—a recognized artist—to draw one's product was a subtle endorsement of the quality of the product. In 1902, *Profitable Advertising* observed that a fundamental and far-reaching change was taking place, what could be called the pictorial trend: "People no longer look through the advertising pages only to discover what advertisers are offering, but also to see in what form the offers are presented."[28]

Advertisers used new printing techniques to introduce vivid paintings and photographic images that challenged the conventional look of black-and-white ads. The creators of these early visual images were among the most skilled of American artists such as Frederic Remington, Maxfield Parrish, Joseph C. Leyendecker, N. C. Wyeth, and Norman Rockwell, among others. They worked variously as designers of magazine covers, creators of literary posters, illustrators of magazine articles, and designers of better advertisements. It should be noted that, from the beginning, being an illustrator or an advertising artist could be extraordinarily profitable, bringing commissions that exceeded the annual salary of a college professor for each ad created or picture drawn.[29] Although the advertising field also offered

Fig. 4.6. Ivory Soap, advertisement, illustrated by J. C. Leyendecker, 1900.

opportunities for talented women such as illustrators Maude Humphrey and Jessica Wilcox Smith, most were hidden in support roles and not credited for their creative contributions.[30]

Certainly Ivory succeeded in getting eminently respectable artists to create and sign the stunning pictures of people washing with Ivory Soap. For example, Joseph C. Leyendecker painted a detailed ad for Ivory Soap (see Fig. 4.6). Leyendecker clearly understood the properly solemn and reverent attitude appropriate to the product; the Byzantine style of illustration clearly made the iconic connection between the Ivory brand and the popular virtue that cleanliness was next to godliness. The ad showed a tall, austere figure wearing the cinctured robe of the Franciscan order, reverently holding a bar of Ivory Soap; the "halo" surrounding his head imprinted upon him a sign of heavenly favor. The ivory-clad figure appeared carefully aligned against a stage-scenery image of the white bathtub and golden tiles. Ivory Soap thus took on a sacral aura, calling to mind purity, cleanliness, and even holiness. Other "name" artists continued to provide Ivory Soap ads with variety and charm. Maude Humphrey, Jessica Wilcox Smith, Elizabeth Shippen Green, and C. Allan Gilbert were among other well-known artists who would not associate their names with products of dubious value.

Other admakers also supported the aesthetic ideal. For pictorial ads, the secret to success was to establish a consistent, appealing style to link with the advertised product. One popular motif captured the attention of most people, especially women: the image of a healthy, happy child involved in everyday activities. If the picture also interested children, and if women exclaimed, "How darling!" it was considered a winner by advertisers.[31] There was a cuteness about them that attracted and pleased, a delightful freshness in the treatment of the subject that made the advertisements notable. The implication of these ads, however, was that the mother was a failure if her children did not measure up to these attractive portrayals. The idealization of the "natural" infant and child occurred, ironically, within a middle class beginning to define itself through consumption. Cute babies and darling children became accepted—indeed, celebrated—as sites of commodity culture. "Idealized images of infants and children that appeared in the arts or other realms of learning were used to display the virtue and competence of the home environment," according to Harvey

The sweetest thing on earth is the face of a little child. Its skin is exquisitely delicate, like the bloom of a ripe peach. Imagine washing a peach with colored and perfumed soap! Next to pure water, Ivory Soap is the purest and most innocent thing for a child's skin. No chemicals! No free alkali! Just a soft, snow-white puff of down, which vanishes instantly when water is applied.

IT FLOATS.

The drawing by Jessie Willcox Smith, reproduced above, was awarded first prize of Six Hundred Dollars in an artists' competition conducted by The Procter & Gamble Co.

Fig. 4.7. Ivory Soap, prize-winning design, illustrated by Jessica Wilcox Smith, *Profitable Advertising*, November 1902.

Green. "In a society in which display was everywhere—architecture, women's dress, and home furnishings—the 'performance' was perhaps the ultimate presentation of middle-class power, influence, and achievement."[32] Thus, the cultivation of children presented adults with a possible avenue to a world of unrealized fantasies and hopes that they might control.

Maude Humphrey and Jessica Wilcox Smith had established a tradition of creating charming ads that portrayed children in everyday activities. Humphrey's graceful images proved especially popular; she illustrated one book after another and created over three hundred covers for the major magazines of the time. Another painting by Jessica Wilcox Smith won first prize of six hundred dollars in an artist's competition sponsored by Procter & Gamble (see Fig. 4.7). It pictured a cute young girl washing her hands with Ivory Soap and gently made the point that the soap was mild enough for the child's skin:

> The sweetest thing on earth is the face of a little child. Its skin is exquisitely delicate like the bloom of ripe peach. Imagine washing a peach with colored and perfumed soap.
>
> Next to pure water, Ivory Soap is the purest and most innocent thing for a child's skin. No chemicals. No free alkali! Just a soft, snow-white puff of down, which vanishes instantly when water is applied.

By the time Smith started doing Ivory Soap ads, she was already known as the person who had illustrated *The Child's Garden of Verses*, *Evangeline*, *Water Babies*, and over two hundred *Good Housekeeping* covers. Smith brought the new interest in Japanese prints, with its clean lines and open spaces filled with colored wash, to her advertising art. These pictorial ads often looked appealing enough to put up on the kitchen wall or to frame for the parlor.

Certainly Harley Procter not only recognized that the child's place in the home was unique, but also aimed advertising toward children. For example, Ivory Soap ran attractive, full-page advertisements in *St. Nicholas*, a magazine for children. One ad suggested an excellent way to amuse children if they must stay indoors, "An Ivory Soap Bubble-Party— for Rainy Afternoons." Another entertained children with a little rhyme about the Three Wise Men of Gotham, making the point "Ivory Soap . . . . . It Floats" (see Fig. 4.8):

Fig. 4.8. Ivory Soap, advertisement, *St. Nicholas* children's
magazine, 1911.

Three wise men of Gotham
Went to sea in a bowl;
'Tis very clear,
Their craft was queer,
And yet they reached their goal.
Since Ivory Soap kept them afloat,
The incident seems quite worthy of note.

Perhaps a child's influence on purchasing decisions was more powerful
than most advertisers cared to admit at the time.

Like Procter, other advertisers believed it was a good investment to
direct their advertising messages to children. "Let's get after the future
business of the country by advertising to the children of today," urged the
trade journal *Advertising & Selling* in 1912. "And right here let us get it
well fixed in our minds that it does not take long for a child to become an

ultimate consumer after he has reached the age when he can read a little."[33]

The notion of the child as "the ultimate consumer" had some basis in reality. At the time, psychologists told advertisers that children formed many of their most important lasting impressions and habits in their early years.[34] This concept spurred the marketing and advertising of products to children. Advertisers were also encouraged to speak to children in the child's language, so he or she could understand the message. If advertisements were written so that the child could grasp them, they were also likely to tell the story so simply that they would have more effect upon the adult mind. Thus, the trade journal concluded that there were three reasons to advertise to children: (1) the immediate sales of children's goods to children, (2) the education of children on the merit of the products being advertised, and (3) the influence children may exert on the parents. Indeed, it paid to advertise to children.

Some manufacturers and many retailers had already shrewdly recognized that children were business assets, integral to their sales strategies. For example, Lion Coffee packed pasteboard animals in packages. A breakfast food manufacturer printed a game on the inside of the package. Even shoe and clothing merchants often gave away a souvenir with each purchase of children's clothes. In the fall, they might give away footballs or balloons with a new suit of clothes; in the spring, a red top or a kite; in summer, a baseball bat; and so on. The idea was that children soon learned that they would always get *something* if they bought their clothes from this particular merchant. These promotions proved successful only because the prices were reasonable and the goods worth what the merchant charged. It was true the merchants gave away something, but the merchant simply applied a basic principle of sales: they *interested* the children. Thus, the advertisement became part of the child's life.[35]

Image Building

Although both Ivory and Pears' Soap possessed a unique characteristic found only in the product itself, there was also a large class of soaps that were difficult or even impossible to present in such a way as to appeal to the consumer's imagination. The ad maker had to get an emotional response

Fig. 4.9. Fairy Soap, advertisement, the *Delineator*, August 1917.

by creating an image that connected with consumers, making them feel that the advertised product would do wonderful things for them. To build an image, placement of the all-important product name and identifying symbols, trademarks, and slogans became important parts of the advertisement.

In particular, Fairy Soap and Packer's Tar Soap provide excellent examples of building a favorable impression for a brand. To do so, N. K. Fairbanks Company brought a trademark to life. The soapmaker hired a New York artist named Paleogue to create an advertising character to distinguish the product from those sold by others. Thus, the Fairy Soap Girl, a pretty and elegantly dressed child sitting on a cake of soap, entered the market with the slogan, "Have you a little fairy in your home?" (see Fig. 4.9). In 1910 *Printers' Ink* recognized the success of the device. "She is calculated to touch the heart and carry the soap into homes on the strength of the admiration she has aroused."[36] This appealing imaginary character would be welcomed into any parlor and made comfortable by a charmed family—yet her every underlying message was "Buy our goods," as the advertisement's clever slogan said.

Like Fairy Soap, Packer's Tar Soap did not possess a unique product feature that differentiated the soap from its competitors. As a result, Packer's advertising did not focus on listing product features; rather, the goal of the ads was to evoke an emotional response in the reader and to build a favorable image for the product. But instead of using the device of an advertising character to distinguish the product from the competition, as did Fairy Soap, the Packer's campaign used striking photographs.

Initially advertised in the medical papers, Packer's Tar Soap eventually expanded its advertising to other general interest periodicals. As early as 1892, Packer's ran full-page ads in a number of magazines, using exquisite line drawings and copy written in rhyme. The transformation of the campaign took place in the mid-1890s, when the ads combined an artistic sensibility and photographic skill. The resulting ads were striking. Among the most fetching of the series was one showing a charming little girl shampooing her brother's hair: "You cannot begin too early"; another showed a cat held up in a human hand with the caption, "Doesn't Scratch."[37]

The advertisements were more than merely attractive; the approach demonstrated the value of the camera in an indisputable manner. In 1902, the trade journal *Profitable Advertising* heralded another Packer's ad as

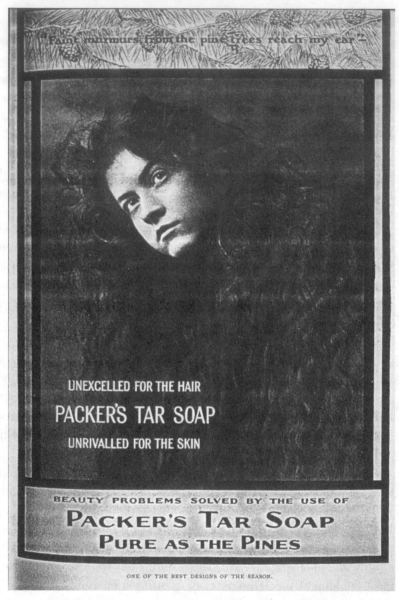

Fig. 4.10. Packer's Soap ad declared "best of the season," *Profitable Advertising*, January 1902.

"season's best."[38] The purity of the soap was trumpeted in a design showing pine boughs artistically arranged with a dramatic picture of a young woman with near-perfect features and lush hair. The headline read simply, "Faint murmurs from the pine trees reach my ear." From an advertising stand-point, the journal explained that the advertisement possessed a double value. It was decidedly artistic in pose and treatment, but it was also an excellent illustration for the catch phrase "unexcelled for hair" (see Fig. 4.10). In retrospect, advertising historian Frank Presbrey claimed, "Packer's showed the way for other advertisers with a series of human-interest photographs that set a standard in effective advertising art."[39]

Thus, the camera had assumed a position of importance in the illustration of advertisements by the turn of the century.[40] One of the key factors in favor of the photographic method was that it provided a faithful repro-duction of the advertised product. Advertisers thought that the photograph must carry with it a sort of guarantee of truthfulness. Because the adver-tisers thought the photo would be more true to life than a hand-drawn illus-tration, they believed that it would also be more persuasive. In the case of the Packer's Soap ad, it was indeed arresting.

However, other admakers recognized the shortcomings of the commer-cial photograph. Although the major appeal of the photograph to admakers was that it conveyed truth, conviction, and exactness, there were other signs that the new technology had limitations. As A. Rowden King of the Etheridge Company explained in 1912: "The great trouble is that the camera is *too* faithful and the photograph is *too* true to reality." Especially when there were human-interest issues and human emotions to be presented, the mechanical camera could not, unlike the artist, develop an emotional bond with the subject. For this subject matter, King observed, "the product of the camera is nearly always tame, spineless, and disappointing."[41] Then there was the business of securing an appropriate model. Not only the face, but also every minute detail, had to be right. The artist with a brush and pen could combine the good features of scores of faces, necks, shoulders, figures, and feet, but the photographer was limited to the models and settings avail-able. Although commercial photographs could be retouched, such work proved not only expensive but often obvious. Also, there was a certain same-ness about to all photographs when half-toned, but there was no end to the shades of treatment a good artist could work into the finished product. Thus, demand for better and cheaper commercial artwork continued, while photography was used less until the end of the 1920s.

ADVERTISING AND THE NEW SCIENCE OF PSYCHOLOGY

As admakers expanded their techniques, approaches, and services, they also developed theories and practices to embrace a more scientific basis for advertising. The ability to capture the public's attention and to influence what people bought became the single largest determinant of success in business. Successful marketers recognized the importance of well-coordinated promotional planning that pushed the sale of particular brands and continually introduced new ones. By the turn of the century, manufacturers routinely introduced new brand-name products with a wave of advertising. As the volume of advertising increased, so did an endless duplication of what appeared. As readers stopped responding, admakers shifted their pitch from jingles, trademark characters, and pretty pictures to harder-selling copy with new appeals. Advertising also gradually became more scientific.

A successful ad works because it creates a connection between the product being advertised and some need or desire that the audience perceives. These links, called "appeals," generally fit into one of two categories: (1) logical or rational, and (2) emotional.[42] Although the advertising appeal refers to the approach used to attract the attention of consumers and/or influence their feelings toward a product, service, or cause, the creative execution refers to the way a particular appeal is turned into an advertising message presented to the consumer.

The underlying content of logical or rational appeals focuses on the consumer's practical, functional, or utilitarian need for the product or service. Initially, soap advertising campaigns focused on a single brand-name identification, using persuasive arguments based on the ethics or integrity of the manufacturer that gave the consumers a logical or rational reason to prefer one brand of soap over another. Manufacturers like B. T. Babbitt, Pears, and Procter & Gamble put their names on the package, their faces in the advertisement, or a picture of their factories in the ad to induce the confidence of the consuming public. The arguments then evolved from simple brand-name identification to selling pitches based on either the product's performance features or its ability to solve a problem. The idea of the sales argument, or "reason-why copy" presenting specific reasons the product was worth buying, rather than brand identification, served as the basis of the sales campaign.

In contrast, emotional appeals base the selling argument on emphasizing the satisfaction that comes from purchasing the product and then owning it or making a gift of it. An extremely strong emotive appeal tells the consumer, "this is *the* product that will meet your needs or fulfill your desires." Such ads provided provocative arguments for improving oneself and aspiring to the lifestyles of richer people. Although fundamental to advertising today, these concepts seemed novel and revolutionary in 1905, especially the idea that the skillful use of emotional appeals could move products faster than any other approach.

Ad makers' growing interest in the reason-why copy approach and emotional appeals coincided with their interest in the new science of psychology. Advertisers had long wanted to understand who their consumers were and what motivated them to purchase one product over another one. A. G. Tansley's 1897 book *The New Psychology and Its Relation to Life* popularized the new science of psychology, and by the 1910s Freud's theories on psychoanalysis entered into American technical and avant-garde literature. Among numerous contributions to psychology, Sigmund Freud created analytic techniques that used free association, dream interpretation, and analysis of resistance and transference to explore mental processes. The theory of psychology founded by Freud revolved around concepts of the unconscious, resistance, repression, sexuality, and the "Oedipus complex," unconscious sexual feelings in a child for the parent of the opposite sex that appeared in early childhood.[43]

Advertising and selling emerged as the first areas in which psychology could be applied. Initially the literature of both psychology and business aimed to develop a salesperson, one who could sell anything by breaking down a prospect's resistance to purchasing the item. Around 1905 the copy style shifted the focus of ads from soft-sell formulas to detailed, straightforward sales arguments designed to overcome any resistance; this was called "reason-why copy."[44] Not an entirely new idea, reason-why copy simply echoed the fundamentals of hard-sell patent medicine techniques such as testimonials, money-back guarantees, specific claims, and attention-getting typographic devices. Yet this hard-sell style contrasted sharply with the single brand-name identification campaigns that brought Pears', Ivory, Fairy, and Packer's soaps to the public. Instead of jingles, soft-sell images, and general claims, proponents of this new style advocated that an advertisement should state in print what the salesperson would say face-to-face to a customer. Thus, it should offer a sensible argument with specific reasons the product was worth buying.

While reason-why copy became an important approach, Walter Dill Scott called attention to a major weakness in the style. This logical approach rationally described the product itself instead of extolling the pleasure it would provide the purchaser. Using a softer selling style, the ad maker could use suggestions or associations to convey the impression of integrity, quality, and prestige. Scott's article "The Psychology of Advertising" appeared in the *Atlantic* in 1904 and in *Modern Advertising* in 1905. *Mahin's Magazine* also served as a showcase for Scott's writing on topics in psychology and advertising; Scott then turned his twenty-six *Mahin's* articles into *The Theory and Practice of Advertising* in 1903 and *The Psychology of Advertising* in 1908.[45] In particular, Scott challenged admakers to associate the advertised product with emotive suggestions to make an impression:

> How many advertisers describe a piano so vividly that the reader can hear it? How many food products are so described that the reader can taste the food? How many advertisements describe a perfume so that the reader can smell it? How many describe an undergarment so that the reader can feel the pleasant contact with his body?

Although Scott advocated the application of psychology to advertising, the idea of studying people's wants and buying behavior was just beginning to take root.

Other evidence of admakers' flirtation with the new psychology also appears throughout the historical record. Scholars published the results of university investigations and experiments in psychology. In 1911, for example, Dr. Edward K. Strong of Columbia University published findings from a study to determine whether psychological tests could be employed to estimate the value of advertisements before they were actually used. He concluded that such an investigation certainly would be valuable, citing the studies of Scott, Harlow Gale, and H. L. Hollingworth. In the same year, *Printers' Ink* reported that Hollingworth presented his scientific analyses to a weekly series of roundtable discussions with advertising men.[46] Advertising textbooks reported similar forays, and occasionally an entire chapter devoted to psychology appeared. Typical of the period, the 1917 textbook *Advertising as a Business Device* emphasized that the purpose of psychology was "to save waste" and went on to define twenty-two instincts that advertising may influence, from the food and clothing instincts to the hoarding and hospitality instincts.

At this time, however, advertising with a psychological appeal mainly revolved around class appeal and gender. As opposed to making an argument based on price or utility, the text, illustrations, and historical allusions often made a subtle appeal to the feminine sentiment for class distinction, suggesting that a share of this distinction would come to the owner or user of the advertised item. Such appeals to the prospect's yearnings for social status were especially appropriate in a society geared toward social mobility. Although men were open to class appeals, it was essentially an "appeal feminine," explained one advertising manager in 1912. "The natural instinct of women makes them study the dress and appointment of those they admire or envy and either imitate or strive to surpass and excel them."[47] Advertisers claimed that women believed that their personality expressed itself in dress, furniture, and all the little appointments of their world. As a rule, however, advertisers found that the more subtly the suggestion was made, the more effective it was. In ads, they frequently used such words as "aristocratic," "exclusive," and "distinguished" to produce the illusion that was the essence of class appeal.

Although hundreds of different appeals are used as the basis of advertising campaigns, the essential emotional appeal, characteristic of modern advertising, did not suddenly appear. Rather, the idea of emotive appeals as the basis of the sales campaign slowly evolved from a subtle approach to more powerful arguments that tapped into basic human drives. In the process, cleansing, beautifying, and consuming became knitted together as the American woman's way.

THREE CAMPAIGNS IN THE MAKING

During the period between 1900 and 1920, three successful advertising campaigns reflected admakers' growing sophistication in using emotive appeals to influence consumers on an emotional level. The information-based Lifebuoy campaign, launched in 1902, illustrates the reason-why copy approach based on logical appeals. Advertising gave consumers strong, rational reasons to buy the product: Lifebuoy Soap was a lifesaver. Around 1910, national advertising for Palmolive combined both information and beauty appeals to suggest that there were both rational and subtle emotional reasons for purchasing the soap. But the turning point came when Woodbury Soap based its 1910s campaign on a more overt emotional appeal. The advertising talked about not only beautification but also romance as key reasons women should use the soap. Such emotive advertising created feelings, images, meanings, and beliefs related to soap that were activated when consumers used the product.

Lifebuoy Soap and the Reason-Why Copy Approach

Lifebuoy Soap was the product of the Boston and Philadelphia facilities of Lever Brothers, Ltd., based in Port Sunlight, England. The British firm already ranked among the largest soap manufacturers, and Lever Brothers products were marketed extensively around the world. In the case of Lifebuoy, the firm set out to utilize up-to-date American methods and hire an American ad maker capable of planning and conducting a vigorous campaign, one that would advertise Lifebuoy as no soap had ever been advertised before. In 1902, the Lifebuoy Soap launch promised to be one of the strongest and most ambitious advertising campaigns yet attempted. To execute the campaign, the British firm appointed Oscar E. Binner, president of the Binner Engraving Company in New York City, as the director of publicity and promotion for Lever Brothers in America. Binner controlled everything connected with the promotion of Lifebuoy Soap, including the advertising designs, copy, engraving, and booklets to establish a consistent, appealing style. Binner did this with astonishing success.

First, Binner planned to create demand for the new soap by reaching American households through extensive advertising in leading magazines, women's publications, and illustrated weeklies. The Lifebuoy advertisements represented the best features of modern advertising at the time, with lavish illustrations, designs, and engravings all produced by Binner's firm. According to Binner, the "household publications come first of all, because I believe that such an article as soap should be advertised principally through such mediums to reach the household." Notices in newspapers, billboards, bulletins, and streetcars would come later.[48]

Using images of the familiar flotation device called a lifesaver, Binner yoked the larger cultural meaning of something that not only preserved life, but also saved it. The name "Lifebuoy" quickly came to evoke images of a life preserver. Indeed, the chief features of the campaign were the strength and consistency of the lifesaving feature of the soap, but perhaps the best conception was the image of an old lifesaver himself. Binner put the lifesaver's portrait on the Lifebuoy Soap package along with the tag line "Sanitary Disinfectant." There was a close connection between this trade character and the ring-shaped life preserver with the health-preserving attributes of Lifebuoy soap, bringing to mind that the use of the soap helped to save lives. For example, one of the 1902 full-page magazine advertisements incorporated the soap carton as part of the design, while the ancient sea dog was provided with a telescope and a medal (see Fig. 4.11). But why a lifesaver? The copy in another ad that same year explained:

> Hidden in this soap is a weapon, which in the hands of the weakest woman, was powerful enough to destroy the unseen seeds of infection. Careful and exhaustive experiments, by some of the world's greatest scientists, have proved that Lifebuoy Soap destroys the living seeds of infection, as it is strongly impregnated with a potent disinfectant. These scientific tests have shown that Lifebuoy Soap destroys the living germs of typhoid, diphtheria, cholera, smallpox, and other infectious diseases. Therefore Lifebuoy soap is the enemy of disease and the friend of health, hence a lifesaver.[49]

Ad after ad stressed the lifesaving features of the soap. It was the friend of health—safe for the body but the enemy of disease.

To appeal to housewives, another series pictured a lady with the lifebuoy, at the entrance to a happy home, suggesting that Lifebuoy Sanitary Cleanser and Disinfectant was the soap for the home.[50] Such ads stressed that Lifebuoy Cleanser and Soap were powerful enough to destroy

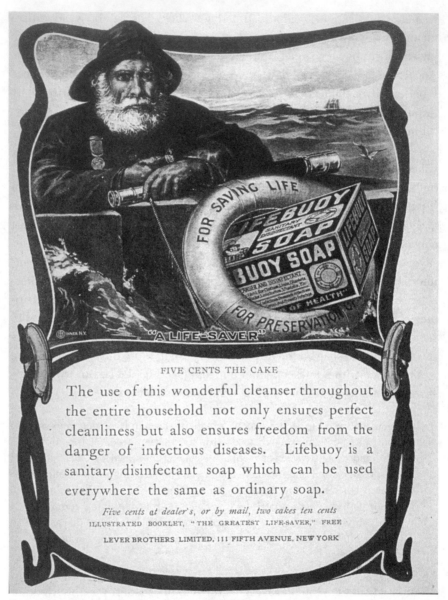

Fig. 4.11. Lifebuoy Soap, advertisement, June 1902.

the infectious germs that threatened people's lives. The picturesque old lifesaver and the lifebuoy became familiar images to magazine readers of the period.

What the actual results of the campaign were cannot be definitively stated; after the campaign had been in place for one year, Binner declined "to make public the facts and figures." Nevertheless, the trade publication *Advertising & Selling* noted that a "substantial success" had been scored.[51] One can only assume that Binner's methods had been successful, as he was promoted to general manager of Lever Brothers' interests in the United States. In 1905 the J. Walter Thompson Agency acquired the Lifebuoy account, but the firm didn't actually place any advertising until late 1908.[52] Well into the following decade, the advertising continued to feature the trademark package with the old lifesaver and to stress the soap's disinfectant properties.

Lever Brothers believed that the advertising was needed to improve Lifebuoy's rank relative to scented toilet soaps. This was especially important because Lifebuoy had a strong odor. The company wanted to convince consumers that this feature was not objectionable, but rather a property of strong cleansing power. Seeking to dispel the association of Lifebuoy with an unpleasant odor, the new ads stressed the fact that the soap had a clean, antiseptic odor "typical of purity and safety." Other copy also touted that the ingredient was unequaled in healing, purifying, and providing antiseptic power.[53] One 1913 ad put it this way: "The first clean whiff of Lifebuoy will assure you of that—but the odor soon disappears, leaving behind it only a faint, refreshing suggestion of whole-some, immaculate cleanliness" (see Fig. 4.12).[54] But the ads were unable to overcome consumer objections, and sales still proved disappointing. So the Thompson agency again asked: Why didn't more people buy Lifebuoy Soap?

In 1918, the agency conducted a market investigation of sales and distribution that focused on this problem. One dealer in Winfield, Kansas, put it this way, "We use Lifebuoy because it's a good soap. But most folks don't like the smell."[55] This research was significant because the agency believed that the buying habits of Winfield fairly represented the buying habits of "ten thousand" other towns across America. In response, the agency created a new series of ads that emphasized the healthful odor of the soap, making this point in attention-getting headlines rather than the text

Yes, take more baths; tomorrow morning, try this kind

Rub Lifebuoy Soap, briskly and thoroughly, deep into the pores of your skin.

Cover your entire body with the refreshing, invigorating lather which springs freely and abundantly, in hot or cold water, from Lifebuoy. It's a glorious sensation and it's due largely to the antiseptic Lifebuoy contains.

Lifebuoy Soap has a clean, antiseptic odor which you will recognize at once as typical of purity and safety. This odor completely disappears from your skin in a few moments.

You will feel cleaner than you ever felt before. Its very odor suggests cleanliness. More than this, you will know, for the first time, just how much energy and animation a bath can give you.

You need — everybody needs — this soap for the bath

Because Lifebuoy Soap is not merely a cleanser — getting clean is only half the battle. Lifebuoy has other qualities which make it unique. It contains cocoanut oil which gives it an agreeable, soft "feel" and an abundant lather. It contains red palm oil which has been famous for centuries for its healing properties. These are combined with the antiseptic solution which not only cleanses the skin, but purifies it.

Lifebuoy is the soap-backed by a $5,000 guaranty of purity.

Send 5c for full size cake

The price is only 5c — at your grocer's or druggist's. If you do not find it readily, send 5c (stamps or coin) for a big, full size cake to Lever Bros. Company, Dept. 8, Cambridge, Mass.

LIFEBUOY
HEALTH SOAP   5c

Lifebuoy saves the health of your skin — that's why it was given its name.

Fig. 4.12. Lifebuoy Soap, advertisement, *Saturday Evening Post*, July 5, 1913.

of the ad. "Gee, doesn't it smell great?"; "The HEALTH SOAP the odor tells why"; and "Odor tells you why Lifebuoy keeps your skin healthy."[56] By tying their product to disinfection, the ads offered consumers a powerful rationale for purchasing their product. As soap manufacturer George Schmidt pointed out, "*proper* advertising, of the great discoveries made in the art of disinfection, would mean fame and fortune for those who undertake this enterprise."[57]

As Lever Brothers did, companies like Lehn & Fink and Johnson & Johnson capitalized on the discovery of disinfection. For example, Lehn & Fink, a druggist supplier, did significant trade by focusing ads on around the single specialty of selling disinfectants. Bearing the trade name Lysol, the powerful germicide was first sold as a disinfectant to physicians and institutions, and then aimed for home protection. When the infantile paralysis epidemic gripped America in 1916, ads for Lysol shifted from informative to a "moderate 'scare' nature" reminding people of its germicidal properties; sales tripled during the period.[58] The following year, the firm introduced two new products, Lysol Antiseptic Toilet Soap and Antiseptic Shaving Cream.

Like Lehn & Fink, Johnson & Johnson, a manufacturer of surgical dressings, also promoted the disinfectant properties of its products. One promotional booklet, the *Household + Handbook*, provided a compendium of useful information along with sales pitches for the company's product line. Using the theme "The Protector of the Home Against Germs," the copy explained how the prevention of the spread of diseases and conservation and promotion of health were within the power of anyone, by simply using the advertised antiseptic products. Products like Synol Soap, Shaving Cream Soap, and others were available at "any first-class drug store."[59]

Palmolive Soap and the Beauty Appeal

Claude Hopkins's Palmolive Soap campaign blended reason-why copy with subtle emotive suggestions that appealed to the feminine sentiment for beauty. This advertising approach transformed Palmolive Soap from a simple skin cleanser to a successful skin care treatment. Also transformed was the creative execution, as alluring, beautiful woman of antiquity supplanted graphic images of health problems.

For over a quarter of a century, health appeals provided the basis for the advertising of Palmolive Soap. Caleb Johnson of the B. J. Johnson Soap Company conceived of the idea of Palmolive Soap, a cleansing agent made entirely from vegetable oils, olive and palm, a formula so mild it could be used on sensitive facial skin. Like Ivory, the soap was a clear improvement over homemade lye soaps, which were notoriously harsh and left the skin red, dry, and chapped. It was also less caustic than the domestically manufactured soaps made from lye, potash, and tree oils.

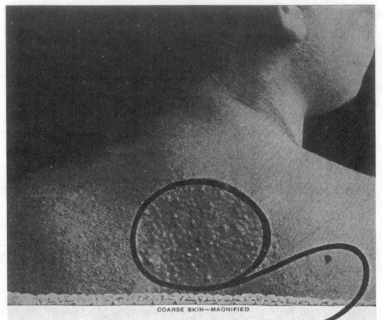

COARSE SKIN—MAGNIFIED

The Grain of the Skin

Every child, without exception, is endowed by nature with a skin as fine in grain and velvety in texture as a rose petal. To retain this fineness of skin permanently requires the constant use of *something more than soap*.

Ordinary soap tends to weaken and coarsen the tissues, depriving them of their natural oils and producing the result shown in the above illustration. PALMOLIVE, *which is more than soap*, builds up the tissues, refines the skin and imparts to the complexion that fine-grained, clear-faced, aristocratic appearance which makes a face, however irregular in feature, good to look upon. And what

PALMOLIVE

does for the complexion it does for the entire surface of the body.

PALMOLIVE does this because it is *much more than soap;* because it is composed of the refining and helpful oils of the palm and olive and cocoa butter, which have been used from time immemorial to cleanse and beautify the skin.

To keep the skin smooth and fine as nature intended, to restore it when coarsened by ill-usage to its original beauty, you should use PALMOLIVE persistently—and enjoy the pleasing results.

Price 15c; two cakes 25c. A liberal sample can be had together with booklet "*Palmolive Culture*," if you will send 5c in stamps to cover postage and mention the name of your dealer.

B. J. JOHNSON SOAP COMPANY, 334 Fowler Street, Milwaukee, Wis.

Fig. 4.13. Palmolive Soap, advertisement, 1904.

Palmolive began advertising in 1904, when the Johnson Soap Company contracted the services of the N. W. Ayer Agency in New York. For Palmolive Soap, the Ayer Agency created a series of ads that graphically showed how ordinary soap tended to weaken and coarsen skin, depriving the epidermis of its natural oils and producing coarse and wrinkled skin, and even brittle nails (see Fig. 4.13). But Palmolive's mild formula would not harm the skin. A "liberal sample" could be had free, together with an illustrated booklet, "Palmolive Culture," if the reader would pay the postage. The booklet featured a treatment for washing, massaging, and rinsing the face. Palmolive was also invaluable for the bath, shampoo, and manicure; the booklet even offered recipes to make "skin food" for a chapped face or a face that needed to be bleached.[60] After three years of consistent and widespread advertising, however, the results were "very small," reported *Printers' Ink* in 1910. That fact caused the Johnson Company's next step to move their Palmolive account to the Lord & Thomas Agency.

Johnson's sales and advertising manager, Charles Pearce, made the acquaintance of Claude Hopkins, one of the most influential copywriters in advertising, as well as a pioneer in providing free samples and using coupons in ads. Pearce and Johnson then met with Claude Hopkins's advertising agency, Lord & Thomas, and laid out a plan to advertise Palmolive Soap nationally. About the toilet soap, Hopkins recounted the following: "At that time, the men around the table only dimly recognized the beauty appeal, though later we were destined to develop on that line some of the greatest advertising successes."[61]

Initially the Palmolive campaign represented a huge sampling effort that was aided by national advertising and retailers. The first ad in the series appeared in the May 1909 *Saturday Evening Post*: "The easy way to beauty—Free." By filling out a coupon in this advertisement, the reader could get a free cake of Palmolive. The dealer, in turn, would return this coupon to the manufacturer for ten-cents cash; or, if the dealer preferred, the stock given away would be replaced at no charge. In either case, the dealer would receive what amounted to a dime profit on every transaction. The soap company redeemed two hundred thousand of these soap coupons. Within one week after the advertisement appeared, the efforts produced $35,000 of business. Another full-page advertisement appeared in the *Ladies' Home Journal* the following November and resulted in the distribution of more than one million new cakes of Palmolive.[62]

The campaign continued in leading national magazines and in local midwestern newspapers in towns of over five thousand people, each offering a coupon good for a free cake of soap redeemable over the dealers' counters. To keep grocers and druggists from padding their margins, the company prominently displayed Palmolive's retail price, which was ten cents. Other promotional devices and methods of getting people to try new Palmolive Soap were also tried. The company included thirty-six postcard coupons with each gross of Palmolive soap. The dealer's instructions were to send the postcards to the best customers. In turn, consumers would come into the store and exchange the coupons for a free bar of Palmolive Soap provided they bought one, an early "buy-one-get-one-free" type of sales promotion.[63]

Sampling was one of the oldest methods of creating demand; however, this effort proved more selective in its distribution than the house-to-house type of giveaway. In this case, the manufacturer gave away full-size cakes of Palmolive only to those who asked for them and so presumably wanted them. Hopkins believed it never paid to give either a sample or full-size package to people who did not request them; the adman called this "promiscuous sampling." Rather, Hopkins maintained that selective sampling offered many advantages over a "free" offer:

> It is much more impressive, for one thing. There is considerable difference in the psychological effect when you offer to buy an article for a woman to try, and pay the dealer his price for it, as compared with offering that article free to all. The "Free" offer cheapens a product. There is a certain resistance when we ask people afterward to pay for a product, which came to them first as a gift. But when we ourselves buy the article, just as the consumer does, we show supreme confidence in the belief that the article will please. "We Will Buy" is much better headline than "10-Cent Cake Free."[64]

The coupon advertisements not only introduced the soap into many new homes, they also led many new dealers to stock up in preparation for the demand that this energetic advertising would create. "If you sell the customer, the dealer will supply the demand," stated Hopkins.[65]

The advertisements told the story of Palmolive soap by bringing out the beauty appeal. Palmolive lent itself well to color advertising as it was made of tropical components, palm and olive oil. Around this single selling point, Hopkins used what is called the "preemptive claim" technique, which established a product's uniqueness.[66] He then gave readers scores of reasons they should want the product. Other soapmakers could make a similar claim that their soaps also contained tropical ingredients like palm, olive, or coconut oils, a standard practice in the industry. Hopkins, however, theorized that if one took a product feature or quality that might be common to the industry and made the claim first, one "owned" it. Above all, Hopkins believed that an ad should be built around a single selling point, the preemptive claim.

Although the advertising focused on the soothing, almost medicinal qualities of the soap, the campaign also established Palmolive as a luxury product. Addressing an urbane, well-heeled consumer, Hopkins opened up a fantasy world of ancient beauties who used palm and olive oils in elegantly appointed baths. The resulting ads conveyed an impression of beauty, luxury, and indulgence. "The luxury-loving Greeks equipped the bath with extravagant accessories—but they lacked Palmolive Soap," claimed one 1916 ad. Later ads used a similar theme, such as "Cleopatra's Vision" and "Buying Palmolive 3,000 years ago."[67] According to the copy, historical ingredients produced its smooth, creamy lather—the famous palm and olive oils that Cleopatra prized (see Fig. 4.14). The ads then had a regimen for washing, massaging, and rinsing.

The Palmolive ads also did much to promote the centrality of beauty to women's identity. Using images of ancient beauties made the iconic connection, linking Palmolive with Greek and Egyptian symbols of women's beauty and allure. The name "Palmolive" added to the mystique by evoking images of palms, olives, and other luxuries of the Mediterranean. Indeed, Hopkins celebrated the Mediterranean and ancient beauty cultures as exotic and universalizing counterpoints. This was not a new idea; late nineteenth-century cosmetic firms had advertised their wares to Americans using images of Egyptian, Turkish, and other exotic enchantresses, observes Kathy Peiss. "Reproductions of Little Egypt, whose dancing caused a furor at the 1893 Columbian Exposition, sold rouge and makeup, while Cleopatra was virtually a cult figure."[68] In addition to the savvy advertising campaign, the agency also combined national advertising of Palmolive Soap with two other Johnson Company products: Galvanic Laundry Soap and Palmolive Toilet Cream. The cross sell spurred sales of Palmolive Soap. Sales doubled and redoubled until trade in one item reached such proportions that the company decided to change its name from the B. J. Johnson Company to the Palmolive Company. This was done in 1917.[69]

Fig. 4.14. Palmolive Soap, advertisement, *Ladies' Home Journal*, 1918.

Woodbury's Facial Soap and Sex Appeal

The 1910s Woodbury's Facial Soap campaign marked the moment when advertising distinctly and powerfully began to appeal to the consumer's emotions. Although the Palmolive campaign embodied the beauty appeal, the Woodbury campaign tapped into a more basic human interest—sex. The style blended soft-sell pictorial images with reason-why copy approaches, but the slogan "A skin you love to touch" suggested softness, sex appeal, and even romance. Woodbury's Facial Soap, however, started out as a skin cure similar to Palmolive Soap.

Woodbury's Facial Soap was the undertaking of Dr. John Woodbury. The soap first appeared on the market in 1885, but over time sales for the product declined as new competition presented itself. Woodbury sold the company to the Andrew Jergens Company, a firm experienced in the toiletries business, in 1900. At first Jergens continued to promote the product on a patent medicine basis, featuring many health appeals and the Woodbury's trademark "neckless head." For example, advertising emphasized that the soap softened calluses yet was cooling, healing, and antiseptic. It thus made an ideal soap for the footbath, or a "wonderful rest-cure for tired feet," as one ad pointed out. To reach a wider audience, however, pretty girls, decorative lettering, and ornate borders took the place of the symptom-and-cure copy. Ads and pages from booklets touted Woodbury's "World Famed Face Culture," pitching the gospel of beauty. That is, "it is possible for anyone willing to take pains and exercise intelligence to be physically attractive, pleasing to look upon, pleasant to think of."[70] But sales still dropped, and the Jergens Company nearly abandoned advertising entirely.

At this point the J. Walter Thompson Company, which specialized in advertising to female consumers, undertook to bring Woodbury's Facial Soap back into the market "by spending every dollar of the advertising appropriation with scientific accuracy."[71] The advertising budget was set at $25,000, "an appropriation so small that it would not even allow a local campaign in one of the larger metropolitan centers."[72] The agency considered objective facts to assess the market and applied "fine psychological reactions and feminine habits of thought" to create the advertising appeals for Woodbury's Facial Soap.[73] The admakers first conducted an investigation of the toilet soap market to determine the distribution and potential marketing for the soap. A preliminary survey showed that distribution of Woodbury's Facial Soap among druggists was extensive but thin due to light consumer demand. As for the largest potential market for the product, it was undoubtedly female. Market research had shown that the largest audience was comprised of women from sixteen to sixty years of age, and of the middle and upper classes throughout the country. Once the audience for the soap was determined to be women, the women's editorial department took over the account.

At the Thompson agency, women wrote all the copy for the firm's beauty accounts. Helen J. Lansdowne, one of the first women in advertising, became a guiding figure. She briefly worked for a Cincinnati toiletry manufacturer, but quickly moved to advertising in the early 1900s. Stanley Resor, later the president of J. Walter Thompson, hired Helen as a copywriter, and they later married in 1917. Helen Lansdowne Resor brought many professional women into the agency to provide the feminine point of view, creating ads that would appeal to female consumers of toiletries, cosmetics, food, and fashion. The women were trained in advertising and held degrees from Barnard, Smith, Vassar, the University of Chicago, and Columbia, among other prestigious colleges.[74] Believing that women would advance further in a single-sex environment, she created separate editorial departments for women and men. This gender division also repackaged age-old stereotypes about women as impulsive and emotional, driven by "inarticulate longings," and easily swayed by flowery French phrases, snobbery, and romantic imagery.[75]

This cadre of skilled women, although small, came to advance what would become key tenets of normative femininity. In selling goods to women, much was made of the "woman's point of view," as 85 percent of all purchases were made by women. It became axiomatic that advertising appeals must be made with the knowledge of the habits and thoughts of women in mind. A corporate advertisement put it this way: "It is a question of establishing *these facts*—in the life of the housewife, the mother, the young girl. It is a question of *knowing* their needs, their desires, their tastes, their prejudices."[76] Caring for one's appearance, they could claim, was part of a larger commitment to women's social participation, self-expression, and dignity—it was a duty.

Thus, the entire women's editorial department devoted the next six months to studying their own reactions to the use of the product. They also consulted one Dr. Broemer, former head of the New York Skin and Cancer Hospital, who was later retained as an advisor.[77] The editorial staff studied over one hundred books and articles on the care and treatment of skin, did a laboratory analysis of the soap, conducted interviews with housewives on how people washed and cared for their skin, and what distinct service Woodbury's Facial Soap performed. Findings showed that even in the simple matter of face washing "there existed all the differences between carelessness and what might be called art." Tests also disclosed definite advantages in the use of Woodbury's for the skin and the company, later developed into a series of treatments for skin troubles; but research also showed that users had to be clearly shown added results and service to justify the twenty-five-cent price. Other soaps also made the same skin treatment claims that Woodbury's did, but these competing products cost 50 to 75 percent less.[78]

The women's viewpoint was apparent in the choice of media and copy appeals for the Woodbury's campaign. The advertising initially appeared exclusively in the important women's magazines with large national circulation, such as the *Ladies' Home Journal*, to reach a middle-class, female audience.[79] As national magazines offered the greatest and most economical coverage of this market, this print media became the backbone of the campaign.

Adopting the selling approach used throughout the cosmetics industry, the first series of ads borrowed beauty culture techniques to transform use of Woodbury's Facial Soap into a daily beauty ritual. The ads mimicked the design and substance of magazine beauty features, in what the J. Walter Thomson copywriters called the "beauty editorial style," featuring a "light and intimate tone" with exhaustive facts and detail.[80] The first revised Woodbury's ad appeared in a 1910 issue of *Saturday Evening Post* featuring "Conspicuous nose pores—how to reduce them." This first campaign stopped the falling sales curve for the first time in fourteen years, and the J. Walter Thompson agency continued work. The following year, the agency changed the packaging considerably, wrapped a booklet of instructions around the cake, and then began the treatment idea with ads headlined "How to Wash." Ads next featured the use of soap for rough, red hands, freckles, and sluggish skin. New treatments introduced "oily skin," "shiny nose," and "how to take make your skin fine in texture."[81]

Fig. 4.15. The earliest form of the famous slogan "A skin you love to touch," *Saturday Evening Post*, May 6, 1911.

The whole educational angle was reinforced by a strong appeal to women's wish to be beautiful and charming, to have a smooth, clear, attractive skin. This appeal was embodied in the slogan "A skin you love to touch," written by Helen Lansdowne Resor, which first appeared in an advertisement in 1911 (see Fig. 4.15).[82] The celebrated ad featured a painting of an attractive couple and a provocative headline that invited the audience to read more about a skin care regimen. Touting the "Woodbury Treatment," ads explained how to cleanse the skin with Woodbury's Facial Soap and hot water, massage the face, and then close the pores with cold water or ice—all skin care treatments long used by beauty culturists. Instead of merely selling soap, the landmark ad also discussed the benefits of using the product, suggesting softness, sex appeal, and even romance.

Later ads in the series appeared with different illustrations but kept that headline with its muted sexuality. In 1916, for instance, Woodbury offered a new Mary Greene Blumenschein painting of an attractive couple reproduced in nine colors, fifteen by nineteen inches, and "no printing or advertising matter appears on it" (see Fig. 4.16). The ad urged the reader to send for the beautiful picture today; it would be a constant reminder that they, too, could have "that greater loveliness which the daily used Woodbury's always brings." The ad went on to inform the reader about the "skin you love to touch" treatment, and closed with an offer of a week's supply of soap, plus the art from the advertisement.[83]

Adapting a running commentary on skin problems, other ads targeted a series of disorders, such as conspicuous nose pores, and solved each one with the Woodbury treatment, giving considerable detail. In 1918, however, the euphemisms of cosmetics had not yet been developed. Instead, the copy simply told it as it was: "the small muscular fibres of the nose have become weakened and do not keep the pores open as they should be. Instead these pores collect dirt, clog up, and become enlarged." The ad recommended the Woodbury treatment, instructing women to "finish by rubbing the nose for thirty seconds with a lump of ice" to free the skin of "tiny, dead, old particles of skin." The beauty regimen, however, did not become as widely accepted as the "A skin you love to touch" slogan.

What the Woodbury ad campaign undertook was to educate women about the nature and working of their skin, the cause of common skin problems, and the way in which these defects could be overcome by the right cleansing method with the advertised product. This whole educational story was then reinforced by a strong emotional appeal to women's desire to be beautiful and charming, to have a smooth, clear, attractive skin, as embodied in the slogan "A skin you love to touch." The association of Woodbury's Facial Soap with this prescriptive program of giving women practical help and instruction in the care of their skin did more to establish its prestige as a skin soap than any mere assertion of its merits. Helen Lansdowne Resor understood why women buy "women's goods" such as soap, cold cream, and shortening, so she presented provocative arguments for improving oneself and aspiring to the lifestyle of wealthier people.

Edith Lewis, a Thompson agency copywriter, later explained that where a product faced great resistance, or where it had strong competition, the ad maker sometimes had to draw on outside sources in order to reinforce the emotional quality. That is, one "has to invent a situation or create an

Fig. 4.16. One of a series of paintings that readers could send away for, titled "A Skin You Love to Touch," by artist Mary Greene Blumenschein, *Ladies' Home Journal*, September 1916.

interest outside the product itself or its uses, in order to awaken an emotional response." By creating situations that powerfully brought before the reader's imagination the social disadvantages of a bad complexion, the ad maker also presented the social incentives for a good one.[84] Clearly, Woodbury's advertising is a case in point. The campaign transformed an unpleasantly stinging soap into a wildly popular beauty aid by dramatizing the product itself, describing it with so much feeling that it seemed attractive and desirable.[85] In the next five years sales of the Woodbury line skyrocketed, from $515,000 in 1915 to $2.58 million in 1920.[86]

Previous ads had exploited sex and pretty women, but none with the effectiveness and persistence of the Woodbury's campaign. About the slogan "A skin you love to touch," the sober *Atlantic Monthly* commented that the "phrase sings itself into your memory." The editorial noted that the "pictures of this famous series have probably been seen by more people at one time than any others ever painted."[87] Helen Lansdowne Resor had added the essential emotional appeal to the sales argument. "I added the feminine point of view," she explained. "I watched the advertising to see that the idea, the wording, and the illustrating were effective for women."[88] The words and visuals embraced women's hope, fears, desires, and dreams regardless of what they did for a living.

The omnipresence of sex in selling had not reached the point where admakers were selling sex to get the reader's attention. It was a time when a mere glimpse of a stocking was shocking. Although the Woodbury's campaign used sex in the copy, it was barely hinted at in the artwork. Since the "concealed" was so exciting, a man's peek under a women's outer clothes to glimpse naked delights was still considered taboo, and presumably this sight was equally arresting to viewers of advertising. An imaginative way around the taboo was the presumably titillating sight of an artist's wind gust lifting the hemline as high as an ankle in an advertising illustration, allowing the viewer a glimpse of stocking. From the 1880s until World War I, this sight could bring readers to a full stop. By 1915, however, silk hose had become accessible to ordinary women, instead of only the rich, and "advertising could reveal a good eighteen inches of stocking without being accused of bad taste," wrote Charles Goodrum.[89]

At the same time, advertisers were occasionally using sex to attract female customers to buy male products. Male nudity was permitted in soap

Fig. 4.17. Ivory Soap, advertisement, *American* magazine, July 1918.

and underwear advertising, since it was used on products bought primarily by women and not as an erotic expression. Ivory Soap, for example, showed pictures of nude youths cooling off in a stream and men showering in the locker room, while meeting the requirements of contemporary good taste in 1916 (see Fig. 4.17).[90] Using artfully placed towels, bodies, and other props, artists creatively maneuvered around the frontal male nudity taboo. Full female nudity would not be introduced until the mid-1930s. In any event, the advertisers would have to learn an entirely new set of rules after World War I.

Fig. 4.18. A metal soap dish found in a typical doughboy pack.

SOAP GOES TO WAR

When the United States entered World War I in 1917, the event marked the transformation of soap from a seldom-used product to an everyday necessity as thousands of soldiers adopted the soap-and-water ritual. In the United States Army, soap had become part of a soldier's regulation gear. In the equipment pack, or "haversack," a soldier was expected to carry his extra rations, means of cooking his food and eating it, clothing, and toilet articles—for toothbrush, comb, and soap were "regulations."[91] The canvas roll, between eight inches and a foot in diameter, was carried by shoulder straps and hung to below the soldier's hips as he marched. It was reported that some soldiers also carried a silver soap dish or something of the sort as a reminder of the folks back home (see Fig. 4.18). One sergeant seemed to have prized his soap dish very much, having taken it with him to the Philippines, China, Mexico, and many other places.[92] Familiar brands like Ivory Soap also accompanied the troops around the world.

While many manufacturers converted from consumer goods to wartime production, others felt constrained from promoting nonessential consumer products during this time of national crisis. Shortages increased "institutional" advertising that kept company names and products in the public eye. Thus, ads often carried the corporate message that these products were helping the fighting men to hang on. One classic 1916 Ivory Soap ad informed readers that the product was the "very joy of living" to American soldiers, and wherever they went, Ivory followed:

> IVORY SOAP follows the flag. Wherever America goes, it goes "among those present." Ivory's use is as unchangeable a part of American life as the practice of cleanliness. Ivory Soap is the very joy of living to Our Boys when they are relieved from the front lines for rest, recreation, clean clothes and a bath.[93]

Another ad from Ivory Soap appeared in 1919 that told the story of the delight of one woman who saw for the first time that Ivory floated in water (see Fig. 4.19). The concept for the ad came from a true story taken from the "Intimate Notes on the Firing Line" column in the *Los Angeles Times* about a group of French civilians who shared a community wash trough with American soldiers. When a cake of Ivory Soap started to slip from a slanting board into the depths of the water, one mademoiselle frantically grabbed to recover the soap. "Il flotte," she delightedly screamed, paraphrasing the well-known advertising slogan, when she found that the soap conveniently floated in the water.[94]

Despite the presence of low-priced soap, for many Europeans soap became a scarcity. Throughout the war, Germany had been practically cut off from importation of the raw materials that go into soap manufacture, including oils, tallows, and many chemicals, which had been largely diverted to ammunition plants and to other wartime needs. As a result of these shortages, soap in some areas took on a new meaning. It emerged as a valuable currency in trade, explained the *Soap Gazette and Perfumer*:

> During the armistice, the desolate land became a literal trading place for the exchange of all manners of souvenirs between erstwhile enemy troops. While the German soldiers evinced some measure in coins, brass buttons and similar trinkets, with American cigarettes in particularly high favor, nothing gratified him quite so much as a cake of soap.[95]

"It Floats!"

Suppose you were to see Ivory Soap
for the first time—wouldn't you
be amazed and delighted to find it
always floating conveniently at hand
in washbowl, dishpan or tub?

IVORY SOAP . . . . 99 44/100 % PURE

Fig. 4.19. Ivory Soap, advertisement, *Saturday Evening Post*, April 19, 1919.

Certainly soap had become a necessity not only in America, but also in many European countries.

After the 1918 armistice ended the war, manufacturers increased their advertising budgets and spurred the return to a consumer economy. In the following decades, new products and consumer patterns would emerge, and far-reaching social changes would occur. After the war new manufacturing systems and technologies produced reliable heating devices, good plumbing, and built-in tubs and sinks, which put convenient bathing within reach of ordinary citizens. The chemistry of soap manufacturing also changed. In response to the World War I-related shortage of fats for making soap, the first "soapless soap," or synthetic detergent, was developed in Germany, put together chemically from a variety of raw materials.

The war also greatly increased the number of working women and filled their purses with wartime earnings. New ads targeted women, tempting them with toilet soaps, cosmetics, and dozens of other new products, as well as promoting daring new fashions. The next chapter examines how the admakers addressed this new audience with emotive forms of advertising.

5

New Shrines of Cleanliness, 1920 to 1940

rguably, the images that bathroom fixture manufacturers employed through the years have reflected American culture even as it has influenced the images in turn. In 1915, advertisements for the "modern" bathroom abounded. Ads consistently pictured simple, utilitarian bathrooms with three standard enamel fixtures: the sink, tub, and toilet. Ten years later, in 1925, bathrooms were still advertised, but the represented space had become a showplace of style and a popular fashion statement. "From a mere utility, the modern bathroom has developed into a spacious shrine of cleanliness and health," Crane bathroom fixtures heralded in one advertisement (see Fig. 5.1).[1]

The advertising images are perhaps more revealing of the change. Before World War I, the bathrooms featured immaculately white fixtures, and tiled floors and walls. Stripped of allegedly microbe-laden furnishings, bathroom interiors were practical and sanitary. All of these images of germ-free white space contrasted with images revolving around indulgent lifestyles employed ten years later. To show the possibilities of bathroom beauty, one 1925 Crane bathroom ad depicted tiled

Fig. 5.1. Crane bathroom, advertisement, *Ladies' Home Journal*, February 1925.

floor and plaster walls with borders of Spanish majolica in primrose, brown, and green. Even more exotic interiors appeared featuring Satara marble slabs brought from Africa and design inspired by Italian art, among other elegant bathrooms. Standard designers "envisioned bathroom fixtures comparable in grace of line and proportion to the finest furniture—baths of sculptural-like quality, lavatories with the charm of dressing tables—fittings wrought in designs of rare distinction."[2] Americans had moved beyond the question of whether "to have or not to have" a modern bathroom, wrote the magazine *House Beautiful* in 1925. "Now the questions are 'how many' and 'how fine.' "[3]

Something happened between the mid-1910s and the mid-1920s. It is both accurate and misleading to claim that advertising was the proximal cause of these visible changes. Other revolutionary movements were already well under way. Following World War I, the economy began a period of rising prosperity as factory assembly lines multiplied, the stock market soared, and industrial production skyrocketed. Higher wages, the availability of credit, and more leisure time also prodded the economy. People's newly acquired affluence provided mass marketers with a ready-made and growing consumer base. This newly affluent population represented a new breed of consumer who no longer made the basic necessities at home, because everything from soap to dresses came premade and prepackaged. Large food, drug, and apparel chain stores provided new places to shop and offered consumers a cornucopia of products and services, and automobiles transported families to stores and shops, as well as to various events and other new diversions.

Americans had long used individuals' consumption choices and physical appearance to help them make judgments about their social identity.[4] As subordinate groups attempted to adopt the status symbols of the middle class and climb up the ladder of social mobility,[5] many also impersonated them by adopting new consumer rituals. Personal cleanliness had become an essential requirement for acceptance into the middle and upper classes. Even children were thought to be instantly improved with a good scrub and a change of clothes. Dirty hands, greasy clothes, and a smelly body would never do. In addition to considering a person's grooming habits, one made inferences about personality based on clothing, home decorating choices, leisure activities, cars, and so on. Objects and personal rituals, however, also acted as a sort of security blanket by reinforcing people's identities, especially in unfamiliar situations. This coping process protected the self from being diluted in a strange environment.[6]

Advertising both reflected and shaped consumers' insecurities about their physical appearance during the 1920s and 1930s, particularly as people motivated by high standards of self-presentation strived to pattern their behavior on the perceived expectations of society. Thus, the next section examines the innovations in bathrooms, the ongoing consumer culture, and the development of new advertising formulas based on powerful emotional appeals.

THE LIBERATION OF THE BATHROOM

Advertising and the fashion system largely fueled the transformation of the bathroom from a prim, utilitarian place to a decorative and indulgent space by associating the functional interior with new symbolic qualities. Crane Company, for example, gave the bathroom a new cultural meaning by associating it with a "shrine of cleanliness." In the process, the bathroom took on a special status, transformed from a sanitary place to a sacred space, a domain of sacred consumption that "set apart" the interior from the normal activities of the rest of the home. The advertised bathroom fixtures, furnishings, and accessories, in turn, imparted their meanings to consumers as they used these facilities to create and express their identities in their daily lives.[7]

American tastes and product preferences in bathrooms were not formed in a vacuum. Their choices were driven by the images presented to them in the mass media, their observations of those around them, and even their desire to live in the fantasy worlds created by admakers. In the 1920s, however, the depiction of opulent bathrooms in motion pictures also represented liberation from nineteenth-century moral restraints as evidenced in the national preoccupation with sheiks, vamps, and sex. An individual could expect to spend six months' salary on the bathroom alone in order to bring it up to Hollywood standards.[8]

In particular, the films of Cecil B. DeMille used bathing and other cleanliness rituals as the perfect opportunity to show partial nudity on the movie screen, supposedly without provoking any sexual associations. Gloria Swanson's bathtub scene in the 1919 film *Male and Female* was perhaps the most memorable thing about the movie, for DeMille not only introduced the bathroom to the screen but also glamorized the bath itself. From then on during the twenties, DeMille's films would come to a halt for a lingering scene in which the heroine, or sometimes the hero, washed in preparation for some event.

Elaborate marble, tile, and chrome characterized DeMille's bathrooms with an occasional bearskin thrown in.[9] Although these movie bathrooms became a national joke, they also prompted thousands of moviegoers to attempt a similar effect, much to the delight of plumbing suppliers. The glamorization of bathrooms led to new movements in interior decorating, transforming the commonplace room from a merely functional room into the most elaborately adorned room in the house.[10] When it comes to the creation of a "rococo bathroom, no one can touch DeMille," wrote Arthur Dennison in *The Filmplay Journal* in 1922. "Why some bathroom fixtures company or specialty shop which wants to build up an enormous trade among nouveau-riche has not engaged him [DeMille] as Extraordinary Advisor is beyond our small comprehension."[11]

At the same time, color and design breakthroughs for bathroom fixtures, accessories, and furnishings occurred in the mid-1920s. Manufacturers and consumers alike increasingly perceived the bathroom as a style, subject to fashion trends and fads that dramatically altered domestic interiors. The simple white bathroom with its standard, immaculately white enamel sink, tub, and toilet seemed decidedly old-fashioned as bright touches appeared on towels, rugs, shower curtains, window hangings, wall treatments, and floor coverings. In keeping with the trend of the increased use of color in home decoration, bathroom fixtures were also now available in color, creating new possibilities for beauty in the bathroom.

The Pittsburgh firm of Standard Sanitary Manufacturing (later American Standard) has been credited with pioneering color in sanitary wares in 1926.[12] Standard's first tentative experiments in colored fixtures offered a palette of sedate, understated pastel tones. The following year, Kohler announced a line of colored bathroom sets, including the tub, toilet, and lavatory. "A new charm enters the bathroom," declared one 1928 ad. "It is the charm of Color, of color not merely in walls and floor, but in the fixtures themselves—the bath tub, the lavatory, the toilet." The booklet *Color Charm Enters the Bathroom*, told more about the lovely fixtures; it opened with this announcement: "We had color in the bathroom; now we have the *bathroom in color* a complete color *ensemble*, a new color charm." As with Standard, the Kohler Colorware bathroom fixtures came in five "lovely, permanent shades": Horizon Blue, Spring Green, Autumn Brown, Lavender, and Old Ivory.[13] How much did this modern bathroom cost? Though Kohler fixtures did cost more than the white ones, the ads reassured consumers that "the expense of color is a minor" one compared to the cost of the finished bathroom.[14] Another ad in the series noted that the pictured bath was only "$16.40 more in color than in white; the lavatory only $12.30 more."[15] Still, another Kohler ad made the point that the company had a bathroom for every pocketbook. It featured two different models with this telling headline: "A $5000 bathroom—and a $500 one.[16]

In 1928, however, Standard's advertising exemplified the turn of the bathroom from a prudish domain to a fashion statement: "The first coming of beauty to the bathroom," proclaimed one ad (see Fig. 5.2). "For forty years we Americans were so engrossed in making the bathroom the ultimate in utility that the beauty was almost forgotten, except for an occasional ostentatious carved tub leg and old-fashioned marble slab which topped the lavatory."[17] But why shouldn't the bathroom be given as much consideration as other rooms in the home?

Standard designers created new possibilities in bathroom beauty, as evident in the company catalog, titled *Color and Style in Bathroom Furnishings and Decoration*. Indeed, Standard fixtures came in a variety of dramatic colors that had been selected by "an artist of international standing" in order to "complement the skin" and to provide a key color for "correct and livable color schemes." The fashionable hues and even the names evoked images of luxurious rooms, indulgent lifestyles, and narcissistic pleasure. The colors included Ming Green, Ionian Black, T'ang Red, Royal Copenhagen Blue, Meissen White, Rose du Barry, Claire de Lune Blue, St. Porschaire Brown, Ivoire de Medici, and Orchid of Vincennes. The model bathrooms shown in the catalog were equally dramatic, with full-color reproductions of works by eminent American painters, while the accompanying copy encouraged consumers "to make your bath livable." It also told them that just "a little extra planning and expenditure [would] develop a

Fig. 5.2. Standard Sanitary Mfg. Co., advertisement, *Ladies' Home Journal*, March 1928.

room of cheer, of beauty, and extra utility."[18] Not to be outdone, the Crane Plumbing catalog *Homes of Comfort* introduced an expanded palette of eighteen colors, of which six were marbleized.[19] Clearly, the striking colors attested to a revolution in bathroom design.

By 1928, the last notes of shining whiteness in the bathroom had been swept away by color, observed *House and Garden* magazine. "As a result, this most intimate recess has been transformed from a room of utilitarian

Fig. 5.3. Standard Plumbing Fixtures' Neo-Angle Bath, from *Plan the Bathroom Wisely*, Standard Mfg. Co. company publication, 1938.

plainness to one of actual beauty and with no sacrifice of sanitary standards." Now bathroom furniture, fixtures, and accessories were available in such a wide range of colors and styles that a room could be created that was both satisfying and practical, "as much as an embodiment of the taste and personality of the owner as his own living room." In the 1930s, however, the range of and design of "rainbow bathrooms" would continue to evolve.[20]

Although the modern bathroom as we know it today was largely defined by the built-in or recessed combination bath, Standard introduced another innovative fixture, the Neo-Angle Bath. To promote the look of modernity, Standard placed an image of the new angled bathtub adjacent to a footed tub, the newest style in the 1860s, in the company catalog titled *Planning Your Plumbing*. From Standard's perspective, the footed model appeared decidedly "old-fashioned-unsightly—an irritation to the family." In contrast, the same room outfitted with the Neo-Angle Bath seventy years later, in 1934, was "Beautiful—modern—clean—inviting—easy to keep spick and span." The angle shape was but one surprising feature. Although it was only four feet square, Standard claimed that "it had more bathing space than the present known five foot types." Thus, the attractive, modern bathroom now included not only the Neo-Angle Bath but a "quiet water closet that doesn't embarrass" and a "lavatory with ample space for toilet articles" (see Fig. 5.3).[21]

Another unexpected feature was a touchy subject. The introductory full-page ad for the Neo-Angle Bath prominently displayed a nude woman, with one breast partially exposed, seated on one of the convenient room seats while washing her foot. Most appropriate for this ad was the headline "At Last America Gets a New Bath Thrill." The copy continued that the tub was "almost square, with the tub set diagonally to provide convenient room seats in two opposite corners. It combines every type of bathing in a single one-piece fixture!" This ad may have been the first one in the history of the plumbing supply magazine *Reeves Journal* to show a plumbing fixture actually being used by a person.[22] However, World War I and the Depression delayed the spread of the design. Like other Art Deco and Art Moderne furnishings, the Neo-Angle Bath did not achieve popularity until the 1950s, twenty years after its debut.

In addition to color and design, bathroom designers began to emphasize comfort, convenience, and safety. These changes meant that less effort was needed to keep the space spotless. For example, chrome-plated brass fittings with a tarnish-free finish came on the market, replacing nickel, which required frequent attention to maintain its shiny appearance. The combined influence of Bauhaus design and economic necessity also rid the bathroom of the ornamentation of the previous decade, substituting fixtures with clean, sleek lines. The deliberate action by designers to develop these plain fixtures was also motivated by the fact that they were not only easier to clean but also less expensive to manufacture. "It was simply cheaper to make things simpler in appearances," explained Paul Duchshere, a historian of architecture and interiors. "The more surfaces, the more ridges and molding, the more dust and dirt can collect. Americans have really been obsessive about cleaning through their history. They've really led the way in kitchen and bath design because of that."[23]

The emphasis on sleek designs also led to the virtual disappearance of the pedestal sink. Instead of this model, bathroom designers began to favor the drop-in basin, mounted in a continuous plastic laminate or tile countertop, or the ubiquitous vanity, which allowed homeowners to trade pedestal styling for handy storage. The recessed bath-and-shower combination also became a standard design, an important factor as bathrooms shrank from spacious chambers to the size of five-foot-square walk-in closets. New designs also included recesses for the sink and "hidden" water closets, niches for towels, ample shelf space, and built-in medicine cabinets. Colored wall tiles and decoratively patterned linoleum, fanciful shower curtains, metal trim, and more extensive use of mirrors added to the look. This break from the sanitized white bathrooms of previous decades encouraged creativity in room plans as well.

To obtain more business, plumbers continued to push for the two-bath home throughout the 1920s and 1930s. Among the numerous advantages, they argued that one bathroom for every two bedrooms would smooth out family difficulties and add to the social accomplishments of the house. Plumbing dealers offered to show people how a model bathroom could be installed in a space as small as five feet by six feet, no larger than a good-sized closet, claiming that this investment would bring enduring satisfaction. One 1923 Kohler ad put it this way: "An additional bathroom often spells the difference between easy, gracious hospitality and embarrassed, apologetic hospitality. And when no guests are present, it adds immeasurably to the comfort and convenience of every member of the family."[24]

The reality was that until this time houses with more than one bathroom had been rare indeed. Rather than adding another bathroom, however, Speakman Showers Company suggested that the homeowners put a shower over the tub. "This makes it possible for more persons to use the bathroom—a shower bath requires only a couple of minutes."[25] Instead of an extra full bath, other plumbers promoted the "powder room," a smaller bathroom with a sink and toilet located in the main living area of the house as opposed to the sleeping area, a feature now common in the American home. Advertising made the point that both family and guests would appreciate this modern convenience. Besides being sociable and comfortable, the powder room also increased the resale value of the home.

The ever-changing bathroom styles illustrated three characteristics of fashion and popular culture: (1) deeper societal trends, (2) interplay between producers and consumers, and (3) fashion-oriented merchandising. Certainly styles are often a reflection of deeper societal trends. For many products, color and design breakthroughs first occurred between 1924 and 1928. Color first showed up on new car models, fountain pens, and cameras; then in the bedroom and the bathroom; and finally, on kitchen cookware, utensils, appliances, and flooring materials.

Such style changes usually originated from the interplay between the deliberate inventions of designers and businesspeople and spontaneous actions by ordinary consumers. Designers, manufacturers, and merchandisers who could anticipate what consumers wanted succeeded in the marketplace. Tying bathroom fixtures and accessories to ever-changing fashions offered companies a powerful rationale for introducing new products and thus inflating prices. A splash of color or a minor design alteration enormously expanded the range of available products, as well as invigorating sales. With the ensemble concept in mind, manufacturers introduced color schemes into towels, floor coverings, and other bathroom accessories. A new shower curtain, towel, or piece of furniture often made everything else in the bathroom seem out of style. Thus, new styles and colors encouraged new purchases.

A case in point: the addition of color transformed the plain white bathroom towel from a utilitarian, absorbent piece of cloth for drying the body to a fashion statement. It also translated into profits. When textile manufacturer Cannon Mills of North Carolina introduced a new towel line in a variety of colors and decorative designs, backing the line with heavy advertising, it charged four times more for the new towels than for plain white ones. Even then Cannon found that consumers would pay for the added value of color and design.

The Cannon campaign provided several reasons to introduce new towels in the bathroom. People could achieve the effect of bathroom renovation merely by purchasing these fashionable towels. "With Cannon Towels, you can redecorate your bathroom every week," explained one 1927 ad. "First, blue or green, with seagulls, or whales, or dolphins, or lighthouses in the marine manner. Then, for a change—rose-colored flamingos or merry orange marmosets, the tropical trend!" If you have children to consider, Cannon suggested a special color for each child's towels. To sell more towels, Cannon also supported the "bath-a-day" habit, not for reasons of comfort and hygiene, but because it increased the number of towels needed and stimulated sales. One ad made this point: because "the first towel absorbs impurities from the skin, it must never (under any circumstances) be used again before washing."[26]

Fig. 5.4. Martex, advertisement for fashion towels, *Ladies' Home Journal*, May 1928.

The copy continued: "Today in the finest bathrooms one seldom sees the old-fashioned all-white towel."

In response, the textile manufacturer Martex followed with a line of fashion towels designed by famous artists that "cost no more than quite undistinguished towels." For use with the colored tiles and new, tinted bathroom equipment, these towels featured motifs from modern artists famous for their posters and paintings, namely Rene Clark, Erté, and Elizabeth Shippen

Green (see Fig. 5.4).[27] Still, many people objected to anything but white in bathroom linen, observed *Vogue* in 1927.[28]

Nevertheless, color transformed utilitarian staples into fashion goods and color-coordinated ensembles, which coaxed people to buy more often and to increase the average size of their purchase. In addition to towels, bathroom sets also took on color, which included a matching mat, a large-size rug, as well as covers for the toilet stool and lid. Bottles of all sizes, shapes, and colors offered to hold such mundane contents as lotions, bath salts, and other toiletries. Other bathroom accessories included drinking tumblers, soap dishes, toothbrush holders, and jars in beautifully shaded colors. Even the bath sponge took on color to add a touch of beauty to any bathroom. Thus, consumers could flaunt their prosperity by accessorizing their bathrooms with fashion-related towels, for which high prices created a high demand and a snob effect. As sales of fashion-oriented products increased, it helped fuel consumer desires by encouraging wider distribution of the items in retail outlets.

This phenomenon of consumption was a relatively new concept in the 1920s. Economist Thorstein Veblen first discussed conspicuous consumption at the turn of the twentieth century, referring to people's desire to provide evidence of their ability to afford luxury goods.[29] Another social analyst, George Simmel, first proposed the trickle-down theory to explain the fashion system in 1904. That is, dominant styles originated with the upper classes and trickled down to those below. Simmel argued that those people in the dominant groups responded to the attempts of lower classes to impersonate or emulate them by adopting even newer fashions.[30] These two processes created a self-perpetuating cycle of change that drove fashion.

THE IMPORTANCE OF KNOWING THE CUSTOMER

Bathroom manufacturers, like soapmakers, faced the challenge of how to present their products, services, and ideas effectively in the media to consumers. The key to a company's prosperity was its ability to attract and to keep customers willing and able to pay for its goods and services, a process we now call marketing. To be successful, marketers needed to know their markets—that is, groups of current or prospective customers—before they started advertising.

They needed to understand what makes potential customers behave the way they do. In order to find the common ground for communication, some early advertisers attempted to get enough relevant market data to develop profiles of buyers. This later developed into the study of buyer behavior—the mental and emotional processes of people who purchased products and services. But the concept of market research was slow to take hold.

Advertisers had more questions—Who is the buying public? What are its tastes and desires? Which ads pull the best?—than answers. To understand their audience, some admakers went into the field to sell the product, observed it in use, or interviewed housewives to acquire a feel for consumer tastes and problems. These early research efforts were primitive by today's standards, but they represented the roots of a vast theory-building enterprise.

Market Segmentation

The process of market segmentation identified groups of consumers who were similar to one another. Market researchers used demographic data to slice up a larger market according to observable measures such as age, gender, social class and income, and geography. These studies proved of great interest to marketers, because the data could be used to locate and predict the size of markets for many products, ranging from soap to automobiles. Ad makers could then devise strategies to appeal to one or more groups, even at the expense of excluding other segments from the firm's target markets.

The J. Walter Thompson Company routinely commissioned market investigations to acquire a feel for consumer tastes and retail problems. One early agency study that was combined with Curtis Publishing's own findings provided a factual base on which future marketing researchers would build. In 1912, Thompson president Stanley Resor commissioned a study entitled "Population and Its Distribution," which listed virtually every store by category and by state. The agency continued to update the research to describe more precisely the consumer population, to track the growth of wholesale and retail stores in large cities, and so on. As marketing research continued to evolve, agencies focused on quantitative market research in order to describe markets factually in terms of population statistics, numbers of outlets, buying-power indices, amount of media coverage, brand preference rankings, and audience profiles by occupation and class.

A MEDIUM-SIZED INDE-
PENDENT REMODELED FOR
SELF-SERVICE.

Fig. 5.5. Interior of a medium-sized independent, self-service grocery store. Courtesy of Pictorial Collection, Hagley Museum and Library, no. 99.215.1.

For example, the Thompson agency conducted a study to find out about the mass market for toilet soap in 1919. The company found that approximately 80 percent of all toilet soap sales were made through grocers, and most of these soaps retailed for a dime a cake.[31] The most popular brands included Lifebuoy, Ivory, Sweetheart, and Palmolive, which were primarily purchased at grocery stores in varying quantities, from one cake to dozens. A new type of self-service grocery stocked shelves with packaged merchandise placed within the customer's reach and with prices clearly marked to allow price comparisons. No longer did customers have to wait for sales clerks to search selves, portion out goods from containers, or tell them the cost of an item (see Fig. 5.5). The grocery chain stores of the 1920s then gave way to large-self service markets, or supermarkets, in the 1930s.[32] Drugstore purchases were special, however, and consumers typically bought their finer toilet soaps here only a few cakes at a time. For example, Woodbury's Facial Soap became commonplace in drugstores, selling for twenty-five cents a cake.[33]

Mail-order response testing emerged as the major form of research that provided a rough idea of consumer preferences. For example, coded advertisements ran with coupons, which readers could cut out and return for information, product samples, booklets, or premiums. In test cities, identical ads appeared in different magazines, and the results were compared. "Split runs" compared different versions in the same edition. From these studies agencies identified the best medium or media for the advertising of a given product. In addition, Robert and Helen Lynd's sociological study *Middletown*, the celebrated 1929 report about the people of Muncie, Indiana, provided agencies with more information on social attitudes for various classes of people.[34]

Other important characteristics that made consumers similar to or different from one another, such as personalities and tastes, were a bit more subtle and could not be objectively measured, yet they were important in influencing product choices. Although demographics and social status certainly did influence a person's choice of products, admakers also began to recognize that an individual's external characteristics were but one part of the puzzle, and underlying characteristics often played a large role in determining purchase behavior.

Buyer Behavior: The New Key to Advertising Strategy

Many approaches to understanding the complex concept of buyer behavior, later known as consumer behavior, can be traced back to psychological theorists who began to develop these perspectives in the early part of the twentieth century. These perspectives were qualitative, in the sense that they were largely based on an analyst's interpretations of a patient's accounts of dreams, traumas, sexual experiences, and so on. By the early 1920s, admakers had adapted some of Sigmund Freud's ideas. In particular, Freud's theories highlighted the potential importance of unconscious motives underlying purchases. The implication was that consumers could not necessarily express their true motivation for choosing a product, even if the researcher devised a sensitive way to ask them directly. The Freudian perspective also hinted that people might channel their desire to gratify their needs into outlets acceptable to the outside world by using products that signify their underlying desires. By acquiring the product, the person was able to experience his or her true goals, which otherwise might be unacceptable or unattainable.[35]

The notion of tapping into unconscious drives was evident in the Woodbury's campaign. The imagery of an attractive couple with the provocative headline "A skin you love to touch" sent a powerful signal to readers. By using the advertised product, you too could find romance or secure a relationship, gratifying a basic sexual desire. What the campaign had accomplished was to create a brand personality, an iconic connection between the advertised product and other symbolic associations. Such inferences about a brand's "personality" can be used by consumers to compare and contrast the perceived characteristics of different brands, so they can choose which product will best fulfill their needs. For example, admakers portrayed Woodbury's Facial Soap as sophisticated, romantic, and sexy. In contrast, the Lifebuoy brand was presented as familiar, comfortable, and practical. In any case, one industry analyst exulted advertisers "to stir up the heart, and the head will blind obey."[36] Thus, the desire to attract a romantic partner, a direct appeal to the sex instinct, appeared to be more effective than a technical discourse on the nonirritant qualities of the soap or the features of rustless steel in corsets.[37]

Freud's work had a huge influence on subsequent theories of personality, as he opened the door to the realization that explanations for behavior may lurk beneath the surface. One of the prominent neo-Freudians was Carl Jung. However, Jung was unable to accept Freud's emphasis on sexual aspects of personality, and he went on to develop a method of psychotherapy that became known as analytical psychology. Jung believed that people are shaped by the cumulative experiences of the past generations. A central part of Jung's perspective was an emphasis on what he called the collective unconsciousness, a storehouse of memories from our ancestral past. For example, Jung would have argued that many people are afraid of the dark because their distant ancestors had good reason to exhibit this fear. These shared memories create archetypes, or universally shared ideas and behavior patterns. Archetypes involved themes such as birth, death, or the devil that frequently appeared in myths, stories, and dreams.[38]

Advertising messages often invoked (at least intuitively) archetypes to link products with underlying meanings. For example, some of the archetypes identified by Jung include the "old wise man" and the "earth mother."[39] These images appeared frequently in advertising messages that used such characters as the revered professional expert and the maternal figure who guided the reader in the most mundane aspects of everyday life.

Other interpretations focused on the quantitative measurements of personality traits, or identifiable characteristics that define a person. For example, people can be distinguished by the degree to which they are outgoing or extroverted opposed to quiet and reserved. One specific trait that admakers had reason to believe was relevant to buyer behavior was "IQ," or intelligence quotient, measurements of which were developed during World War I. In fact, psychologists in the 1920s repeatedly reminded admakers that most people "have the mind of a child of ten."[40] Thus, advertising people such as Thompson copywriter William L. Day believed that the "message should be so constructed that it is graspable by the lowest sort of mind."[41]

Another well-known behavior psychologist was John B. Watson, who claimed to have discovered basic techniques for predicting and manipulating human behavior. In 1920, Watson resigned from John Hopkins University and went to work for the Thompson agency. According to Watson, advertisers needed to tap into fundamental human drives (such as love, fear, sex, and rage) and repeatedly associate the given stimuli with their products. In one of his early successes, Watson conducted a controlled blindfold test that revealed that people could not recognize their favorite brand of cigarettes. Based on this finding, Watson concluded that cigarettes and other products could not be advertised by logical appeals.[42] Although the use of psychology in advertising was oversold at this time, the movement laid the foundation for what Americans now know as advertising.

The science of psychology held a great interest for two reasons. First, it provided information about the instincts, drives, and wants of people. Second, it suggested new ways in which they might be controlled.[43] "Out of this change," wrote Abram Lipsky in 1925, "has sprung the universal interest in psychoanalysis, mob psychology, salesmanship—all connoting a technique with which one may control the minds of others."[44] As for advertising, the study of psychology offered a key to overcoming consumers' objections to purchasing the promoted product. Instead of accepting people as rational beings who knew what they wanted, admakers began to examine what triggered people to make choices such as to buy or not buy a bathroom sink or to choose one brand of soap over another. Armed with this information, advertisers could make the their products more appealing. Here, the focus of advertisers was clearly on the middle class, who had the means to buy the advertised products, and the prime target of all this promotion was women.

New Insights into the Women's Market

From the very start, the advertising world made women the prime target of their efforts, since women read most ads and purchased most products. According to the *Ladies' Home Journal*, women controlled an estimated 80 to 85 percent of household spending in 1929.[45] Ad makers drew on a long tradition that assumed a woman's place was in the home, believing that women were only concerned with "their desire to look young and sexually appealing."[46]

Although economic prosperity had been extended to a larger segment of the population than ever before, this newly acquired affluence was also accompanied by an anxious concern for external appearance, social acceptance, and approval. The literature of advice of the period emphasized not only the need for self-confidence, but also the dangers of feeling inadequate. Special books and courses sought to develop poise and charm—voice control, conversation, and public speaking, among other topics. All stressed exercise, sound eating habits, good complexion, and grooming, as well as clothing, appearance, and good manners. For many Americans, the emphasis on a clean, genial personality was linked to a striving for acceptance, social approval, and popularity. Those who defined success largely as the consequence of appearance and sociability shared similar ideas of the business world. At the time, good grooming and a congenial personality became more valued than individualism as large U.S. organizations became increasingly bureaucratic and required cooperation action.[47]

The role of advertising in this revolution in American values cannot be exaggerated. It was both cause and effect. Just as advertising originated in the need to persuade more and more purchasers to acquire more and more material goods, it also provided women with a version of reality that reflected the changing values and beliefs of consumers. The pages of popular women's magazines, such as *Ladies' Home Journal*, *Good Housekeeping*, and *True Story*, and general periodicals like *Saturday Evening Post*, vividly set forth the vision of the "good life." Thus, admakers appealed to yearnings for social status that coincided with a society geared to social mobility. Ads of the time were quite explicit about the route to improved social status, persuading more and more consumers to acquire more and more material things.

World War I had a lasting influence on most American women's lives, and many from the younger generation repudiated the moralistic idealism of the prior century. The war had opened up unprecedented career opportunities for women. In 1900, an estimated one out of five American women worked outside the home, but most found themselves miserably exploited in sweatshops. As America became more office-oriented, the number of working women reached 25 percent by 1920. Women made up half the financial community's employees, accounting for 90 percent of all the clerks and typists.[48] Their wages amounted to considerably more than "pin money," or pocket change.

Young working women also made it clear in many ways that they wanted the same freedoms men had. The flapper emerged as the symbol of this spirit of liberation.[49] Women threw away their corsets, bound their breasts for a flat-chested look, raised their skirts to the knee, replaced their cotton underwear with rayon and silk, bobbed their hair, plucked their eyebrows, and painted their lips; some also used shocking words, drank on occasion, and publicly smoked. In the spirit of liberation, the "petting question" was also anxiously addressed in the ladies' magazines and elsewhere. The earlier rule had been that a nice girl did not allow a man to kiss her unless they were engaged or married. About this trend, the *Pittsburgh Observer* reported in 1922 "a change for the worse during the past year in feminine dress, dancing, manners, and general moral standards."[50] Indeed, a new philosophy had become part of the younger generation's culture—no more austerity and sacrifice, but rather an emphasis on leisure and enjoyment.

Once admakers recognized that their audience was overwhelmingly female, strategies for copy content and selling appeal seemed evident. Ad makers, who considered women more emotionally vulnerable than men, often manipulated women's hidden desires to be sought after and well liked and to join the successful middle class. Although more Americans had more money to spend than ever before, they also spent more time worrying about social acceptance and approval. "The advertising culture, more than the culture at large, acknowledged that one of the things that linked women was a persuasive discontent," writes Jennifer Scanlon. "Women found their inarticulate longings for sensuality, financial independence, and emotional fulfillment channeled through what Jackson Lears calls an 'unconscious collaboration,' rather than a conspiracy."[51]

In linking those "inarticulate longings" to consumption, emotive advertising campaigns appealed to yearnings for social acceptance that coincided with an American society geared to social mobility. Ads of the time were quite explicit about how products and activities helped to define different social roles. Individuals' clothing, jewelry, furniture, cars, and so on helped to determine how people perceived themselves, as well as how they imagined others perceived them. The use of consumption to define the self was especially important when people filled new and unfamiliar roles, as young working women did after Word War I. The symbolic self-completion theory lends support to this point. Symbolic self-completion theory suggests that people complete their identity by acquiring and displaying symbols associated with it.[52] Thus, when flappers began to shorten their skirts, applied makeup, and smoked cigarettes to bolster their identity in reaction to traditional gender roles, advertising could parlay these symbols into a wider market. Just as individuals contribute symbols to advertising, so advertising adds meanings back to people's lives.

Advertising also acknowledged the new mass media that was shaping the values of a younger generation, including movies, radio, glossy magazines, and tabloid newspapers. Hollywood film stars usually embodied the ideal, which was presented to the nation through the movies and reinforced by magazine photographs, articles, and advertisements featuring models and pinup girls. Dominant styles originating with the upper classes, or elite fashion, had been largely replaced by mass fashion because media exposure to the latest style trends in magazines, film, and ads permitted many people to become aware of a style at the same time. They exchanged old possessions for new ones for no other reason than they had gone out of style. In particular, American women spared little effort or expense trying to make themselves over according to the ideals set forth in the national media. By 1929, expenditures on perfumes, makeup, and toiletries were more than ten times the amount spent per capita twenty years earlier.[53]

In particular, two popular culture phenomena provided admakers with new insights into the female market: tabloid newspapers and confession magazines. Following publication of the *Illustrated Daily News* in 1919, the concept of "tabloid copy for tabloid minds" gained credibility as the tabloid newspapers quickly gained widespread circulation.[54] Although smaller in size than normal newspapers, the lively tabloids had something for everyone—advice for the lovelorn, outrageous scandals, gruesome murders, and sensational stories. Photographs dominated the news presentations and

left little to the imagination; the accompanying text provided fast-paced tit-
illation. The term "tabloid audience" came to characterize the reading
tastes of average men and women.[55]

Like the tabloids, cheap confession magazines also attracted a vast
audience. It started with *True Story* magazine, which Bernard McFadden
launched in 1919. The editors of McFadden's *Physical Culture* health and
exercise magazine had been flooded with unsolicited letters recounting
intimate experiences, and they decided to publish the narratives. The confession magazine featured first-person confessional stories aimed at young
working women, offering dramatic personal accounts of tragic adventures,
temptations, and romantic triangles such as "The Primitive Lover," "Her
Life Secret," and "How to Keep the Thrill in Marriage." The primary appeal
of such periodicals was often the candid autobiographic segments that featured experiences like the readers' own; the resolution of the dramatic con-
flicts provided inspiration on how they could solve their own problems. Certainly the popularity of *True Story* lends support to this point. By 1926, the
confession magazine achieved a circulation of almost two million, a remarkable achievement considering that the mainstream *Saturday Evening Post*
enjoyed a circulation of about three million in the mid-1930s.[56]

McFadden also went on to publish *True Romances* and *Modern Marriage*. At the same time, motion pictures also reflected the national preoccupation with sheiks, vamps, and sex goddesses. Movies with titles like
Cheap Kisses, *Soiled*, and *Sinners in Silk* attracted large numbers of
patrons.[57] As Gilbert M. Ostrander noted, two of the most popular themes for
American women readers had always been those of religion and seduction.[58]

Madison Avenue began to recognize that the female readers of tabloids
and confession magazines offered new opportunities for advertisers. The new
publications had fashioned, in effect, a female market that had plenty of
money to spend for products like clothing, cosmetics, and soap. Poor,
working-class, and black women, largely ignored by national advertisers and
magazines, joined the affluent in the market for beauty and fashion. Although
some agencies expressed no interest in these new ideas, others, like J. Walter
Thompson, became involved in discovering and then exploiting the secrets of
human nature. The agency helped popularize campaigns based on psychological appeals aimed at the largely female buying public.

THREE FORMULAS IN THE MAKING, 1920s

Advertising content and style had changed gradually but decisively by the 1920s. In retrospect, *Printers' Ink* marked this important change as a shift from the "factory viewpoint" to concern with "the mental processes of the consumer," from the "objective to the subjective," from "descriptive data" to "talk in terms of ultimate buying motives."[59] But it was the J. Walter Thompson Company that pioneered the dramatic shift away from merely describing and picturing goods and services to using well-known psychological devices to entice customers. In order to reach what the agency perceived as a tabloid audience, the admakers replaced the rational selling arguments with a complex blend of psychology, human-interest visuals, and sophisticated copy. The resulting ads appealed to the powerful emotions of fear and sex and the motive of emulation.

Looking at the whole range of emotional selling arguments in the 1920s, there are three advertising formulas under which a majority of the soap ads can be subsumed: (1) first-impression, (2) romance, and (3) emulation.

The First-Impression Formula

Fear appeals emphasized the negative consequences that would occur unless the consumer changed a behavior or an attitude. A multitude of products and services capitalized on people's insecurities and desire to be well liked, because many consumers in this era went to great lengths to alter or maintain aspects of their physical self in order to present a desirable appearance. Fear strategies were widely used in advertising, attempting to "scare" the audience into purchasing a specific product. These appeals were often based on legitimate concerns such as disease germs. However, appeals were also based on irrational fears. Soap ads aimed at both people's vanity and their fear of social disgrace. The advertisements painted a gloomy picture of the possible consequences of not having the featured product, and they recommended a specific action for reducing the threat.

The central story of the "first-impression" formula involved a hero or heroine who overcame some obstacle or personal or domestic disaster simply by using the advertised product.[60] The wrong soap could ruin a new chiffon dress, irritate the tender skin of a baby, and so on. Whereas the early advertising-by-fear campaigns had dealt with physical disasters of some sort, the new "scare" or "whisper copy" went to new lengths to grab the reader's attention and evoke broader ranges of human response.[61] Instead of facing real-life challenges such as an actual physical accident or illness, the men and women who starred in these ads faced dramatic social situations, what has been called the "slice of life" approach to communication.[62] For example, an advertisement might address people's concerns about losing their romantic partners, their jobs, or their social standing.

The successful Listerine "Halitosis" campaign, which first sold the general antiseptic as a "breath deodorant" in 1922, initially spurred the popular use of the negative slant.[63] Installments of the dramatic fear campaign created new anxieties, they depicted the product as a way to avert social disasters, from missed invitations to ruined marriages, occasioned by unpleasant breath or "halitosis," the medical-sounding word that the agency used to talk about bad breath in polite company. Annual earnings jumped from around $115,000 in 1921 to over $8 million in 1928.[64] Although fundamental to advertising today, Listerine's idea of jolting consumers into a new consciousness seemed novel at the time and proved that the skillful use of emotional appeals could move products faster than any other approach.

Soap ads pictured case after case of women committing unforgivable social offenses, because their complexion, hands, or laundry didn't measure up. The cumulative effect likely reinforced readers' impression of being surrounded by a host of accusing eyes and unspoken comments. Often the ads left readers feeling guilty and anxious, worrying about how their friends and acquaintances perceived their personal appearance. The right image was a simple matter of using the advertised product. Thus, the ads began to look more like public service messages from the soap manufacturers.

The first-impression formula appeared fully developed in a series of advertisements for Lifebuoy Soap, the "Body Odor" campaign. The Thompson agency originally promoted Lifebuoy as the soap that cleans, disinfects, and purifies, all in one operation, so the principal focus was as a family soap for general health and toilet purposes. By the 1920s, however, the company had softened the appeal. The campaign then suggested that the entire family use the soap frequently for washing the hands, face, and

Fig. 5.6. Lifebuoy Soap, advertisement, 1925.

body to protect against disease germs, which were on almost everything they touched.

The slogan "Use Lifebuoy Health Soap" and different "protect the children" messages were aimed at men, women, and children with the goal of making washing with Lifebuoy a health habit. Ads urged homemakers to stock up on the product with attention-getting headlines: "Mothers—for the health of your children and husband—keep a cake of Lifebuoy soap at every place where there is running water"; "Train children and husband to use Lifebuoy regularly"; and "Isn't Their Health Worth Guarding, too?" (see Fig. 5.6).[65] As part of their coming-home-after-work ritual, fathers were urged to first wash with Lifebuoy even before embracing their wife or playing with the children. "Let Daddy wash up—*first!*" followed by, "Wise Daddy. No dangerous city dirt passes from his hands to his loved ones."[66]

The agency shifted the selling argument from points about health care to social disgrace in 1926. Print ads dramatically made the point with the slogan "Lifebuoy Health Soap stops body odor." One ad portrayed "Poor Uncle Ed" as a "half-failure—too bad he never suspected 'B.O.' [Body Odor]."

> People never liked him. Despite his geniality, even men had denied him friendship. For all his ability, real success had always evaded him. Now he was past middle age—a lonely man—unpopular, just a half-way success—and all for the same unpardonable failing—"B.O."[67]

The insidious thing about body odor, the ad continued, was that the offender was the last to know. Even one's closest friends would not tell the individual; however, the friendly Lifebuoy advisor could. Lifebuoy gave "the marvelous freshness that lasts for hours, with never a hint of 'B.O.' "

Further installments of the dramatic Lifebuoy campaign presented other social disasters from lost business to ruined romances (see Fig. 5.7). On later radio shows, a foghorn boomed "BEEE-O-O-O-O-O!" Fortunately, Lifebuoy Soap would "protect" its users. As these stop-smelling pitches ran, business boomed for Lever Brothers. The Lifebuoy campaign worked because the ad maker struck a responsive chord with the public. The J. Walter Thompson Company recognized the value of promoting consumer products as solutions for fearful individuals in a hostile world. The inferiority complex had become a "valuable thing in advertising," explained executive William Esty at an agency meeting in 1930.[68] Instead of being

Fig. 5.7. Lifebuoy Soap,
advertisement, *Silver
Screen*, March 1934.

frightened into buying a product, the prospect was shamed and ridiculed. Social threat appeals in soap ads proved an effective strategy.

Other whisper copy in Woodbury's Facial Soap ads also revolved around unspoken comments. Soap and water may be clean, but one still might not be above reproach. Such ads made it clear that while "personal daintiness" began with cleanliness, it did not end there. "Nothing has more influence on your appearance than the condition of your skin," claimed a series of Woodbury's Facial Soap ads. In fact, one's whole popularity supposedly was determined by this crucial first impression. Such ads simply started out, "His unspoken thoughts when he looks into your face—what are they?" or, "All around you people are judging you silently."[69] Thus, all of these women's grooming efforts were for naught. Not even the prettiest clothes, charm of manner, or highest character could counteract the first impression of neglect and carelessness about their appearance.

The first-impression formula sold a lot more than just soap. The premise also successfully pitched everything from deodorant to etiquette books. Many of these ads suggested that one of the most important effects of using the advertised products was the self-confidence it created in the consumer. The strategy underlying the first-impression theme was obvious. Appearance and material goods had a significant impact in the context of a mobile, urban society. People increasingly conceived of the details of their personal appearance and that of their home as an index of their true character. By presenting a desirable image, they also avoided the ridicule, guilt, and other forms of emotional distress that resulted from being seen or revealed as deviating from the norm. Indeed, the first-impression formula provided admakers with a powerful new selling tool. In fact, negative emotional appeals in advertisements of foods, toilet articles, medicine, and sanitary napkins nearly doubled over the decade, occurring in 10 percent of the advertisements in 1922 and in 19 percent of the ads five years later.[70]

Did fear work? Most research on this topic has indicated that negative appeals were usually most effective when only a moderate threat was used and when a solution to the problem was presented. Otherwise, consumers would dismiss the ad, since they could do nothing to solve the problem.[71] This approach also worked better when there was sufficient elaboration of the harmful consequences that enhanced credibility.[72] More precise measures of actual fear responses are still needed, however, before definite conclusions can be drawn about the impact of such appeals on consumption decisions.

The Romance Formula

Under the assumption that "sex sells," many admakers incorporated erotic suggestions ranging from subtle hints to blatant displays of skin. In the case of the romance formula, the crucial defining characteristic was not that it starred a female, but that the organizing action involved the advertised product bringing two potential lovers together in a deeper, more secure relationship. The Woodbury's Facial Soap campaign "A skin you love to touch" had already demonstrated that sex could sell a lot of soap. The advertisements featured three essential elements: (1) a romantic man-and-woman situation; (2) a dominant sex appeal, focused on "a skin you love to touch" as key to desirable charm; and (3) the famous Woodbury treatment for overcoming skin problems.

Instead of merely selling soap, the Woodbury campaign had discussed the benefits of using the product, suggesting softness, sex appeal, and even romance. These advertisements also employed fantasy appeals, which allowed women to extend their vision of themselves by permitting them to escape from problems in the real world and "try on" interesting or provocative roles. Emulating the Woodbury approach, Palmolive launched a campaign that focused on the romance formula. To differentiate soap from Woodbury's Facial Soap, when both personal soaps were so much alike, the copy emphasized aging: "Keep that schoolgirl complexion." Ads featured the modern women staying young with her husband at eighteen, at thirty, and at fifty, with exactly the same face as in her youth.[73] The beauty appeal also reinforced the notion that all women shared identical desires—to remain magically young forever—so that they could not only capture a man, but also keep him by staying attractive. Thus, the ads showed women how the Palmolive "simple beauty ritual" could help them retain their freshness of youth. The suggestion of romance is implicit in one 1928 ad with the headline "He remembered"; it was left to the imagination of the viewer what unexplicable thing brought about the note and bouquet of fragrant roses for the woman in the illustration:

Fig. 5.8. Palmolive Soap, advertisement, *Ladies' Home Journal*, August 1928.

He remembered—That Schoolgirl complexion. The beauty that men admire—and remember—is *natural* beauty. And that may be yours whether you use powder and rouge—or not—if you observe one simple beauty ritual. Washing the face for beauty is the recommendation of all the leading skin specialists.[74]

The readers could only guess at what the soap would do in their own lives (see Fig. 5.8). The slogan "That Schoolgirl Complexion" was effective, running for several decades.

Did sex sell? Although the use of sex appeal did appear to draw attention to an ad, its use may sometimes also have been counterproductive for the ad maker. Ironically, a provocative picture could be too effective if it attracted so much attention that it hindered the consumer's processing and recall of the ad's content. Sexual appeals appeared to be ineffective when used as a "trick" to grab attention. They appeared to work, however, when the product itself was related to sex.[75]

In the case of Woodbury and Palmolive, the ads convinced women that the advertised soaps could beautify and soften the skin and thus persuaded them that they would become more attractive to the opposite sex. Still, the Woodbury and Palmolive campaigns only hinted at sex in the artwork and copy. The themes had been "you can keep your man if you keep your skin as attractive as it was when you captured him," "The skin you love to touch" and "Keep that school girl complexion!"[76]

What is important here is that the romance formula offered a pliable advertising concept to reach both the women of the smart salon trade and working women from the factory. The advertising invoked the mythic expectation of romantic love. According to one version of the romantic love myth, for each individual there is one perfect partner who, once found, will make life complete; the logical extension is the myth of the nuclear family. That is, the continued use of the advertised product will not only bring romance, but will lead to marriage replete with children and a well-appointed home.

Thus, the Woodbury and Palmolive campaigns, among others, continued to repackage nineteenth-century ideals and gender roles. In this view, a woman's place was in the home; and her beauty, not her accomplishments, measured her worth. "Through beauty woman can enter into her kingdom—woman's kingdom—where, as friend, sweetheart, wife, mother, she reigns in serene majesty and infinite power," explained one Palmolive ad. Moreover, beauty was not just a birthright; it was a duty.

> Given an attractive heart and mind, a woman must be totally deficient in some womanly qualities who calmly accepts pimples, moles, obnoxious hair upon the face or unsightly features with what she deems becoming resignation, and views the effort to rid herself of such disfigurements as a sinful pandering to feminine vanity.[77]

Indeed, the romance formula in advertising further legitimated women's pursuit of beauty.

The Emulation Formula

Advertising appeals with the concept of emulation in mind resulted in quite different messages from the first-impression and romance formulas. Ad makers gave an aura of truth to the advertisements by including testimonials of supposedly satisfied users of the product. In 1920s, the Thompson agency introduced an upscale version of the testimonial, giving the old form credibility by using famous people, not just ordinary satisfied people, to endorse a product. Prominent people, celebrities, and professional experts told consumers that to be socially acceptable they had to buy the "right" soap, the "right" fashions, and the "right" car.

The emulation formula generated remarkable results for Lux Toilet Soap with the famous "Hollywood" campaign. When the agency introduced Lux Toilet Form, the first white, French-milled toilet soap with a reasonable price in America, the ad campaign had been preceded by years of tests. Women had already extended the use of Lux Flakes laundry soap to the general realm of toilet soap; that is, they used Lux in flake form for their hands, baths, babies, and shampoos.[78] Surveys also showed that women wanted a white toilet soap that would not cost the fifty cents to two dollars that French soaps cost.[79] Selling for a dime, the Lux soap cake directly competed with such best-selling brands as Ivory, Fairy, and Palmolive.[80] However, Lever Brothers believed that Lux Toilet Form would compete too closely with another of its own products, Lux Flakes, so sales could be cannibalized. That is, the two brands would take sales away from each other, rather than from competing brands. In fact, since the "profit on Lux Flakes per package is equal to the profit of two cakes of Toilet Form, it would be the poorest form of business policy," explained F. A. Countway, then president of Lever Brothers. He added that Lux Toilet Form should be placed on a "pinnacle, removed from any suggestion of laundry or dishpan use."[81] Thus, the Lux Toilet Form campaign was launched in 1925.

To create an aura of luxury, Lever Brothers packaged the soap in pastel colors, adopted "French-type" ideas in advertising to render the soap feminine, and aimed to reach all social classes with its message.[82] Even the

Fig. 5.9. Lux Toilet Soap, advertisement, *Ladies' Home Journal*, May 1927.

Already America has bought tens of millions of cakes

From France
The gift of a Smooth Skin

BEAUTY-WISE France! The country that can make any woman lovely. For hundreds of years all the world has looked to France for petal-smooth skin, for the magic of her fine toilet soaps.

Costly, extravagant—French soaps! But today, *by the very method France uses for her finest toilet soaps,* Lux Toilet Soap, white, delicious, is made in America!

That creamy smoothness you loved in French soap—that firm, fine textured cake! The instant, luxurious lather of Lux Toilet Soap tends your skin the true French way. It even lasts like French soap!

France, with her passion for perfection—America, with her genius for achievement! For Lux Toilet Soap is but 10c. Lever Bros. Co., Cambridge, Mass.

LUX TOILET SOAP

name "Lux," a form of *luxe*, implied sumptuousness and luxury. Headlines underscored the idea that Lux offered a fine white soap made in the same way as the finest French soap. "'Please—an exquisite soap we can love like French soaps'" women pleaded." "From France—the gift of a smooth skin." And, "So captivating—so Parisian."[83] "French-type" pictures also commanded attention (see Fig. 5.9). Inspired illustrators drew on new Art Deco design ideas and rendered highly stylized line drawings with a wide variety of exotic motifs such as oriental, Egyptian, Aztec, and other international styles. While now a commonplace style, the drawings appeared ultrasmart at the time. Finally, Lux used a variety of copy appeals to reach a broad audience. For perfumed soap users, the product offered a delightful fragrance. To those who preferred lather, a generous froth was generated almost at the touch of water. To those who were economy minded, the soap wore wafer-thin. And for those not satisfied with the soap they were using or who were eager to try something new, a change that met exacting demands.[84]

The following year, in 1926, Lever Brothers began national distribution of Lux Toilet Form and boosted advertising by adding magazines to the newspaper campaign. Coupons were distributed on a large scale, while car cards, or transit advertisements, appeared inside streetcars and buses. With a change in the brand name, from Lux Toilet Form to Lux Toilet Soap, Lever extended the advertising campaign to include acceptance by men in the family. For example, one ad in the series declared, "It has captivated those sternest of critics—*THE MEN*." Next came use by the entire family, not only husband but also sons, daughters, and the baby, with headlines like "My entire family insists on it."[85]

Having successfully introduced Lux as a fine toilet soap at a reasonable price, the advertising abruptly changed face in 1927. Photographs of real people replaced the stylized line drawings.[86] The agency provided two reasons for this marked change in advertising strategy. First, the media plan increased the amount spent on advertising in small towns and in farming communities and reduced the amount spent on color. So the campaign shifted from drawings to actual photographs for "far more of an air of conviction."[87] Second, the drawings had several drawbacks. According to agency executive William Esty, some ads were successful and others were not because "the very best in drawings falls short of reality in portraying real people."[88]

The Lux "Hollywood" campaign exemplified the turn to photography. It began with the goal of making Lux Toilet Soap the best-selling soap in Hollywood. Although the Thompson agency could not accomplish that goal within the given time frame, the admakers did ensure that all the studios and a large majority of actresses used Lux Toilet Soap and nothing else. In order to get such widespread representation, the agency enlisted the backing of Mr. Quirk, president of *Photoplay*, a magazine that had tremendous influence on the people in Hollywood. Next, the agency set up an elaborate machinery, not only making sure the studios and the actresses used the soap, but also that they received a supply of the soap at regular intervals. The agency even had liquid soap machines removed from the dressing rooms, replacing them with Lux cake soap. "Very quickly it became impossible to wash your hands in Hollywood unless you used Lux Toilet Soap," explained Esty.[89]

The second phase of the Lux "Hollywood" campaign involved an intensive campaign to secure celebrity endorsements; the hope was that the stars' popularity would transfer to the product. To secure the famous names, Danny Danker, a Thompson representative in Hollywood, signed up unknown actresses hankering for publicity, who gave their names in exchange for a crateful of Lux. If they became famous, Danker put them in Lux ads for no further expense.[90] An ad featuring actress Doris Kenyon appeared in 1928, and other celebrity endorsement soon followed. Later that year, the famous slogan "9 out of 10 Screen Stars care for their Skin with Lux Toilet Soap" ran as a headline after an investigation showed that 96 percent of the stars supposedly used Lux (see Fig. 5.10).[91]

However, movie stars like Joan Crawford ("Never have I had anything like it for keeping the skin smooth"), Janet Gaynor ("Lux Soap has a caressing quality"), Clara Bow, and others only appeared to testify for Lux. That is, the actresses did not actually speak the words attributed to them; and if they used the product at all, they did not necessarily prefer it to all others. Nevertheless, sales for Lux Toilet Soap nearly doubled in 1928 alone.[92]

To increase the atmosphere of glamour, the agency photographers posed the stars in beautiful bathrooms specially designed for them. In Hollywood studios, the agency built twenty-five different bathrooms ranging from classic Greek to ultramodern designs, all luxurious and impressive. "Graceful silver swan faucets and the glittering crystal chandelier are bril-

Fig. 5.10. Lux Toilet Soap, advertisement, 1928.

liant notes in a black and white bathroom conceived so appropriately as a setting for Mary McAvoy's delicate beauty," noted one 1928 ad. Similar striking bathroom designs were inspired by popular stars such as Phyllis Haver, Esther Ralston, and Janet Gaynor.[93] Many of the bathrooms actually had water piped into the baths, showers, and wash bowls, with no expense spared to make them absolutely right. Still, the cost of the photography and custom sets added up to no more than the drawings that were used for the prior year.[94]

In response, Palmolive challenged the statement that nine out of ten stars used Lux and that it was the official soap used in Hollywood dressing rooms. The agency sent the famous publicity agent Harry Rickenbah and even the president of Lord & Thomas agency to Los Angeles to make offers of $2,500 to $25,000 each for broadcast stars, but they secured few names.[95] Palmolive countered not with a similar Hollywood testimonial campaign the following year, but with endorsements from celebrated beauty specialists—namely, Lisa Cavalieri, Masse of Paris, and Fontaine of Brussels—who advocated a twice-a-day treatment with soap to keep skin lovely.[96] Although successful, the famous Palmolive ad campaign never achieved the same success as the Hollywood campaign for Lux Toilet Soap, but it did force Lever Brothers to intensify its advertising efforts. Thompson had linked Lux with fashion and rode it through years of success, as the "Hollywood" campaign continued for the next twenty years.[97]

A fine opportunity for advertising women's personal care products came when women first embraced the movies in the 1920s. The movies, with their highly made-up stars, glamorous lighting, and close-ups, influenced the way American women and men looked at women. Female fans took pleasure in actresses, who were always clad in the latest fashions, and copied their appearance and gestures.[98] Soaps, cosmetics, and other toiletries played an essential part in the new look of glamour. Tapping into popular tastes, the J. Walter Thompson Company glamorized motion picture stars and blatantly appealed to women's desire to emulate their appearance. At an agency meeting, Mrs. Devree put it this way: It was "exploited . . . as something magical, mysterious, and in some way synonymous with fashion. Fashion and style, always belonging to the upper class, were becoming the prerogatives of the middle class."[99]

At the same time, soap ads exalted advice from other "personalities"— professional experts such as doctors, scientists, and other specialists. For example, Procter & Gamble's new toilet soap, called Camay, featured a series of ads with the "woman's angle." The one thing that women most especially wanted to know was whether the soap helped keep their skin fresh and lovely. As with Ivory Soap, Procter & Gamble had found a way of saying that its soap was exceptional by emphasizing that it was mild enough for even the

71
famous skin specialists said:

"Those 282 Chicago girls have the right idea about complexions"

DID you *really* come all the way from New York just for that?" a young Chicago housewife asked me in utter surprise. She could hardly believe I had traveled a thousand miles just to ask her and several hundred other girls about their complexions and this fragrant new Camay!

But I had! I'm a consultant about women and their ways. Various manufacturers call me in for advice, just as you might call in an architect or an interior decorator.

I knew all about Camay's gentleness, of course, from the way it felt on my own skin. And I loved its firm, clear whiteness and its delicate wildflower fragrance.

But just my experience wasn't enough, I felt. So, among other things, I went out to Chicago and talked to women and girls—282 in all, my note book reminds me.

What Chicago girls told me

"There just never was a soap like Camay for *my* skin," one young woman out in Evanston said. "It makes my complexion look so smooth and fresh."

"Camay feels gentler on my skin than any other soap I ever used," and the head of the toilet goods department of a well-known shop who told me this, has a *very* wide soap acquaintance!

I met enthusiasm like this for Camay's gentleness from girl after girl, in every part of town.

71 leading American skin specialists gave Camay their unanimous approval as the kind of soap they would recommend for the daily cleansing of the most delicate complexions—something no other complexion soap in history has ever had!

Then I decided to go farther. I took my idea to the editor of the official journal of the dermatologists of the United States, himself one of the best-known skin specialists in the country

Why 71 leading skin specialists approve Camay

He agreed to have Camay analyzed, and to test it thoroughly in use. He did this, and Camay came through without a single question-mark. And he did much more! He sent copies of Camay's analysis to 70 dermatologists whom he regards as outstanding in their profession today and asked *them* to examine it and test Camay, too. Most of these men are heads of the department of dermatology in the largest universities and hospitals in the country.

And now I am very happy to tell

CAMAY IS 10¢ A CAKE

CAMAY

you that all these skin specialists approved Camay's formula and Camay's gentle way of cleansing even the most delicate feminine skins. This is the first time in history that any perfumed soap has ever had such approval.

So every time you cleanse your face with Camay's snowflake lather, you can know that you are using just the kind of soap these skin specialists would recommend to you if you asked their best advice about a soap for *your* complexion.

Could any soap say more?

Free Booklet: There isn't space here for all the things I learned about complexions from the 71 famous skin specialists. But I've put everything into a booklet—their advice about dry skins; oily skins; care with hard water and soft; diet; sleep; exercise; cosmetics and many other things so important to beauty.

I shall be glad to send you this booklet without charge if you will write to me at 509 Fifth Avenue, Dept. YJ-79, New York City.

Helen Chase

CAMAY IS A PROCTER & GAMBLE SOAP

Fig. 5.11. Camay Soap, advertisement, *Ladies' Home Journal*, July 1929.

most delicate complexions. Sixty-nine leading dermatologists analyzed the soap, tested it thoroughly, and bestowed on Camay their unanimous approval—"something no other perfumed complexion soap in history ever had."[100] This endorsement became the basis for the 1929 Camay campaign (see Fig. 5.11). Other ads invited readers to write to confidential advisor Helen Chase for a free booklet about the things she had learned from these skin specialists about complexions, including their advice about dry skin, oily skin, diet, sleep, exercise, cosmetics, and many other beauty issues. Ad makers soon advocated anything from a bar of soap to yeast for everything from a woman's youthful look to the consummation of a happy marriage.

Although these campaigns featured hundreds of endorsers, none of whom were paid, others used statements purchased for money and publicity.[101] Stanley Resor believed that using paid endorsements in advertisements would not abuse the confidence of readers and eventually lessen their belief in advertising. When only testimonials of people who enthusiastically used the product were employed, payment had no effect on their opinions, claimed Resor. Rather, readers would read them because they liked to read to about prominent people. In addition to choosing credible spokespeople, he also believed "very little that is worth while in this world is secured without solic-itation," and as a result, readers developed an increased interest in adver-tising. Despite the fact that many spokespersons received payment for their product endorsements, the Thompson testimonials were "no more honest than others of the period," concluded historian Stephen Fox.[102]

Stanley Resor's use of famous people acknowledged a fundamental aspect of human behavior: people read about other people out of curiosity. People wanted to know how the other half lived—whether it was movie fans reading what their idols ate for breakfast or the socialite who enjoyed plays and stories in which the humbler aspects of life were depicted. Resor also felt that people continually searched for authority figures, what he called "personalities," and copied those whom they deemed superior in taste and knowledge.[103] In particular, Resor claimed that the desire to emulate was stronger in women than in men, avidly confirming the observations of the celebrated Italian psychologist Gina Lombroso.[104] According to Lombroso, a woman's self-fulfillment derived from the objects and people immediately about her, unlike men, who gained their satisfaction from within, from more abstract and impersonal subjects.[105] This psychological factor could explain why a woman would be motivated to use toilet soap or cold cream that a princess, a movie queen, or other prominent person recommended.

When it came to who people seriously listened to, Stanley Resor observed that the public generally had both little discrimination and an insistent hunger for personalities. This tendency was evidenced in the newly popular tabloid newspapers, confession magazines, success magazines, decorating magazines, and motion pictures. Clearly, the public wanted its news, education, and entertainment conveyed through the medium of personalities whom they regarded as authorities in their respective fields. Thus, Resor concluded that since prominent people had become an integral feature of almost every editorial program, it seemed logical for advertising to present its messages through people to whom the public would listen with interest and respect.[106]

What is important here is that Stanley Resor had recognized three key ideas about the role of "personalities" in the modern consumer experience. In advertising, "personalities" could function as one of the following: (1) opinion leaders, (2) sacred people, and (3) archetypes. Although consumers acquired information from personal sources, they tended to value people who were knowledgeable about products and whose advice was taken seriously by others. These individuals have been called opinion leaders, persons who frequently were able to influence other people's attitudes or behaviors.[107] As a result, each interpretive community also had its own fashion innovators who determined fashion trends and its own opinion leaders. Thus, the emulation advertising formula achieved the aura of truth by including credible opinion leaders such as professional experts, socialites, and even celebrities.

Stanley Resor had accurately observed that celebrities shared a certain specialness that "set them apart" from normal activities. In this perspective, celebrities could be considered sacred when they were idolized, set apart from the masses, and treated with some degree of awe or respect. Souvenirs, memorabilia, and even mundane items perceived to be used by famous people took on special meanings and acquired value in their own right. If a woman purchased Lux Toilet Soap, for example, she would be using the same toilet soap that stars put on their face. Indeed, the Lux campaign using the emulation formulation tapped into consumers' desires for products associated with celebrities, a common practice in today's advertising that features movie stars and popular athletes to endorse products.

In addition to opinion leaders and archetypes, Stanley Resor's concept of "personality" advertising, or testimonials from famous people, often invoked archetypes identified by Jung and his followers. These included images of the "old wise man" and the "earth mother,"[108] who appeared as professional experts, authority figures, and confidential advisors to convince people of the merits of products. Images of the old wise man proliferated in the form of scientists, physicians, dermatologists, druggists, and Hollywood producers, among others. Then, too, ads depicted the earth mother as a beauty expert, confidential advisor, and even the friendly next-door neighbor.

Ultimately, consumers identified with authority figures, celebrities, and upscale settings rather than reflecting on their actual realities. As a result, admakers paid special attention to choosing attractive, credible endorsers and showcased products in elegant settings. Such high-society models and high-class scenes created an image of the social elite that recognized products of quality, "the good things in life," and admakers calculated that their taste would trickle down to the masses. Thus, the ads using appeals to fear, sex, and emulation portrayed an ideal modern life and beauty type, one to which young working women and those readers in the upper middle class both presumably aspired, but also ones specifically designed through the vision of the admakers. Still, these popular advertising formulas were not merely a projection of beliefs and values onto society; rather, they drew legitimacy from dominant cultural myths, beliefs, and values in America.

ADVERTISING GETS ENTERTAINING, 1930s

In the general climate of the Great Depression, admakers worked hard to promote products that Americans could not afford or were hesitant to purchase. At the same time, advertisers found a scientific basis for their image of the public as a tabloid audience that responded to unsophisticated, sensational, and frivolous entertainment. It began with the work of George Gallup, a professor of journalism and advertising, who provided admakers with new insights into the popular tastes of the American audience. Along with the J. Walter Thompson agency, Young & Rubicam was among the first advertising agencies to incorporate research as part of the creative process by bringing in Gallup.

Gallup had begun to poll readers about what they noticed most in newspapers and magazines in the 1920s. The newspaper studies covered some fourteen newspapers and forty thousand readers. The results showed that 85 percent of the respondents noticed the picture pages, 70 percent the comics, and 40 to 50 percent the editorial cartoons—a far greater share than the front-page story. Predictably women read the society and cooking sections, and men the sports.[109] Gallup's 1931 survey of magazine readership yielded a few more surprises. The researcher first ranked appeals by the number of times they appeared in advertisements. Economy and efficiency ranked first and quality fifth, while sex and vanity tied for ninth. Interviewers then rang doorbells, asking some fifteen thousand people which ads they remembered reading. It turned out that men noticed the ads with quality appeals first, and then sex; women responded most to ads that featured sex, vanity, and quality. Interestingly, the economy appeal that appeared most frequently in ads drew the least attention from the public.[110] According to Gallup's research, readers also preferred that lengthy blocks of copy be broken into short paragraphs and that type devices be employed, such as italics, boldface, and subheads. Gallup also found that people liked to read the comic strips, which reached an estimated 95 percent of families.

Gallup's findings strongly influenced admakers in the 1930s. To create copy and illustrations that would appeal to the tabloid audience, admakers tried to more closely associate entertainment with the product to gain attention, so the customer would be in the mood to be entertained—what Stanley Resor called "entertainment advertising." Thus, admakers creatively adopted the popular first-impression, romance, and emulation formulas to new ad forms that incorporated such elements as dramatic photographs, motion picture themes, and even the comics to get attention.

Realism and Drama

Photography in advertising had progressed gradually, from quite commonplace reproductions to dramatic realism in the 1930s. In this era photographic compositions differed markedly from the earlier pictures, in which actors posed stiffly in unreal situations and in obviously superficial sets. Following the success of the tabloid newspapers, picture-filled magazines emerged. *Life* debuted in 1935, featuring a dramatic photograph on the

cover and dozens of pictures inside chronicling current events and entertainment news; photo-filled *Look* came out two years later. Some of the
photos seemed almost clipped from a reel of movie film, with a new sense
of beauty, realism, and drama.

Two of the moving forces behind popularizing picture-filled advertising
were New York adman J. Stirling Getchell and fine art photographer
Edward J. Steichen. Remarkably, the Getchell agency dynamically expanded even as hard times and economic upheavals weeded out many other
firms. After working for leading agencies Lord & Thomas, Barton Durstine
& Osborne (BBDO), and J. Walter Thompson, Getchell opened his own
agency in 1931. As Getchell attracted new accounts, he developed and
refined a distinctive photojournalistic style, a cheaper alternative to beautifully painted and hand-drawn illustrations. He presented the ads in a
tabloid format, with rectilinear layouts, sensational headlines, and punchy
copy built around realistic, attention-getting photographs. Getchell sold
everything from cars to Ritz crackers. "It's the same thing we used in our
early days before beauty got to be in fashion," commented copywriter Helen
Woodward. The sales appeal was the same. "What is new in the Getchell
idea is his able use of modern action photographs. . . . This screaming
direct, ugly stuff hits the public as hard as ever."[111] Soon scores of other
advertisers were making the dynamic use of photographs as illustrations.
Soap ads were no exception.

In this era, however, admakers began to offer new visions of women's
beauty that challenged what had seemed to be fixed and unshakable codes
in the early twentieth century. The line between fine art and risqué blurred
more and more. Although sex had been used in copy before, illustrations
had barely hinted at it. Scantily clad women, formerly encountered mostly
in lingerie ads, now sold bathroom, household, and even industrial products. In the trade magazines, advertisers often used images of nude women
because there they could be reasonably certain the viewer would be male.
For example, a 1937 Simoniz car wax ad portrayed an unclad woman with
the headline "Your car is no nudist."

What was new in the mid-1930s, however, was the use of such images
in popular magazines addressed to middle- and upper-class women who
read fashion magazines. A new Cannon Mills towel campaign introduced the
approach in 1936. Initially Charles Coiner, art director at the N. W. Ayer

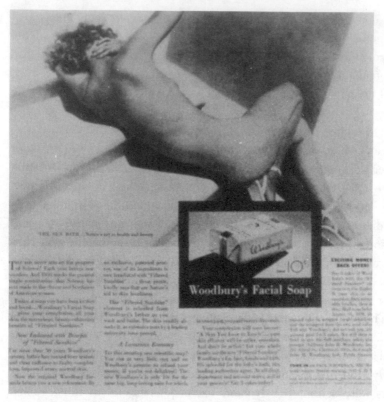

Fig. 5.12. Woodbury's Facial Soap, advertisement, 1936.

agency, commissioned the fine art photographer Edward Steichen to develop a series of nude studies. The models were shown relaxing after the bath or attending to their personal grooming with towels placed in their usual setting. The images were printed in sepia tones, yielding a softer look than the more obvious photographic black and white. They also tacitly affirmed that Steichen's photographs were fine art. Arguing that good art attracted readers' attention, the advertising trade press hailed the Cannon ads a success. Yet Steichen's nude studies were only one element of the overall advertising strategy of the Cannon campaign. The appearance of Steichen's nudes for Cannon towels in *Vogue* and *Harper's Bazaar* underscored the admakers' goal of targeting middle-class women, while the *Ladies' Home Journal* advertisements pictured attractive but fully-clothed housewives.

Using women's bodies to attract attention and market products appears to have been the hot new idea for 1936. Woodbury's Facial Soap and Camay

Soap followed Cannon Mills with a similar series of nude studies. Through
the Lennen and Mitchell agency, however, Woodbury hired Steichen to give
its advertising the veneer of fine art.

In the Woodbury nude series photographed by Steichen, an unclothed
model wearing only sandals and lounging near a swimming pool emerged as
the most prominent image in the campaign (see Fig. 5.12). Soap in a swimming pool? Sunbathing in ankle-strap sandals? However, the copy provided
an explanation of how this soap packed "Filtered Sunshine" into every bar to
give the consumer "all the benefits of a sun bath." The other images in the
campaign referenced classical nude studies. In one a sundial on a classical
column partially obscured the model; and in another, a women shown from the
back from the waist up was draped over a large urn. Nevertheless, it appeared
that the woman's body was there mainly to attract attention. Where as Steichen's Woodbury ads seemed overworked, a series of Cashmere Bouquet
soap ads by an unknown photographer presented a woman's body in more natural ways attending to the bath or her personal grooming (see Fig. 5.13).

Given the magazines where the ads were placed, the implication was
that the nude female body no longer shocked and offended when it
appeared in a commercial context. The Woodbury ads appeared in magazines such as *Good Housekeeping*, *Ladies' Home Journal*, and *True Story*, all
aimed at a middle- and even working-class audience, both proper housewives and shopgirls. By the mid-1930s, one could run nude studies inside
a magazine if not on the cover, observes historian Patricia Johnston. "What
seems new in the advertising agencies' strategies for Cannon and Woodbury
was their commissioning a well-known photographer to design photographs
of female nudes that clearly referred to the history of Western art and
appealed to the upright middle-class consumer."[112] Indeed, these ads went
far beyond the standards of acceptability established in the previous
decade, when most people considered displaying the backs of the knees a
taboo.[113]

With the popularity of motion picture drama, the Thompson agency
found that the Hollywood campaign for Lux Toilet Soap was as effective in
the 1930s as it had been in the previous decade. However, the admakers
made two slight modifications. First, the ads specifically talked not about
Hollywood stars in general, but about specific stars such Bette Davis,
Carole Lombard, and Ginger Rogers. Thus, the new ads proclaimed that

Fig. 5.13. Cashmere Bouquet, advertisement, *McCall's*, 1936.

Fig. 5.14. Lux Toilet Soap, advertisement, 1937.

nine out of ten Hollywood stars used Lux Toilet Soap to keep their complexions lovely. This enabled the advertising messages to more closely associate Lux with Hollywood, the entertainment center of the world. Second, Lever Brothers asked that the advertisements also begin to sell the product as a bath soap, and not solely as a complexion and beauty soap. Two types of advertisements made up these presentations, according to an agency executive (see Fig. 5.14):

In one, a woman comes home tired, is going out for the evening, and doesn't know what to do about it. She takes a Lux Bath, however, and here she is fresh and fragrant, ready for the big evening. The other situation is again romance, winning her man by being dainty, sweet, and with a lovely skin.[114]

The "perfectly legitimate extension" of the use of Lux Toilet Soap into the bathtub contributed to the increased sales in 1936 and again in 1937, compared to the two previous years when the number of bath advertisements was negligible.[115] Instead of the photographer or the celebrity, however, it would be the comic artist who took full advantage of the possibilities of advertising using humor, drama, suspense, and sheer entertainment.

Fig. 5.15. Lifebuoy Soap, advertisement, early 1930s.

It's Fun to Be Fooled

The comic strip technique or "adstrips" achieved high popularity in consumer advertising during the Depression.[116] These ads featured cartoon panels superimposed with speech balloons, which created a minidrama with an aura of realism. Such ads contained three to a dozen individual frames. Then, too, the adstrip proved an inexpensive technique.

It began in the late 1920s, when the Ruthrauff & Ryan agency experimented with proven symptom-and-cure copy and cartoon strip ads for Lifebuoy and Rinso soaps made by Lever Brothers. For Lifebuoy, the agency dramatically pictured the social disgraces of "B.O.," using scare tactics in the new adstrip format. One campaign featured a series titled "True B.O. Experience," which were based on thousands of letters "telling of *real* people who unknowingly let 'B.O.' offend." One such story told how a newly married woman, who "scrubbed, baked, and cooked from morn to night," soon noticed that her husband's greetings were hasty kisses and later asked him: "Doesn't the house look clean and neat?" Her husband replied, "It always does but it is more important to have his wife sweet and dainty." That was the clue: trying to be a perfect housewife, she neglected herself. She then learned that bathing regularly with Lifebuoy Soap was a sure means of stopping body odor. And before long, her husband was again smothering her with kisses (see Fig. 5.15). By 1933, *Advertising and Selling* had proposed a "21-gun salute" to Ruthrauff & Ryan and its cartoon strip campaign for the "public service" of "scaring so many about B.O."[117]

A great deal of interest in the comic strip technique had been identified by the Gallup surveys and the Hearst publishing salespeople, as well as by advertisers who tried it. The Gallup polls showed that the comic section proved a better read than the main news story. Similarly the Hearst people reported that a significant number of people complained when the comic strips were missing from their issue—880 people out of 1000 recipients of three issues of their Sunday papers, compared to only 45 complaints when the main news section was omitted.[118] Without a doubt, the modern comics proved a reliable circulation builder. Of the square formats, Indoor Sports, Wobster's Bridge, and the Toonerville folks were among the most successful. Of the comic strips, people enjoyed Krazy Kat, Mutt and Jeff, Bringing Up Father, and Little Orphan Annie.

Hence, admakers began to experiment with the popular comic graphic and copy formats. Adstrips appeared in places that featured comics like the *Comic Weekly*, the *Metropolitan Comics*, and the *Sunday Magazine* of the *New York Times*, as well as other monthly periodicals. Of the various early advertisers who made use of a modified form of the comic strip, the readership of the best Rinso adstrip was estimated at 80 to 100 percent of its circulation, nearly four times greater than that of ads, which were estimated at 25 percent of its circulation.[119] Procter & Gamble also reported outstanding results. Half of the circulation of the *American Weekly* ran a traditional ad with a coupon, and the other half ran an adstrip with a coupon almost the same size; the comic format pulled three times as many coupons as the other ad.[120] Although certain advertisers had increased their sales through the use of comic advertising, with others the superiority of this form over standard forms had yet to prove itself.

The appeal of comic strip advertising goes deeper than the physical way in which the cartoon panels and speech balloon panels were presented, explained *Printers' Ink* in 1938. People liked to hear other people talk; they liked humor; they liked drama, suspense, and action—and they liked the funnies because they contained all of those elements. People liked the

Fig. 5.16. Palmolive Soap, newspaper advertisement, 1938. Courtesy of Walter J. Thompson Archives, John W. Hartman Center for Sales, Advertising, and Marketing History, Duke University Rare Book and Special Collections Library.

movies and the theater because there was plenty of conversation and action; similarly they liked to read novels and stories, especially the dialogue, but would often pass over long descriptive passages. The comic strip technique had all of these appeals and allowed an ad maker to get away from the long, didactic copy in which the advertiser did all the talking and in which the advertiser also tended to lecture readers.[121] However, Ruth Waldo, a J. Walter Thompson copywriter, had another theory about the popularity of comic strips, the peculiar power of what she called the "progressive technique." This was the hypnotic factor, in which one of the squares led to the next; people either read all of them or none at all. Or, as *Advertising & Selling* wryly observed about advertising gone comic strip, it "gets down to the market," and eventually it would sell to an enormous class of readers who could not read at all.[122]

The funny papers, from which this technique derived, had educated people to expect only a few characters, action, a brief story told succinctly, and suspense until the end of the conversation or the last frame of the comic strip. In the conversations, then, the product was brought in naturally and not forced. In 1938, *Printers' Ink* observed that the conversational copy could be classified into six categories similar to other advertisements of the period: (1) testimonials, (2) before and after, (3) domestic harmony, (4) personal popularity, (5) indirect criticism, and (6) social success. A description of several advertisements shows how soap advertisers adopted the comic strip technique to their own specific use.

One of the most popular and simpler adoptions was the use of a question-and-answer theme with the questions and answers printed or lettered

Fig. 5.17. Cashmere Bouquet, advertisement, *Ladies' Home Journal*, 1939.

in balloons. Three 1938 advertisements for Palmolive Soap exemplified this technique with headlines that echoed the popular confession magazines (see Fig. 5.16). "Need Marriage Kill Romance? Not for the clever wife who guarded against 'middle-age' skin!" "But what good is a figure like that when a girl has 'middle-age' skin?" And, "LOVE blooms for Sue since she learned how to get rid of middle-age skin!"[123] With a bit of conversation and five panels, the ads briefly told a dramatic story revolving around the consequences of using the wrong soap and the benefits of changing to Palmolive. They all ended happily with a wife who looked marvelous, a young ingenue who became popular, or another woman falling in love, all because Palmolive Soap had left their complexions so radiant and lovely.

The balloon had become a mainstay of the comic strip technique, but here and there an advertiser avoided circling the conversation from the speaker's mouth and merely set the conversation off in type at an angle that achieved the same effect but avoided what was now a commonplace technique. Other advertisers varied the size and shape of the balloon, had the conversation printed white against black, or merely encircled the conversation halfway in order to give variety to the balloons. Ad makers even managed to combine sex appeal with the funny paper format in the nude series campaign for Cashmere Bouquet (see Fig. 5.17).

What was significant in these uses of realism and drama, entertainment, nudity, and comic strip advertising was the growing consensus about audience emotionality. In particular, popular convention further defined emotion as particularly characteristic of women. The next chapter will examine the resulting beauty types, stereotypes, and other ideal behaviors that advertising both shaped and reflected.

6

Soap, Sex, and Society, 1920 to 1940

dvertising had become important to the way American people saw themselves. They looked at ads to see how to dress, what to eat, how their household should appear, and, in the case of women, what they should do and how they should act. Americans knew, to be sure, that clean bodies, clean clothing, and clean homes were essential for success in this culture. Often, given the racism, sexism, and narcissism of the culture, their personal happiness and economic security paradoxically depended on it. In 1927, *Printers' Ink* observed that advertisers in one representative woman's magazine had the position situation sized up properly:

> . . . all women need nowadays is the right soap and the right toothpaste, and the world is theirs in a cellophane wrapper. Foreign potentates will kiss their hands; casting directors will allot them the rich and juicy parts; manufacturers will pay them big sums to endorse their products; adoring maids, preferably with foreign accents, will lay caressing fingers on the silken luster of their gowns; husbands, after fifteen years, will continue to pay them compliments; and children with

their charming naivete of early adolescence, will stroke the crinkly softness of their hair, and tell them just how really beautiful, or cute they are.

And if they don't use the right toothpaste, or soap, the frankness, or,
bad manners (according to the taste of the reader) of their friends would
inform them of their mistakes.[1]

Thus, Americans began to disregard the significance of cleanliness in its
relation to health and to think more about its aesthetic value.[2]

The soap industry, too, hastened to absorb, foster, and profit from the
virtue of cleanliness, and it did so using the images of the body it promul-
gated as stereotypes. For decades, the advertising world had thought it was
telling its female audience what it wanted to hear, endlessly propagandizing
the woman into believing that she had no choice other than to be a better
housekeeper, a better mother, and more caring wife. Having pictured
women in this role, advertisers either deliberately or inadvertently created
images of women to fit that ideal or prescribed an appropriate role for them.
But at the heart of this business was women.

Problematic as this may seem, it is crucial to recognize that women, in
part, were responsible for the development of mass cultural representations
of femininity, masculinity, beauty, and success—images of the prevailing
sexist ideals against which feminists later protested. Agencies had explicitly declared the importance of women, estimating that they made 80 to 85
percent of all retail purchases. "Woman is the purchasing agent, always
was, always will be."[3] With this in mind, agencies such as the Thompson
Company and George Batten specialized in the women's market and hired
women to cover the women's viewpoint. Thus, this discussion turns to exam-
ining the degree to which women colluded in sustaining sexism and sexist
stereotypes. These connections will then also link to the soap industry's formation of the Cleanliness Institute and creation of radio soap operas, which
also concern the gendrification of cleanliness.

WOMEN COMPOSE THE SELLING PROSE

Although the period from 1920 to 1940 saw more varied images of women
than the prior decade, it also ended by reinforcing narrow gender stereotypes of both women's and men's roles in society. White women were the

audience for national advertising that tied beautification to broad cultural concerns over female mores and sexual mores.

To reach American women, advertisers drew upon an array of existing images representing modern American industrial society. Men ran the offices or worked at the factories, while women created the home as a retreat from the stresses of the man's world and built a haven in which to nurture the children. Within these boundaries, admakers challenged the traditional role of women. There was the homemaker, the smartly dressed wife, the occasional working woman, the coed, the sporting woman, the actress, the socialite, and the clubwoman, among others. Yet for all the talk of social revolution and women's freedom, the range of these roles quickly narrowed and became more conventional, inspiring what would become key tenets of normative femininity in the twentieth century.

Advertising was again both the cause and the effect. The beauty appeal had effaced differences among women and also reinforced the notion that all women shared identical desires, including the hope to remain magically young forever so that they could not only capture a man, but also keep him by being an attractive partner. In a little more than a decade, notions of women's freedom and modernity had narrowed. As advertisers primarily sought to reach the affluent female audience through national advertising, their efforts often resulted in portrayals of women and men as exaggerated stereotypes, especially in light of the society's actual diverse population.

Who, then, was writing these ads? Although there were a few well-known women in the advertising field, most were hidden in support roles and not credited for their contributions.[4] Based on a study of the 1931 *Who's Who in Advertising*, Roland Marchand concluded that 99 percent of the writers and designers in ad agencies were white men, with few women employed above the secretarial level in advertising.[5] Although women generally had limited influence in producing advertising, nonwhite ethnic and racial groups had even less. Another study of major ad agencies showed that the midlevel salaries of the experienced professionals were five times the national average, that 66 percent of the copywriters had servants in their homes, and that the majority had an Ivy League education.[6] Clearly distinctive characteristics of class, culture, education, gender, and ethnicity separated ad creators from their audience. But this is only a partial view.

In the beauty and fashion industries, there were significant numbers of professional women working in marketing, advertising, sales, and media. Women began to write specifically to women, concentrating on women's products. The woman's page in newspapers appeared, and women learned to write copy that women would read—that is, copy from the woman's viewpoint. The women's magazines also began to flourish about this time, furnishing more media for reaching women. Store advertising and mail-order houses provided other opportunities as women wrote reams of fashion copy. The field of cosmetics and toiletries also offered one of the greatest opportunities for women who entered advertising. Women headed several large cosmetic companies, served as advertising managers, wrote advertising and promotional copy, and demonstrated and sold their goods.[7]

When the first women's advertising club formed in 1911, there were about two hundred advertising women in America.[8] Between World War I and World War II, however, the number increased to three thousand, which might seem a large number until compared to the thirty-two thousand men in advertising during the same period.[9]

At the same time, advertising work became more segregated. According to copywriter Dorothy Dignam, men wrote the earliest ads for beauty products and toiletries, but "when face powder began to come out in shades and creams could 'beautify overnight' and perfumes were all moonlight-and-roses men got fed up and women began to compose the selling prose."[10] Although men could and did write very successful copy aimed at women, most had a harder job and more to overcome, according to the trade. For example, Roy Dickinson explained that it would be a "most difficult task" for the man, who wrote about roofing, paint, stained shingles, vacuum cleaners, and water heaters, to write for the season of weddings and that the product had good use as a wedding gift.[11] One common explanation for why men found it difficult to sell to women was their lack of background or experience from the earliest years in washing dishes, setting the table, running errands, dressmaking, and other household tasks.[12]

Thus, women were disproportionately assigned accounts for women's products in advertising, supplying the feminine point of view for soap, cosmetics, food, and fashion ads; retail advertising also provided new opportunities.[13] Such pioneers as Helen Woodward, Helen Lansdowne Resor, Francis Maule, and Dorothy Dignam, among others, developed major national campaigns, while many others worked on advertising in local agencies, department stores, cosmetic firms, and mail-order businesses.

More important, the women who wrote the soap ads, even those who identified themselves as feminists, had to deal with contradictory impulses. They repackaged age-old stereotypes about women as emotional and with their place in the home. A similar view of narrow gender roles occasionally surfaced in the writings of women who worked in the advertising industry. On advertising to women, for example, suffragist J. Walter Thompson copywriter Maule suggested that a woman was more qualified than a man to write copy directed especially to women.[14]

> Practically "every normal woman" has an innate, instinctive sympathy with the needs of the home and of children that cause them to think more deeply on these subjects than do most men. Occasionally, however, a man will produce copy on what is usually conceived to be a "women's subject" as true and as sympathetic in feeling as any that could be produced by a woman.[15]

The women's viewpoint was further justified by the notion that the psychology of the female buyer was far more subtle than the average male could grasp.[16] Another Thompson copywriter, Lois Ardery, put it this way: "Women of course have certain known wants; certain vulnerable points of appeal—vanity, appetite, economy, health. . . . But women also have another set of wants—unexpressed and unrecognized even by themselves. *Inarticulate longings!*"[17]

When it came to writing, advertisers thought women naturally used those little phrases and intimate ways of talking that rang true with a housewife, since they sympathetic to the needs of the home and of children. Marian Hertha Clarke, of Albert Frank & Company, observed that women spoke "a particular and peculiar language of their own." In Clarke's view, women were not "technically-minded as a rule," while men were more interested in facts and figures. Thus, many times men made the mistake of thinking that price was the dominant factor in a woman's buying decision. Clarke noted:

> If a woman is convinced that what you have to sell will help to make her life easier and happier—if it will add anything to the health and well-being of her family—she will find a way to afford it even if she goes without so many other things to do so.

For advertising to be successful, Clarke continued, "sell her the idea of a better home, better things for her family, healthier children, improved surroundings."[18] Awareness of style trends had also became vital to businesses. When it came to style, many thought only women had the necessary appreciation of what was good taste, of what was appropriate and artistic.[19]

Of course, here one encountered the problem that was to distress the subsequent women's movement of the 1960s, the matter of stereotypes. In the case of female stereotypes, not only the adman but also the adwoman perpetuated the long-standing assumption that women's minds were akin "vats of frothy pink irrationality."[20] For instance, feminist Christine Frederick, a home economist and advertising counselor, presented a sad view of the average American women in the 1929 book *Selling Mrs. Consumer*.[21] Frederick contended that woman could not be expected to be wholly reasonable for three reasons. First, woman's nature was to be emotional. "She therefore lives a life *closer to instinct* than man." Second, women were born as "second fiddle to man." Paradoxically, a woman's role was "how to be independent, though inexorably dependent; how to be demure and 'feminine' and yet aggressively attain her ends." Finally, women, unlike men, were not persuaded by logic and reason. In fact, Frederick inferred that Mrs. Consumer was mentally deficient with a "vocabulary of only about 1,200 words"; her schooling consisted approximately of a sixth-grade education and a fourteen-year-old mentality, if that as much.[22]

Indeed, these advertising women may have recognized women's narrow role in modern society, but given these constraints they could have claimed that caring for one's appearance, especially one's personal cleanliness, affected a woman's popularity and success. Thus, this appeal, call it vanity if you will, emerged as a more powerful selling tool than price or health. Women spent hundreds of million dollars a year for something called "beauty." They bought such "beauty aids" as creams, cosmetics, hand lotions, soaps, shampoos, bath accessories, and other toiletries.[23] Certainly beauty aids had become important to many women. As film star Mary Pickford aptly observed, "They act just like a moral cocktail."[24]

For that matter, the mass production of beauty aids created many new opportunities for women, but the ad world had in mind a certain kind of person essential to the field. A common axiom among mass-market manufacturers and advertisers was that when selling to women, nothing succeeded like a woman's viewpoint.[25] In the 1939 *Advertising Careers for Women*, N. W. Ayer copywriter Elizabeth Colt Kidd gave this list of ten questions to find out whether one had the makings of a good advertising woman:

I.   Have you changed your hair-style at least once in the last five years?

II.   When you were feeling very "down" did you ever buy a new hat just to cheer yourself up? (Did it?)

III.   In a train, bus, or streetcar, would you rather study the people around you than read even the most exciting new book?

IV.   Did you ever speculate—just once—on how false eyelashes would look on you?

V.   Do you read "Advice to the Lovelorn" in your daily papers?

VI.   Do you like women—at least as well as you do men?

VII.   Can you think of at least one way to improve the appearance of each of your five best friends?

VIII.   Are you as interested in *why* people do things as in *what* they do? (Are you also interested in *what they do?*)

IX.   Do you think requited love should be the most important aim of most women?

X.   Have you ever, that you remember, spoken to a stranger in an emergency, a shared emotion, a sudden excess of friendliness— and enjoyed it?[26]

If a woman answered six or more questions with a "yes," Kidd suggested that she could earn a living at cosmetics writing, but a score of eight or more meant that she had makings of a good advertising woman. Naturally, other factors entered in, such as intelligence, education, and ability to get along with people. But what these questions enabled a woman to determine was another matter: Was she truly "feminine"? That is, if she held beauty to be a personal pleasure as well as an ideal, she would have more in common with the audience for beauty aids, and thus, she could more likely connect with other women who expressed interest in their personal appearance. That said, were the advertisers simply reflecting women as the women saw themselves, or were they telling women what they should be and do and how they should see themselves?

BEAUTY TYPES

Advertising and other forms of mass media play a significant role in determining which forms of beauty, maleness, and femaleness are considered desirable at any point in time. More than anything else, the imagery in advertising was that of idealized human beings. Advertisers, having learned that this was what consumers wanted to look at, converted their hopes into its forms. Advertising distilled from a variety of human appearances the few that could be accepted as glorified examples and returned them as iconography to an audience desiring to see such interpretive forms. Thus, advertisers responded to vague preferences by promoting certain standards of attractiveness.

Throughout history, many women worked diligently to attain some ideal of beauty. They have starved themselves, cinched their corsets, painted their faces, and spent countless hours in front of mirrors to alter their appearance to meet what they perceived as their society's expectations of what a beautiful woman should look like. In retrospect, many eras in history can be characterized by a specific "look," or an ideal of beauty that prevailed during that period. Recent history can be described in terms of a succession of dominant ideals. In contrast to today's emphasis on vim and vigor, in the early 1800s it was fashionable for a woman to appear delicate to the point of looking ill. The poet Keats described the ideal woman of that time as "a milk white lamb that bleats for men's protection." Other looks have included the voluptuous, lusty woman epitomized in the late 1800s by Lillian Russell, who tipped the scales at 175 pounds; the athletic Gibson Girl of the 1890s; and the slim, boyish flapper of the 1920s as exemplified by Clara Bow.[27] One can also distinguish among ideals of beauty for men in terms of facial features, musculature, and facial hair.

Advertising, too, was actively involved in the process of making and remaking ideals of beauty. Ad imagery offered up formulaic and endlessly reproduced "beautiful" women and men. Glamorous screen stars, chic Parisians, aristocratic beauties, and breezy flappers all became familiar faces. Similarly, the images and tastes of popular culture, appearing in films, novels, and magazine stories, helped Americans assume appropriate appearances and fill appropriate gender roles for the new industrial society. In particular, the 1920s marked the point when mass-produced images distinctly and powerfully began to influence men's and, especially, women's self-conception. Images in photo-filled newspapers and glossy magazines, and on billboards and the big screen derived their power from their conscious design, visual resonance, and widespread circulation.

Exposure to advertising like Woodbury's and Palmolive's that featured beauty appeals could also have triggered a process of "social comparison," whereby readers tried to evaluate themselves by comparison to these artificial images.[28] A consumer might have asked, "Am I as attractive as I would like to be?" This form of close scrutiny appears to be a basic human motive, and many soap advertisers tapped into this need by supplying images of happy, attractive people who just happened to be using the product. Although the gender depictions forwarded by the media were narrow representations of what it was to be a female or to be a male, the viewers could situate themselves close to the stereotype or reject these particular ideals.[29]

Stereotypes: The Depiction of Women in Advertising

Some well-intentioned advertisers struggled to envision a New Woman who challenged popular clichés. A number of women at the J. Walter Thompson Company, both market researchers and feminists, argued against stereotyping female consumers. Frances Maule, for example, a Thompson copywriter and veteran of the women's movement, criticized advertisers for relying too much on the "the good old conventional 'angel-idiot' conception of women," and she urged them to remember the "old suffrage slogan—that Women are People." She emphasized that, "it is just as impossible to pick out a single feminine type and call it 'woman,' as it is to pick out a single masculine type and call it 'man.'"

Instead of one type of female consumer, Maule identified four categories in the 1920s, each responding to different appeals: (1) housewives concerned with a well-stocked and well-run home; (2) society women oriented to fashion and leisure, the chief purchaser of fashion, cosmetics, toiletries, and other luxuries; (3) a new class of women purchasers, or the clubwomen interested in the politics of consumption; and (4) the working women, an ever-increasing class with an entirely different set of needs, looking for fashion and style at a reasonable price.[30] Hence, modern advertising strategies continued to build on older iconographic conventions and also made efforts to imagine an alternative feminine appeal.

Looking at the whole range of formulaic representations, six popular stereotypes broadly defined women in the 1920s advertisements: (1) the *home-maker*, (2) the *temptress*, (3) the *tutor*, (4) the *modern woman*, (5) the *independent woman*, and (6) the *superwoman*. Yet underlying the celebration of variety was the belief that the true American face was still a white face, as mass marketers conscientiously avoided black imagery in advertising targeted for white demographics, a matter discussed at length in the next chapter.

The *homemaker* made the home a haven in a heartless world, and her work set the standards for respectable housekeeping.[31] Judging by the copy and the illustrations in soap ads, the admakers exalted homemaking as a career and suggested how women could become good companions and partners to their modern husbands. They also tried to convince her that one of her major responsibilities was to remain magically young and attractive by purchasing the correct soap; this would help her keep her man by keeping her skin as attractive as it was when she captured him.

The *temptress* transferred eroticism to the product; daring poses and suggestive promises showed women how to build up their confidence and find enduring love. Instead of portraying scantily clad models to attract attention, admakers used dignified sexual content in the copy but only hinted at sexual imagery. Alluring actresses and screen stars glamorized a made-up look once associated with prostitution, "images that countered the values of prudish middle-class respectability," explains Kathy Peiss.[32] Close-up photographs of the female face, painted with lipstick and darkened with eye makeup, projected a provocative but no longer sinful eroticism. This strategy allowed readers to extend their vision and escape from problems in the real world, by placing them in exciting situations that permitted them to "try on" provocative roles, to be sought after and well liked.

The third character type, called the *tutor,* scolded, befriended, and guided readers. In this strategy, maternal figures, celebrities, lovers, and professional experts gave directions for the most mundane aspects of everyday life. All suggested how women could be better wives and mothers. Other advertisements aimed at women also tried to undermine the readers' confidence in traditional sources of advice and authority such as mothers, friends, and neighbors, so they would rely on the assertions of the ads themselves. For example, the insidious thing about body odor or bad breath was that the offender was the last to know; even a woman's closest friends would not tell her, but the friendly advertising tutor could. In the 1920s, however, advertisers found a

Fig. 6.1. Yardley Soap, advertisement, *Ladies' Home Journal*, October 1928.

new archetypal form in the confidential advisor, similar to the authorities featured in the advice-to-the-lovelorn columns in popular magazines like *True Story* and the tabloid newspapers. Thousands of women wrote letters seeking advice and inevitably received "personally signed" replies from fictive "Helen Chase" for Camay Soap, "Marjorie Mills" for Lux Soap Flakes, and "Betty Crocker" for General Mills. Ad writers had realized that such personalized, conversational copy effectively reached readers one person at a time.

Some well-intentioned advertisers also struggled to envision the New Woman in ways that challenged popular clichés. These views had an appeal in the wake of women's campaigns for suffrage, higher education, and professional opportunities. A variety of popular images showed this New Woman as the modern woman, the independent woman, and the superwoman. Thus, ads urged the *modern woman* to adopt a look that had been increasingly defined by abstract portrayals of high-fashion women in modernistic illustrations—what Maule identified as the society women oriented to fashion and leisure. For instance, Yardley Soap distinctively portrayed modern women in fashionable playgrounds of the world, settings like Deauville and the Riviera, where the wealthy gathered and played (see Fig. 6.1). Advertising artists distorted and reshaped women's bodies, transforming them into Art Deco figurines, particularly in the illustrations of the late 1920s. In the process, such advertising illustrations reinforced the "decorative" role as natural and appropriate for women.

The *independent woman* appeared only sporadically, as if admakers were unsure how independent their female target markets might be. This stereotype appeared in diverse images, ranging from the free-spirited outdoor girl to the businesswomen and secretaries who made their own way in the world. At the time, however, such portrayals of professional women were relatively few. One ad for Palmolive Soap that appeared in 1927 pictured a working woman with the headline "The Business Girl knows the dollar-and-cents value of a schoolgirl complexion"[33] (see Fig. 6.2). While hardworking women seldom appeared in the ads, when they did, admakers depicted them as glamorous professionals or as laundresses and maids.

The *superwoman* first emerged as the assertive flapper of the 1920s, the fashionable woman who had it all; she nurtured, seduced, and competed. Judging from the creations, the young, short-skirted flapper was more at home in metropolitan settings than small town—what Maule called the younger society women oriented to fashion and leisure. For her, there were not enough hours in the day. Whether or not she worked outside the home, this character type had come to value greater independence, and she responded positively to marketing campaigns that featured active, confident women who had the freedom to make their own lifestyle decisions.

Thus, advertisers constructed ads in ways that reinforced the images of gender most familiar to their target audience. In the imagination of advertisers

The Business Girl Knows

The Dollars-and-Cents Value of
"That Schoolgirl Complexion"

THE universal rule for daily skin cleansing with soap and water is founded on one important factor: *A true complexion soap is meant.*

Thus millions use Palmolive, a soap made for ONE purpose ONLY; to safeguard and protect the skin. Remember this when purchasing soap for facial use.

AS beauty is rated a dollars-and-cents asset by women of the stage and screen, so too it is rated today by women in the business world. Note there the lovely complexions that you see.

The rule for *gaining* a good complexion is the same as for *keeping* one—soap and water, as advised by virtually every leading authority on skin care. This to keep the skin and pores clean and free of beauty-impairing accumulations.

The one secret is in the *kind of soap* one uses. Only a true complexion soap can be wisely employed on the skin. Other soaps may be too harsh.

*The rule for
"That Schoolgirl Complexion"*

Thus millions use Palmolive, in this way—a soap made for ONE purpose only, to safeguard the skin. A good complexion is worth too much for experiment.

Wash your face gently with soothing Palmolive Soap, massaging the lather softly into the skin. Rinse thoroughly, first with warm water, then with cold. If your skin is inclined to be dry, apply a touch of good cold cream—that is all.

Do this regularly, and particularly in the evening. Use powder and rouge if you wish. But never leave them on over night. They clog the pores, often enlarge them. Blackheads and disfigurements often follow. They must be washed away.

Avoid this mistake

Do not use ordinary soaps in the treatment given above. Do not think any green soap, or one represented as of olive and palm oils, is the same as Palmolive.

It costs but 10c the cake! So little that millions let it do for their bodies what it does for their faces. Obtain a cake, then note the difference one week makes. The Palmolive-Peet Co., Chicago, Illinois.

Retail Price
10c   1623
Palmolive Soap is untouched by human hands until you break the wrapper—it is never sold unwrapped

KEEP THAT SCHOOLGIRL COMPLEXION

No. 3623—finished—Page Photoplay, Nov., 1927 Forecast, Nov., 1927 EFH AMR 19760—1

Fig. 6.2. Palmolive Soap, advertisement, *Photoplay*, November 1927. Courtesy of Foote Cone & Belding Collection, State Historical Society of Wisconsin, reel 37.

and advice givers, an animated world of romantic interludes, leisure activities, social encounters, and narcissistic pleasure was built on commercial exchange. It appears from this vantage point that until World War II the female consumer either accepted or agreed with the way she was pictured in ads. Feminists may be quick to criticize some of these caricatures as limiting or even demeaning but may forget that men were also rendered as one-dimensional.

Stereotypes of Men for Women: The Depiction of Men in Advertising

In contrast to the varied character types of women displayed in the soap ads, the images of men tended to conform to a single stereotype, *Mr. Everyman*. Soap ads invariably depicted men as businessmen rather than as blue-collar professionals; they did not show feelings and certainly did not get involved in cooking, cleaning, and parenting. Men also rarely assumed decorative poses or exaggerated bodily proportions, but they frequently appeared as success objects—that is, as the reward for women using the advertised product. As *Advertising & Selling* observed in 1933, men had been portrayed as inferior partners to women as "only the morganatic consort; a blurry, indefinite background prop."[34]

Interestingly, Christine Frederick did suggest a provocative appeal for women. Why didn't advertising exploit men's physical beauty, what she delicately called "male pulchritude"? To Frederick, perhaps the strongest appeal would consist of the depiction of a "handsome *gentlemen* [sic], immaculately attired in a dress suit, and smilingly operating the 'Lily White' washer without once dampening his glossy vest." At least, she reasoned, pretty women were used as "bait" in advertising; it logically followed that attractive men would attract women's attention.[35] But the feminist was far ahead of her time, and images of gender-role reversal would not become prevalent until the 1980s.

As gender roles for men evolved, formerly "feminine" products such as fragrances and toilet soap were marketed to men. Although shaving soap had become a big business, high-priced toilet soaps for the male market did not appear in leading department stores until the 1930s.[36] Among the best-selling cake shaving soaps were Williams Barber' s Bar, Williams Mug Soap, Colgate Cup Soap, and Palmolive Shave Tablet. Among the leading toilet soap brands were Yardley and Morny, imported from England, and Roger &

a new kind of tonic for Mrs. Spinock

Mrs. Spinock is tired. Tired of washing. Tired of cleaning. Tired of trying to keep up to odd American ideals of living that make so much added drudgery for her.

It may relieve that tired feeling and improve her house-keeping too, if you prescribe *extra* help. And as far as washing and cleaning go, Fels-Naptha Soap will give it to her. The *extra* help of good golden soap and plentiful naptha, working hand-in-hand. Together, they loosen the most stubborn dirt—quickly, easily. Mrs. Spinock needn't waste her energy with hard rubbing, and she needn't worry when hot water is scarce. Fels-Naptha gets things beautifully clean, even in cool water.

Write Fels & Company, Philadelphia, Pa., for a sample bar of Fels-Naptha, mentioning the Survey Graphic.

THE GOLDEN BAR WITH THE CLEAN NAPTHA ODOR

FELS-NAPTHA

Fig. 6.3 Fels-Naptha Soap, advertisement, *Survey*, 1931.

Gallet which came from France. Yardley sported an attractive wrapper with its trademark; and the others came individually wrapped in cellophane, sealed inconspicuously at the bottom with the sticker carrying the trademark. Still, women made most purchases of men's toilet goods. In fact, manufacturers assumed that mainly women purchased groceries, drugs, and toilet goods.[37] Hence, the simplistic stereotypes of men were really intended as a sales pitch for women.

Stereotypes: The Depiction of American Immigrants

If alternate visions of gender roles were not in evidence, the soap mass-market industry did challenge some perceptions about social class, which had seemed fixed and unshakable in the nineteenth century. Although advertising primarily targeted the middle-class female audience, on occasion ads seemingly addressed women of disparate ethnic backgrounds. The poor obviously had less money to spend than did the rich, but they had the same basic needs as everyone else. Low-income families purchased staples such as milk, tea, bread, and soap at the same rates as average-income families. Many of these working-class people considered toilet soap a luxury, so they often used a less expensive, all-purpose soap for everything from general household use to washing the body.

Although most marketers had largely ignored poor people, some developed soap products especially for low-income consumers. These products sold for a nickel or less a cake, half the price of the popular brands like Ivory or Palmolive that sold for a dime. In some cases, these strategies may also have reinforced the stereotype of immigrants as the "great unwashed," as when Procter & Gamble advertised Fels-Naptha Soap in *Survey* magazine, a professional journal aimed at social workers.

During the 1920s and 1930s, the Fels-Naptha ad campaign recounted the travails of American immigrants, who felt much pressure from advertisers to adopt the American standard of cleanliness. One ad read: "Mrs. Kominski is wearing a hat. She's folded away her old-country shawl. She's folding away other things, too—old-country customs, old-country ideals. Yes, Mrs. Kominski wants to be American. And one way you can help her realize that ambition is to teach her American methods of keeping house." Another ad read: "Mrs. Spinock is tired. Tired of washing. Tired of cleaning. Tired of trying to keep up to odd American ideals of living that make so much drudgery for her" (see Fig. 6.3). Other ads talked about the hardships of Mrs. Panzella, Mrs. Cebrelli, and Mrs. Torkowitz, among others. Despite the patronizing and insulting tone of the ads, immigrants took them to heart and worked hard to be as clean and prosperous as Americans. In all the ads, Fels-Naptha brings "*extra* help" to ease the cleaning task and to help immigrants attain better living conditions.[38] Clearly, cleanliness had become an indicator that some individuals were morally superior, of better character, or more civilized than others.

Still, the foreign-born had not come clean enough, reasoned the soap-makers. To reach this group, soap and detergent manufacturers collaborated with public health officials, schools, and women to find new ways to present middle-class models of personal cleanliness rituals as the American way, harnessing both public spirit and the profit motive.

THE CLEANLINESS INSTITUTE, 1927 TO 1932

The Cleanliness Institute was established to teach the public the importance of keeping clean. In 1927, the big soapmakers—Lever Brothers, Palmolive, Procter & Gamble, Colgate, Kirk, and Swift—along with other members of the Association of Soap and Detergent Manufacturers formed the institute, with cooperative sales promotion as its chief function.

The manufacturers exemplified a model of a large-scale cooperative organization. The soap manufacturers had some experience with organization. As early as 1899, rumors circulated about the soap manufacturers forming a trust to include every large soap manufacturing firm. By consolidating their efforts, they would save millions of dollars annually in "gift schemes" to advertise different brands of soap.[39] Then, during World War I, the government encouraged industry cooperation to produce glycerin, since this by-product of soap manufacture was essential to dynamite production. This experience led to some practical discoveries, more efficient methods of production, and experiments with controlling prices. Then, in the 1920s, the manufacturers turned toward the idea of cooperative ventures to protect their markets and promote consumption for their soap products, which was becoming a common practice in many fields.

According to Sidney M. Colgate, president of the organization, the aim of the Cleanliness Institute was to "promote public welfare, efficiency and health by research directed at problems of the community, industry and personal cleanliness in the United States through educational work in the schools and cooperation with the leading social agencies of the country."[40] Headquarters were established in New York City. Among the trained staff three women held influential positions: Julia B. Tappan, director of the School Department; C. Margaret Munson, research librarian; and Sally Lucas Jean, consultant for the School Department, a school nurse who had formed the national Child Health Organization (CHO).[41]

The assumptions behind the formation of the Cleanliness Institute were arresting. For twentieth-century Americans, public welfare and industry were polar opposites, and the presence or absence of the profit motive marked the divide. The organization appeared to have been accepted for what it was—a "public service" initiated by the soap industry, selling the world on cleanliness. The organization received letters of approval from more than one thousand public welfare leaders and more than 250 congratulatory editorials.[42] Among them, the *New York Times* heralded the effort as "a new public welfare organization of national scope." On the other hand, Chicago soap manufacturer George Schmidt called it "laughable" that a number of "big fellows" would form a private association of their own.[43] William Esty, a Thompson agency executive, went so far as to refer to the efforts of the Cleanliness Institute as "propaganda work."[44] Needless to say, selling more soap was at the heart of the institute's efforts. At the inauguration of the organization, Colgate reminded soapmakers that Americans spent more than $1 billion annually to keep clean.[45] Cleanliness made good business. Important to American standards of living, health, and social welfare, promoting cleanliness boosted sales and guaranteed a future for the soapmakers' products, a potential source of enormous profits.

Like many trade organizations, the Cleanliness Institute grappled with common problems of ensuring distribution, creating brand recognition, and increasing demand. Although many trade associations agreed on the conventional Code of Ethics as their first matter of business, the soapmakers initially adopted a platform covering the two concerns that brought them together—protecting their markets and getting people to use more soap. Explained Colgate:

> The soap industry is an industry today at the mercy of a certain rate of soap used here in America, that is not sufficient to consume all that the industry is equipped to produce. Thus, the association work should look to this basic work of developing new users of soap and larger use by all who already are the consuming public."[46]

Surprising as it may seem, the soapmakers had some reason for concern.

Historian Vincent Vinikas argues that competition for consumer dollars became more intense as more products flooded the market than people could use or afford.[47] As the business of the beauty culture emerged in the 1920s, soapmakers also came into direct competition with cosmetics manufacturers, who promoted products like face creams as a substitute for soap in cleansing the face. Soapmakers also faced stiff competition from cosmetics that would truly beautify and give immediate results compared to soap products, whose advertisements offered only an elusive promise of future loveliness. Indeed, women spent a great deal more money on cosmetics than on soap as they prospered. The widespread practice of relying on plain old soap and water for a woman's beauty ritual became almost extinct in the cities, especially among the "comfortable levels." In fact, cosmetic sales tripled between 1919 and 1929. This amounted to an annual expenditure of $53 per woman for cosmetics and other beauty products and services, four times the annual soap expenditures of $13.88 per family.[48]

Yet for all the talk of protecting its markets, "competitive advertising" had not reached the soap industry, wrote the trade journal *Advertising & Selling* in 1928. While America used more soap per capita than any other nation in the world, the most casual survey revealed that millions used soap so rarely that they constituted "an almost virgin market."[49] In sum, the soap industry had to interest the population not in soap, but in cleanliness, which in one form or another motivated all soap purchases. Thus, the leaders of the industry recognized that the main problem was not a commercial one but a social one.[50] There were certain reasons some people were cleaner than others, and there were certain factors that induced people to want to become clean. Cleanliness had an ethical value; it was allied "with self-respect, pride, with behavior, with manners, with bodily comfort, and well-being, with optimism, tolerance, and all the higher values of life."[51] It was this broad aspect of encouraging cleanliness that the Cleanliness Institute adopted as its mission. The question then became how to crystallize the idea and make it feasible.

Cleanliness Sermonettes

The Cleanliness Institute emphasized the importance of reaching broad sections of the public that were not touched by the printed word. This idea of more cleanliness applied to the entire population, from infancy to old age; in turn, the problem of communication involved practically the whole population.[52] There were still millions who did not read the newspaper. "We will get to them through the motion pictures, health departments, women's clubs, and other agencies," explained institute director Roscoe Edlund. "We will hammer it into them that bathing is permissible during the winter months, that soap is nothing to be feared and that if they wish to get ahead they must wash behind their ears."[53]

The platform of the Cleanliness Institute translated into the central idea of "More Cleanliness." It divided the population of the country into three strata, in terms of the ease by which each class could be reached through various means of communication: (1) For the hard-to-reach illiterates, semi-illiterates, and foreign-born, as well as schoolchildren, the institute directed its work through health departments, women's clubs, and public welfare organizations. (2) For the "midsection," powerful arguments for higher standards of cleanliness aimed to make individuals realize that the things they hoped to achieve were based on cleanliness. (3) To reach the "intelligent minority," however, communications avoided any inference that these people were still unclean; rather, they learned of new standards through the work of the institute for other groups.[54] With the three-point plan, the Cleanliness Institute quickly paved the way for large-scale cooperation between soap manufacturers, health officials, educators, publicists, heads of social service organizations, and representatives of women's clubs. One Institute spokesperson went so far as to observe that the " 'slovenly folk' who have been going on the theory that they can take a bath or leave it are to be brought to their senses."[55]

Magazine advertising and radio broadcasts appeared to be the most obvious way to teach Americans the importance of cleanliness. To create the advertising campaign, the Cleanliness Institute contracted with Newell-Emmett Company to spend some $350,000 annually for a period of three years to induce people to use more soap. The campaign, starting in 1928, represented the first time in the history of cooperative advertising that the participants were such large advertisers. They advertised as a group not because it was the only way they could afford a national campaign, but because the campaign would differ from their own advertising. The advertising schedule aimed at national coverage through an almost equal division among newspapers and magazines; radio was also part of the program. The magazine list included popular men's and women's magazines, industrial journals, and periodicals devoted to the fields of health, social service, and education.[56]

An important part of the campaign was publicity, elaborately and intelligently organized by the Cleanliness Institute. Tying together the efforts of the Cleanliness Institute with social and educational organizations already

At 3 months a success; at 30 years...?

Of course every baby is a success. Freshly bathed and dressed, baby is a picture of spotless perfection.

Any mother knows that the lesson of personal cleanliness, if taught well enough, will exert a powerful influence for clean living all through the years . . . But sometimes it isn't taught and sometimes it isn't learned.

Sometimes the man grows up to reap the results of untidy habits.

He is simply Help Not Wanted.

"You can't keep a clean man down" — SOAP & WATER

PUBLISHED BY THE ASSOCIATION OF AMERICAN SOAP AND GLYCERINE PRODUCERS, INC., TO AID THE WORK OF *CLEANLINESS INSTITUTI*

Fig. 6.4. Cleanliness Institute, advertisement, *Ladies' Home Journal*, 1928.

set up enabled the trade organization to execute the publicity program with a minimum of effort and expense. As most people already used soap on a regular basis, the primary objective of the Cleanliness Institute was to get Americans to use more of an already familiar commodity—that is, to encourage people to wear a clean shirt or dress every day instead of every other day, wash their hands more often, take more baths, and so on. The institute also recognized the importance of the mother's role in establishing a good home-training program to instill the right habits; after all, she was the primary user and purchaser of soap products.

From classroom to advertising copy, the goal of this educational advertising was to reach the masses of readers whose cleanliness habits could use improvement. Inducements to liberally use soap appeared regularly in news releases, educational materials, and advertisements in Sunday magazine sections, women's magazines, and general interest magazines. These advertisements appealed to normal, everyday desires to get a better job, to achieve a better social position, to attain attractiveness and popularity, to "keep up with the Joneses," and to give one's children the most advantages.[57] The attainment of these desires was intimately bound up with cleanliness as the copy claimed. Instead of urging women to "Wash! Clean! Scrub!" the institute based its campaign platform on three appeals: (1) social approval, (2) material benefits, and (3) romantic value. Health issues were entirely omitted; the idea was to associate soap with pleasant thoughts, not household drudgery.[58]

Ads depicting social aspects of soap and water incorporated powerful emotional appeals. For example, one ad opened with the headline "One dirty corner breeds another," suggesting that criminals were often the product of their environments. Another ad showed hoboes, "The only Successful Men who do not use Soap and Water," implying that if the men washed up, they would be taken out of this classification. Still another ad provided a powerful reinforcement with the headline "At 3 months a success; at 30 years . . . ?" (see Fig. 6.4). It pictured the sharp contrast between a baby of "spotless perfection" and a derelict man who had grown up to "reap the benefits of untidy habits." "He is simply Help Not Wanted." It closed with a message of moral uplift: "You can't keep a clean man down." Together these ads dramatically argued that soap and water would make the world a better place in which to live.[59]

Fig. 6.5. Cleanliness Institute, advertisement, *Ladies' Home Journal*, April 1928.

Another series of advertisements employed the first-impression formula that appealed to the basic fear of giving offense, which successfully sold products like Lifebuoy Soap. First impressions counted as people made almost instantaneous judgments about one's character based on one's appearance, and such encounters constantly occurred. For example, one ad showed an everyday scene in a typical family neighborhood. It pictured a housewife looking out a window at her grimy-faced children at play in the yard; in turn, she is the object of the disapproving gaze of both her neighbors and husband. "What do the neighbors think of the children?" headlined the ad. "For people have a way of associating unclean clothes and faces with other questionable characteristics" (see Fig. 6.5). The ad closed, "There's character in soap & water."[60] Clearly, the ad made the point that the hands and clothes of one's children often determined their standing in

Fig. 6.6. Cleanliness Institute, advertisement, *Ladies' Home Journal*, October 1928.

the neighborhood. Such ads powerfully reminded the readers of the kinds of people that their neighbors and employers liked to have around, as well as the ones that made the best life partners.

Other ads also graphically reminded readers that there was a material benefit in adopting the soap-and-water ritual. These ads reinforced the notion of the American myth of success—that anyone with character, clean linen, and clean hands could succeed. For example, one ad dramatically reminded readers of the consequence of the failure to bathe and shave: It was why one salesperson could not "put it over," and this inability to close the deal could cost him his job.[61] By appearing neat and not having dirty cuffs, a person made a favorable impression in business, while to neglect cleanliness was to court disaster. Another ad claimed that women benefited from providing their spouses with a clean shirt every day: "If the wife increases the weekly laundry the chances are that her husband's position will be bettered."[62]

The theme of the material value of cleanliness appeared fully developed in a 1928 ad with the headline "A Kit for Climbers" (see Fig. 6.6). The illustration depicted a crowd of men, climbing over one another to reach some summit. At the top of this mass stood one figure with outstretched arms, reaching for the sun, whose rays spelled out the words "Heart's Desire." The copy advised:

> Hard work, courage, common sense will prove stout aids on your way up in the world. But don't overlook another, one that is tied up with good manners—cleanliness.
>
> Any way you look at it, clean habits, clean homes, clean linen have a value socially and commercially. How many successful men and women were not constantly careful of personal appearance and personal cleanliness?
>
> In any path of life, that long way to the top is hard enough—so make the going easier with soap and water.
>
> For Health and Wealth use Soap & Water.[63]

Certainly this advertisement made the point that a clean appearance would provide an advantage in the scramble for success; after all, those with clean collars get the best jobs. By appearing neat and not having dirty cuffs, one placed oneself socially and made a favorable impression in business.

Another effort of the Cleanliness Institute was the *Cleanliness Journal*. The sixteen-page booklet aimed "to circulate brief articles, stories, quotations, experiences, and plans gathered from many sources—all relating to the some aspect of cleanliness."[64] For example, one issue suggested that a close connection existed between physical cleanliness and mental health; another described how industrial workers subject to skin ailments could escape them.[65] The publication was furnished to sixty-five hundred public health leaders and social service and home economic workers upon request; they in turn spread this message to the general public.[66] In addition to the *Journal*, the institute produced numerous other booklets and pamphlets prepared especially for professional use; written by authorities on medicine and public health, they suggested new methods of presenting the facts about cleanliness. All of this literature was described in the pamphlet *Better Health Through Cleanliness*. Ads in professional periodicals included a coupon to request a

As *guardians of its health* . . .
you will teach it CLEANLINESS

As a reader of this publication you know how important cleanliness is. Every physician, nurse and welfare worker recognizes cleanliness as an important ally of modern preventive medicine.

But to convince the public of its importance isn't always such a simple matter.

To convince the Browns, the Jones, the Jalofskis of the important relationship between cleanliness and good health! Most health and welfare workers feel the need for assistance in that task. And it is to meet this need that the Health Service of Cleanliness Institute exists.

Here health workers will find many publications to help them in their work—many booklets and pamphlets prepared especially for their use, written by authorities on medicine and public health. All of these booklets suggest new methods of presenting the facts about cleanliness—methods so simple and understandable that even the Browns and Jalofskis can be convinced.

All of this literature is listed and described in our most recent pamphlet, *Better Health Through Cleanliness*.

A request will bring you a free copy of this catalog. Use coupon below.

CLEANLINESS INSTITUTE

Established to promote public welfare by teaching the value of cleanliness

CLEANLINESS INSTITUTE, Dept. 10D
45 East 17th Street, New York, N. Y.
Please send me free of all cost a copy of "Better Health Through Cleanliness."

Name ....
Position and organization ....
Address ....
City .... State ....

(*In answering advertisements please mention* THE SURVEY)
73

Fig. 6.7. Cleanliness Institute, advertisement, *Survey*, April 1930.

free copy. One ad appeared in a 1930 issue of *Survey* with the headline "As *guardians of its health* . . . you will teach it CLEANLINESS"; so health work could "convince the Browns, the Jones [*sic*], the Jalofskis of the important relationship between cleanliness and good health" (see Fig. 6.7).[67]

As a result of the work undertaken by the soap industry through the Cleanliness Institute, other industries whose products were closely related to cleanliness also expressed an interest in developing plans of their own or for cooperative work. For example, cleanliness had become a feature in the advertising of gas companies and in the program of the American Gas Association. A towel manufacturer instituted a $150,000 advertising campaign. Insurance companies and industrial and health organizations reprinted Cleanliness Institute posters. In turn, the Cleanliness Institute developed services specifically for the National Linen Supply Association of America to further publicize the cleanliness appeal.[68] Thus, the efforts of the united soap industry were multiplied many times over by what other important industries developed along similar lines.

Please, Send Me Absolutely Free . . .

The Cleanliness Institute sought to monitor the effectiveness of its advertising messages by using a coupon campaign to measure response. Although advertisers typically targeted a largely urban, middle-class group of women, even the poorer working-class woman could not escape the proliferation of cleanliness messages. To reach the young working women, ads appeared in the popular *True Story* magazine, where the institute ran almost all of its coupon ads. Overall, the institute spent an estimated half million dollars, using twenty-one different periodicals and a variety of layouts, to carry its message that cleanliness was within the reach of everyone. Upon request, the institute issued a number of publications for readers and for professional workers.

What was remarkable about the coupon campaign was not the amount spent but the number of Americans who actually responded to the advertising.[69] Consumers returned coupons cut from the ads or soap packages for free booklets that offered help on cleanliness problems from personal grooming to household cleaning. The institute received over 685,000 requests for over a million booklets, some 40 percent better than the typical rate of return on a similar promotion.[70]

The successful coupon ad campaign embodied three basic themes: (1) loveliness, (2) the bath, and (3) household cleaning. However, "For a More Beautiful Complexion" proved the most popular of seven "loveliness" ads that appeared in seventeen women's magazines. The ad offered respondents the booklet *The Thirty Day Loveliness Test*, holding out the promise of loveliness with measurable results in a month. Another ad in the series pictured a woman alone versus a woman surrounded by six admiring men; it simply asked, "Will YOU be a lovelier person by Dec. 15?" Other ads made similar promises. Every woman could become a lovelier and more likeable, happier person if she was willing to commit to the daily soap-and-water ritual. The reward for such attention and diligence was not simply cleanliness, but also popularity and self-esteem.

The second most popular group of appeals focused on the bath, while the cleaning ads proved the least successful of the three promotions. Naturally, the institute recognized that another way to promote consumption of soap products was to provide consumers with good reasons to indulge in more than one bath a day; thus, they would use more soap. *The Book about Baths* offered basics on what type of water to use and when to bathe, and also featured a variety of different baths, including cold, tepid, and hot baths to improve looks; morning baths; and after-work baths, among others. "There's more to baths than keeping clean," emphasized the little book. "It is becoming in America, more and more a part of good breading, good business, and good health for everyone."[71] The institute also offered two cartoon booklets free upon request—for girls ten to sixteen years of age, *The Smart Thing to Do*, and for boys of the same age, *Learn the Art of Magic*.[72]

In the crusade for a cleaner America, the Cleanliness Institute supplemented the public relations and print media campaign with radio advertising. Like the campaigns targeting children, radio broke through the privacy of the family circle with powerful messages about cleanliness that reached even those who bought no magazines or knew only a little English. In 1930, the institute staff delivered a series of formal radio addresses that aired in as many as thirty-six metropolitan areas, including "A Doctor Looks at Cleanliness and Health," "Summer Camps and Cleanliness," and "The Search for Beauty," among others. For the housewife, the target of this array of daytime programs, the institute also created the "Homeville Club" and broadcast messages about the American woman caring for the home while loving every minute, with topics such as "Houseworking Your Way to Good Looks."[73]

All of these publications and activities concentrated on a few simple, clear messages, highlighting the new virtues that cleanliness had given the United States as it became more industrial, urban, and ethnically diverse.

Cleanliness had become a marker of individuals who were not only morally superior, of better character, or more civilized than others, but also more attractive. According to the Cleanliness Institute, those with clean collars not only got the best jobs, but they proved more successful in them. Why? Because clean people had more self-respect; they also appeared more confident, efficient, and congenial, and they had a more pleasing appearance. Such was the logic of this constantly iterated narrative.

Our First Concern Is for the Children

In 1931, the Cleanliness Institute conducted a study to investigate the extent to which soap was used in schools and the resources that were available for cleanliness education. The institute asked a number of questions. What interest did teachers have in encouraging children to wash their hands with soap and water? What cleanliness facilities were available in the schoolhouses? What time and opportunity for cleanliness education were available? What encouragement did the teachers give to the development of personal cleanliness rituals?

The findings were startling but useful for the soap industry. Of the 145 representative schools studied in fifteen states, the report concluded that less than one in three schools provided schoolchildren with hot and cold water, soap, and towels. Even more surprising was the fact that in only one school did children thoroughly wash their hands before meals and after using the toilet.[74] The report concluded that the construction of washing facilities was not enough; they must be used. To instill cleanliness behaviors, the report recommended that an organization be formed to create both teacher and student interest and that the school program permit time for proper supervision of hand washing and teaching of cleanliness practices.

Once the Cleanliness Institute discovered how few American schoolchildren were truly clean in its view, the primary objective of the cleanliness teaching became the establishment of lifelong habits. With this in mind, the institute prepared a curriculum for teaching cleanliness that showed educators how to instill bathing and grooming practices in children from kindergarten to high school. "Shake Hands Often with Soap" typified the kind of advice. The objective was not merely to make children clean, but to make them love to be clean.

The institute primarily targeted children as it infiltrated classrooms

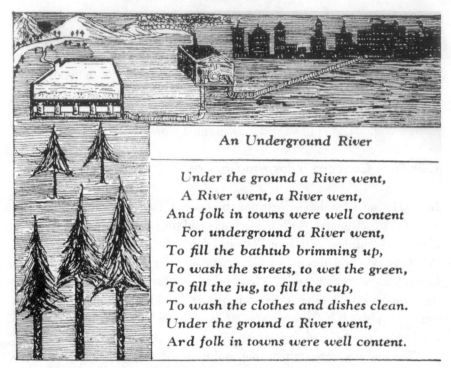

An Underground River

Under the ground a River went,
A River went, a River went,
And folk in towns were well content
For underground a River went,
To fill the bathtub brimming up,
To wash the streets, to wet the green,
To fill the jug, to fill the cup,
To wash the clothes and dishes clean.
Under the ground a River went,
Ard folk in towns were well content.

Fig. 6.8. Soap and pure water supplies become available to the poor as well as the rich, illustration from *A Tale of Soap and Water*, 1928.

with educational materials that dispensed advice on personal hygiene. The program planners reasoned that people learned habits in early life, and such habits generally lasted a lifetime. From the institute's perspective, children had to learn habits of personal cleanliness such as washing their hands after using the toilet and before eating; these personal cleanliness rituals were not instinctual. Schoolchildren, educated in their youth to use soap liberally, would rarely lose the habit as they grew older. Once youths adopted the soap-and-water ritual, they would guarantee a continuing market for years to come. These businesspeople were shrewd enough to recognize that school organizations could carry out the educational work of teaching schoolchildren to wash their hands with soap and water.

Hundreds of thousands of textbooks and storybooks were sold at cost to convey the message. One, a storybook titled *A Tale of Soap and Water*, both written and illustrated by Grace T. Hallock, told the story of the historical progress of cleanliness since ancient times (see Fig. 6.8). How people kept their clothes and their surroundings clean was told in a story form that made cleanliness a part of a well-ordered life. Hallock concluded:

> We know, as [Benjamin] Franklin knew long ago, that to be clean in body, clothes, and habitation increases our chances, because we gain thereby in self-respect and in the respect and liking of others. Most of us want the good and beautiful and worthwhile things of lie. Soap and water alone cannot give them to us, but we know that they help.[75]

Thousands of pamphlets, posters, flyers, and teacher's guides supplemented the crusade, all emphasizing in one way or another the applications of personal cleanliness rituals to everyday life. Morning games and gentle encouragement also served as part of the conditioning process. In addition, the institute distributed bibliographies on cleanliness to hundreds of libraries. Other outreach efforts included lectures by institute representatives before associations, societies, clubs, schools, and other civic organizations in order to reach those group leaders who could influence the cleanliness habits of yet more Americans.[76]

This outpouring of guidance also delineated specific objectives for every stage of a child's education. At the end of the third grade, for example, ideal students washed their hands before meals and after using the toilet, kept their faces clean, took an all-over bath twice a week, and wore both clean socks and underwear after bathing. By the end of the sixth grade, children cared for their clothes, bathed themselves, and unconsciously covered sneezes as the emphasis shifted to making them want to be clean. By the end of the ninth grade, the socialization process thus attuned children not merely to want to be clean but to feel uncomfortable when they or others did not pay proper attention to personal hygiene. The pupils would then provide a ready market for soap as long as they maintained the habit of washing their hands at least twice during the school day, before lunch and after toilet.[77] Clearly, the education programs of the Cleanliness Institute served to meet the soap industry objective to sell more soap, ensuring customers for the present and the future.

Fig. 6.9. Lifebuoy Soap Clean Hands Campaign, advertisement, early 1930s.

The Impact of the Cleanliness Institute

Advertising independent of the Cleanliness Institute also provided constant reinforcement of the cleanliness message. Advertisements for brand-name soap, mouthwash, toothpaste, and deodorant in mass-circulation magazines showed working men and women how to cleanse themselves and become part

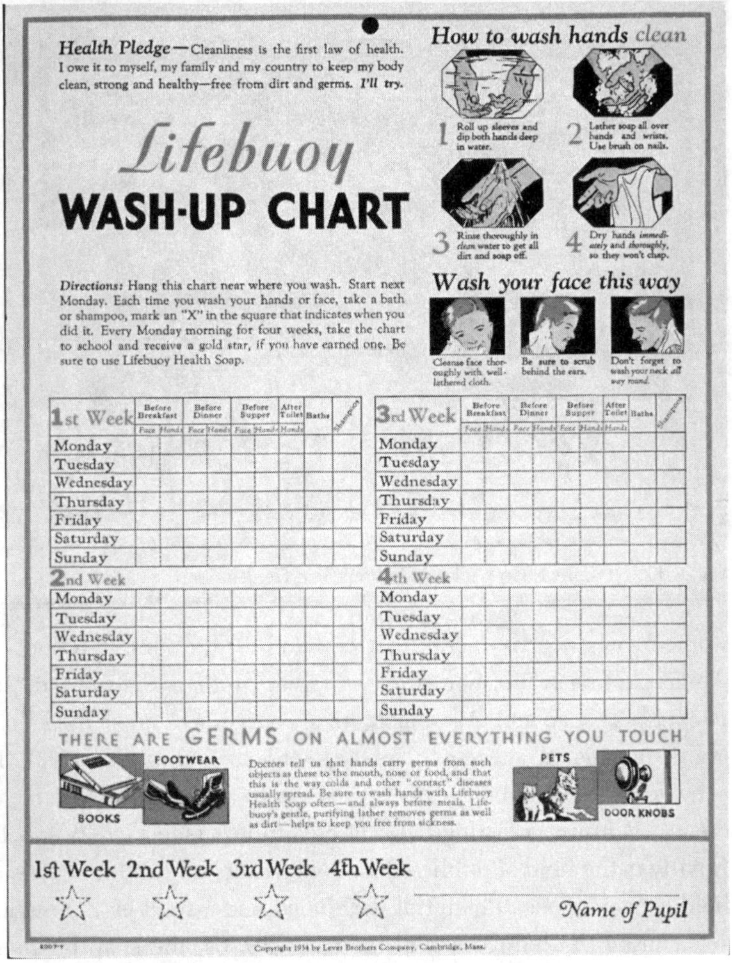

Fig. 6.10. Lifebuoy Soap Wash-Up Chart, 1934.

of the increasingly sweatless, odorless, and successful business class. Nevertheless, hard times forced the Cleanliness Institute to shut down in 1932.

Did the Cleanliness Institute succeed in its aim to sell more soap? It remains unclear whether it was the united promotional efforts of the soap trade or the individual efforts of soap manufacturers that encouraged Americans to use more soap. After the institute closed, however, the soapmakers' messages of personal cleanliness continued to reach the public even as the nation slid into the Depression. At school, children still heard about how they should keep clean and wash their hands to avoid germs, while men and

Fig. 6.11. Lifebuoy Soap package, School Size Health Soap.

women saw advertisements that equated cleanliness with success and the American way of life. For example, Lever Brothers distributed "school size" packages of soap and urged mothers to "carry on at home the Lifebuoy Clean Hands campaign started in 39,000 schools to guard health." They could send for a free Lifebuoy Wash-up Chart to make "a jolly game of keeping clean" and form a lasting habit of cleanliness (see Figs. 6.9, 6.10, 6.11).[78] Finally in the field of public education, writers on health, beauty, and household economics used material developed and issued by the institute.

During the hard times of the early 1930s, the soap business held up remarkably well to the heightened competition and to the Depression, since soapmakers had aggressively protected their markets and promoted consumption of their products. The greatest decline for the period was an apparent decrease in soap sales of 22 percent, comparing the federal census figures for 1933 with those for 1931. Even then the decline was not nearly as great as in the average manufacturing realm. In several instances, however, the quantity sold was even larger than in the previous year. In fact, the lower selling prices caused a lower total sales volume to be reported in 1931. Thus, while the sales of toilet soap were $9 million less for 1933 than for 1931, the quantity sold was between four and five million pounds greater.[79] This also proved true for soap chips and flakes, while shaving soap and powder remained approximately the same in quantity. Soap-making continued to be a profitable enterprise.

Thus, the culture of cleanliness had become institutionalized, rein-forcing a mix of private and public values in a unique cultural enterprise. At the same time, Procter & Gamble, Colgate, and Lever Brothers began to creatively employ the new medium of radio, ushering in another American institution—the soap opera.

SOAP OPERAS AND SOAP

Initially, many broadcast advertisers simply filled entire segments of leased time with promotional messages. Others experimented with creating pro-grams relevant to their product; for example, Gillette hosted a talk show on fashions in beards to generate sales for its shaving equipment and supplies. A mere 20 percent of radio programs had sponsors as of 1927.

The development of regular weekly programs, rather than one-time efforts, gradually convinced advertisers that the new medium deserved their backing. To fill program segments, radio producers picked up popular vaudeville shows that featured song-and-dance teams, singers, and ethnic and blackface comics. The agencies created company-sponsored programs that proved to be the most potent vehicle for advertising during the 1930s and 1940s—in what has been called the Golden Era of Radio. The agen-cies best achieved the underwriter's identification when they worked the advertiser's name into one particular program title or time slot over a long run. Thus, the early commercial programs were actually musical variety shows sponsored by advertisers such as the *Palmolive Hour* for the Palmo-live Company (later Colgate-Palmolive), *The A & P Gypsies* for A & P gro-cery stores, or the *Eveready Battery Hour* for Eveready batteries.

Radio struck a chord with Americans of all classes. By 1930 almost 40 percent of the homes had radios, and the number continued to rise as more low-income families acquired them, preferring the radio to magazines as a source of information on how to run their homes and improve themselves. Although briefly shaken by the Depression, radio quickly rebounded, expanding its number of stations and attracting new listeners and adver-tisers. With the motion picture industry slumping, show business talent flocked to radio, along with listeners and sponsors. Listening to radio became the nation's favorite pastime during the Depression. "Destitute families, forced to give up an icebox or furniture or bedding, clung to the radio as to a last link to humanity," noted historian Erik Barnouw.[80] This success encouraged agencies and advertisers to use the personal contact angle that the medium provided. Initially, Lord & Thomas, J. Walter Thompson, and Young & Rubicam emerged as the most dominant agencies in radio.

Still, daytime radio initially attracted few sponsors because many advertisers thought that housewives had no time to listen to the radio.[81] Inspired by the success of the nighttime program *Amos 'n' Andy*, Chicago station WGN in 1930 aired Irma Phillip's *Painted Dreams*. This is considered to be the first daytime serial script—a mix of philosophy, music, and poetry with continuing characters. The program ran for nearly a year without a sponsor for the unproven format. When Procter & Gamble moved into the new medium of daytime radio the same year, the first Ivory radio show, *Mrs. Reilly*, was broadcast over sixty-two radio stations; it delivered dissertations on baby care for Ivory Soap.[82] Procter & Gamble's consumer attitude researchers reported, however, that "the listeners want to be entertained, not instructed." As a result, the soap-maker's program planners went on to develop radio's first daytime serials, dubbed "soap operas" because of the sponsorship of Procter & Gamble and other soapmakers.[83] Among them Frank and Ann Hummert of the Blackett-Sample-Hummert agency in Chicago, subsequently the most prolific producers of daytime serials, developed the highly successful *Ma Perkins* show and possibly the best sponsor identification, in part due to the show's twenty-seven-year association with Procter & Gamble's Oxydol laundry detergent.

Women played an active role in creating the stories and continuing characters of daytime soap operas. Female writers such as Irma Phillips and Ann Hummert selected the bits of homey philosophy and music, as well as stories of romance, love, and adventure to be incorporated into the scripts. They were creating material that they thought was what their female audience wanted to hear. Actually, audiences did not always listen to the program from beginning to end, as they might watch a movie. Since many soap opera listeners simultaneously cleaned house, read, or ate, they did not always pay full attention to the aesthetic creation. Even so, the housewives controlled the radio dials and responded to offers of small premiums and sales promotions. Thus, women determined which daytime programs would continue and which promotional messages would be heard.

This leads to the question of what, if anything, the people who were sponsoring the broadcast got for their money. A 1930 study concluded that the radio-advertised brands were used in a larger proportion of homes with radio than without radios. In the case of Gold Medal Flour, a consistent and effective user of radio, the rate of use in radio homes was 22 percent greater than in households without radios; and for Palmolive Soap, it was 10.8 percent higher than in nonradio homes.[84] Thus, while the radio soap operas communicated with sound alone, this was sufficient to communicate the essential repetition of the sponsor's name, which was then assimilated into the purchasing patterns of listeners.

Lever Brothers was somewhat slow to take up the use of radio compared to the other large national advertisers, showing little interest until 1934. What the firm did initially sponsor was *Lux Radio Theatre*. The Thompson agency, which handled the Lux account at the time, identified one niche that was not yet filled by any major program. Therefore, the program offered a special opportunity to air a full-hour dramatic show, and subsequently to do full-length plays with competent actors and actresses, including some of the best and brightest screen stars of the 1930s and 1940s—Helen Hayes, Tyrone Power, and Barbara Stanwyck.[85] The program ran on Sunday afternoons for nearly a year before being moved to an available evening hour, airing on Columbia Broadcasting. The program was designed to promote Lux Toilet Soap, a natural for this product, as movie stars had been used as background for the product advertising for many years. The agency concluded that, on the basis of ratings, the audience increased in relation to increased ad spending and length of time on the air. In fact, the audience ratings grew nearly fourfold during a period when radio appropriations more or less doubled, from $550,000 a year in 1934 to $1,250,000 in 1937.[86]

Like Lever Brothers, other advertisers became more radio-minded. In 1938 radio surpassed magazines as a source of advertising revenue for the first time.[87] In this year, Procter & Gamble spent over $6 million for the purchase of radio time; an average of five hours per day were taken up by nineteen regular daytime programs and two evening broadcasts. On the basis of time expenditures, the Procter & Gamble Company emerged as the world's largest radio advertiser, having spent nearly $1 million more than General Foods and $3 million more than Lever Brothers.[88]

7

White Soap and Black Consumer Culture

African American consumer culture and personal cleanliness rituals emerged in a pattern similar to that of white Americans, but a fervid debate about the politics of appearance clouded the picture.[1] Nineteenth-century Americans had inherited racist attitudes established over two centuries that had hardly been eradicated by the abolition of slavery. African American labor continued to carry a different status from white labor. In many instances, African Americans received no greater rights or privileges than had the slaves. They could not vote. In many cases, they could not even own property. Although slavery was now illegal, the dictum that "Negroes have no rights" continued to prevail in American life.[2]

Old social barriers also remained practically intact, particularly when, in 1881, they received reinforcement by new segregation laws. Tennessee, quickly followed by the other southern states, passed the first Jim Crow laws requiring separation of the races on public conveyances and in public places. Laws went even further in establishing separate schools for blacks and whites. Although residential segregation ordinances had been declared unconstitutional in 1917, another form of discrimination kept African Americans out of white neighborhoods by restrictive convenants—agreements by property owners in a neighborhood not to sell or rent their property to African Americans for a certain period of time.[3] The desire of many people to live among family and friends also created African American sections in every large community. Many African American communities had various social clubs in addition to those organized in churches, and these were regularly reported in the society columns of the national and local black press.[4]

While segregation imposed many injustices, it also drove African Americans to strive for a high degree of self-sufficiency. The denial of the right to eat in restaurants run by whites forced them to establish their own restaurants. Mutual benefit societies, resulting from their separate social life, formed the basis for black insurance companies. Funds from insurance companies then encouraged the establishment of African American banks, managed by professional businesspeople trained in African American universities, who in turn profited, in most instances, from an African American clientele. This clientele worked as manufacturers, general merchandisers, grocers, clothiers, druggists, publishers, barbers, cleaners, undertakers, landlords, taxicab drivers, owners of filling stations, and so on—just like whites. Some of them contributed to African American schools and invested in other enterprises, which in turn gave employment to many more African Americans.[5]

Around 1900, the average black family no longer confined its expenditures to "necessities," such as food, clothing, and shelter; they also allocated a significant share of their income to churches, fraternal lodges, consumer durables, travel, amusements, and savings. Improvements in hygiene, diet, and housing also reflected the rising standard of living.[6] Although many families lived in ramshackle rural cabins and squalid urban tenements, an increasing number slowly came to own spacious and comfortable homes. Conservative estimates indicated black income per capita more than doubled between 1867 and the turn of the century. By 1900, the average annual income per capita for rural blacks was between $49 and $80, and for urban black dwellers between $75 and $125.[7] Yet the average African American remained desperately poor relative to poor whites. At the time, it was estimated that a family of five needed $15 a week just to buy the necessities of life.[8] For African American families to manage, it was customary for several members of the family to work for wages, as did immigrant families.

It was not until the beginning of the twentieth century, however, that any record appears of African Americans advertising to black business consumers on a national scale.[9] There were, of course, large white manufacturers doing business among whites that also enjoyed a limited trade with African American consumers.

AFRICAN AMERICANS AND PERSONAL CARE ENTERPRISE

One of the most striking examples of African American enterprise in the mass market can be found in the personal care field. The black enterprises of Madame C. J. Walker, Poro, Overton Hygienic, and Kashmir Chemical did a nationwide business in soaps, cosmetics, and hair-care systems. As F. B. Ransom, the general manager for the Walker Company put it in 1923, they "not only gave the colored business man a new rating in the commercial world, but it brought the colored press into prominence as a medium of reaching the largest number of colored people."[10]

In the toiletry trade, the term "mass market" implies both a standardized product and a standardized consumer. The term, however, conceals important differences along racial lines, not only in Americans' buying habits, but also in their response to the culture of consumption. For African Americans, appearance was not only an aesthetic, psychological, and social marker, but from the outset, explicitly a problem of politics. Soap was never far removed from the fact of white supremacy, the goal of racial progress, and the question of emulation. Unlike mass-circulation magazines aimed at white audiences, African American periodicals often debated the political meaning of exploitative industry, gullible consumers, and a white-dominated society that imposed its own beauty standards.

Advertisers, manufacturers, and advice writers, all part of a black consumer culture, defended the personal care trade with their own claims, ranging from a definite economic benefit to an appeal to racial pride. The doctrine of the "double-duty dollar" was preached in the black press and many church pulpits as part of the weekly sermon with specific businesses often singled out as being worthy of support. The idea here was to buy from black-owned businesses to make the dollar do "double-duty" by both purchasing a commodity and advancing the race. In its most extreme form, the dream was to control the African American market as a completely separate black economy, wholly independent of the white race. Not surprisingly, African American businesspeople and community leaders stressed the theme of racial solidarity in an effort to amass capital and patronage. Though African Americans found it extremely difficult to compete on the basis of price and services in the general merchandising field, business owners like undertakers, barbers, and beauticians operated within a closed market, competing only among themselves.[11] Thus, African American leaders elevated the concepts of the double-duty dollar and the rewards of investing in a black-owned venture into a demonstration of racial solidarity. Despite this dream, African Americans still spent most of their money with white firms, and black businesspeople often complained that their own people did not support them.

A public dialogue involving the meaning of personal grooming and beautifying practices accompanied the entry of African Americans into the consumer culture. In particular, a woman would greatly limit her opportunities if she did not make use of hairdressing, manicuring, and cleansing with facial massages. "Not only is there utility from [a]esthetic improvement; there are also sound hygienic and sanitary advantages," explained the *Messenger* in 1918. Cleansing the body, opening the pores of the skin, and removing germs from under the nails was healthful. If white women spent millions of dollars a year to beautify themselves, "there is no reason why black women should not use every effort to make themselves attractive and comely, and consequently more desirable in every walk of life."[12] While many African American women fashioned their appearances by following in some measure the aesthetic of European beauty, other extreme race loyalists felt that their appearance should be "natural." As a result, soap and water, like cosmetics, became the battleground in a contest of cultural visions, political concerns, and individual desires.

THE POLITICS OF APPEARANCE

Even before the emergence of a black consumer culture in the twentieth century, African Americans had begun to speak about the political meanings of appearance. A legacy of racist attitudes had been established over two centuries, and a distinctly new voice emerged to contest it. In the nineteenth century, however, notions of Anglo-Saxon beauty, cleanliness, and superiority in relation to people of color were central to American culture. Because appearance and character were considered to be commensurate, the beauty of white skin and soap-and-water rituals expressed Anglo-Saxon virtues and civilization and marked a distinction within social classes. Among African Americans, the body itself—the physical features, cleanliness, and demeanor—had become an issue in the debate over collective identity and action.

The Nineteenth Century

Aesthetic conventions reinforced a noxious, national racial taxonomy in nineteenth-century American culture. Alexander Walker, for example, argued in the 1845 book *Beauty* that ancients had long regarded whiteness as the distinctive characteristic of beauty. People of antiquity valued this trait so highly that the name of Venus, from the Celtic *ven, ben,* or *ban,* signified white or whiteness; and Venus herself was said to be fair and golden-haired. In the nineteenth century, whiteness of skin continued to dominate tastes. Hence, metaphoric references to lily white or to complexions as white as the new-fallen snow and smooth as marble or alabaster, and other poetic images were already prevalent and available to advertisers to target woman eager to satisfy longstanding norms of beauty. So greatly did whiteness contribute to women's beauty, observed Walker, "that many women deemed beautiful, have little right to that epithet, except what they derive from a beautiful skin."

No one personified the polar opposite of the dominant American beauty ideal more starkly than African Americans did. White men and women had long invoked stereotypes dehumanizing African Americans and denying them social and political participation.

By cleansing and grooming themselves, African Americans could defiantly claim recognition as individuals, as well as define themselves as modern and self-respecting, when not to do so was a negation of personal, social, and intrinsic identity. Black reformers, educators, intellectuals, and journalists began to speak up about the politics of appearance, both rejecting and embracing Euro-American aesthetic standards. Earlier nineteenth-century sermons focusing on the connection between moral and physical cleanliness circulated in editorials, letters to the editor, and articles published in the black press. However, few African Americans could read. Despite these limitations, notions of Anglo-American cleanliness were continually asserted in relation to people of color. In 1837, for example, one letter to the editor of the New York *Colored American* captured the view on the moral effects of dress; it was simply signed "Augustine":

> In the United States much attention is paid to dress. And it is a custom, which I believe prevails in every part of the Union to determine the rank of person by their dress, and treat them accordingly. . . . And I have often wondered if much of the indignity and contempt with which we, as a body of people are treated, in this country, does not arise from our want of proper attention to cleanliness and neatness of dress.[13]

The following year, an article by the president of a theological seminary in the *Colored American* also stressed the importance of cleanliness: "The charge of filthy habits effectually bars us from respectable society. . . . With it, we are honored; without it, we are disgraced."[14] Continually made aware of the social significance of appearance, nineteenth-century African Americans understood the power and pleasures of looking fine in the face of destructive stereotypes.

Claiming personal cleanliness and neatness of dress contained a cruel irony. After the Civil War, many blacks endured much the same harsh living and working environments that they had faced in slavery. Many African Americans lived enslaved on plantations without a single provision of any kind for cleanliness, reported the New York *North Star* in 1850. Their beds and clothing were seldom washed in any manner, with generally one suit allotted per slave each year; "from the neglect and want of proper cleanliness and care very few become men and women."[15] In fact, the most arresting feature of the health of blacks was the scant change it had undergone in the long period from the late slavery era to the start of the Great

Depression. As late as 1930 in the rural South, some 55 percent of African American housing remained "squalid and often overcrowded, with sanitary facilities and clean water in short supply." Work, too, remained as physically demanding as before.[16]

Various "scientific" studies reinforced the image of African Americans as less than human. Evolutionary science fitted African American bodies into new classifications of inferiority based on facial angles and physiognomic measurements. Most social scientists during the late nineteenth and early twentieth centuries believed African Americans to be inferior to white Americans; for some, measures of intelligence did not adequately describe the differences. Earlier psychological studies argued that African Americans had stronger emotions, greater volatility, and defective morals.[17] Images of exaggerated racial differences circulated throughout American culture as emblems of this new "scientific" basis for perpetuating racist stereotypes. For white Americans, sustaining a visual distinction between white and black masked an uncomfortable truth that some Africans and Europeans had become genetically mixed, with their histories and destinies irrevocably intertwined.[18]

The abundance of low-priced soap and new cosmetic preparations promised relief from such stereotypes. Yet many white and, later, black soap manufacturers were not yet ready to endorse the idea of racial solidarity (see Fig. 7.1). Some manufacturers issued advertising that could be seen as reinforcing racial bigotry because they advertised their soap as no ordinary cleansing agent. Using the right product could not transform one race into the other, but it could offer comforting evidence of one's belonging to the right sort of group. This idea appeared in a series of seven advertising trade cards for Higgins Soap, one for each day of the week. The wise African American woman made sure her entire family worked during the week, took a bath on Saturday, and dressed for Sunday church, achieving an aura of middle-class respectability—"An it all comes—using dat Higgins Soap" (see Fig. 7.2). Using Higgins Soap crassly promised to transform the stereotyped countenances of a plantation slave family to that of a genteel white one.

Other ad campaigns claimed an even more dramatic transformation, suggesting that the featured soap product could even turn the skin of African Americans white, or many shades lighter. For example, the sixteen-page booklet titled "Light and Shade use Dreydoppel Soap" featured

Fig. 7.1. Fairy Soap, trade card, 1898. N. K. Fairbanks and Company also offered this picture as a premium offer.

product information and a picture story that carried a general promise of light, clear skin (see Fig. 7.3). As the story went, "A mite of queer humanity, as dark as a cloudy night" wished to change his complexion from black to white. He rubbed and scrubbed with soaps and strong acids, sam-

Fig. 7.2. Two of a set of seven trade cards for Higgins Soap.

pled all the medicine that was ever made, tried to eat little food, sweated it out, and even soaked in sulfur springs, all in the hope he would bleach. He then spied a signboard for Dreydoppel Soap and thought it could do the job "One trial was all he needed," the story concluded. "Realized was his fondest hope. His face was as white as white could be." Certainly, there was nothing like Dreydoppel Soap.[19]

These advertisements were only a small sample of the extensive literature of the period that advanced the notions of white superiority, black inferiority, and the threat to civilization posed by inferior peoples, including those who were white but in some way inferior to "Nordic" or "Aryan" peoples. The influential racist works of the period included: Houston Stewart Chamberlain's *Foundations of the Nineteenth Century*; D. W. Griffith's landmark film of 1915, *Birth of a Nation*, based on Thomas Dixon's bigoted novel, *The Clansman*; Madison Grant's *The Passing of the Great Race*; Clinton Stoddard Burr's *America's Race Heritage*; and Lothrop Stoddard's *The Revolt Against Civilization: The Menace of the Under Man*.

It became a time to fight, not only for rights, but for appearance as well.

A mite of queer humanity,
    As dark as a cloudy night,
Was displeased with his complexion,
    And wished to change from black to white.

Fig. 7.3. Two pages from *Light and Shade*, Dreydoppel Soap booklet, 1892.

One trial was all he needed;

Realized was his fondest hope;

His face was as white as white could be;

There's nothing like Dreydoppel Soap.

Leading the intellectual fight against doctrines of white supremacy, anthropologist Franz Boas, whose ideas concerning cultural relativism were expressed in *The Mind of Primitive Men*, emerged as an important part of the movement to reappraise American culture. At the same time, black writers rejected the connection between looks and character as long as white Americans were setting the aesthetic standards. Morality had no color, they argued, and racial definitions based on the "one drop" rule of African "blood" relegated African Americans to a life of degradation. In response, black reformers, educators, intellectuals, and journalists began to frame a "New Negro" to counter the plantation and minstrel stereotypes, envisioning a figure of modernity who embodied changed historical circumstances and future prospects.

The New Negro

In an era when black people were virtually shut off from participation in white society, promotion of the health and welfare of the race offered one of the few outlets for black leadership, along with education and religion, that had sympathy if not support from some whites. Aware that their people could make no progress unless they first survived, black leaders across the South, a large proportion of them women, strove to reduce sickness and death from such ills as tuberculosis and venereal diseases and to reduce the staggering mortality rate of black mothers and infants. The United States Public Health Service, state departments of health, and the National Urban League, as well as national and health organizations, undertook special campaigns to uplift the African American race. One of the best-known programs that sought to reach the great mass of American blacks was the Negro Health Week movement, launched in 1915 by Booker T. Washington with the support of other national groups and institutions.[20]

Washington insisted that the most helpful lesson he received at the Hampton Institute was "in the use and value of the bath."[21] The Hampton Normal and Agricultural Institute, located in Hampton, Virginia, opened in 1868; in less than a decade, it grew in size from twenty to more than a thousand students. Hampton's monthly publication, the *Southern Workman*, reminded students, friends, and supporters regularly of the importance of cleanliness. "Remember," instructed an 1875 issue, "that one thing above all others which Society insists upon is 'cleanliness,' and that this cleanliness must begin with your skin and the clothes which you wear."[22] With the Hampton Institute as model, Washington set out to educate young people and build character; in 1881, he opened the Tuskegee Institute in Alabama. Thus, while Washington insisted that Tuskegee students learn the manual skills needed to succeed in an industrializing nation, he also taught them how to bathe and care for their teeth, clothing, and rooms, so the graduates would appear more attractive to benevolent white employers.

In a similar vein, black women's groups were equally active in public health and municipal housekeeping campaigns of the late nineteenth and early twentieth centuries. White females in the late nineteenth century were still expected to function within a separate sphere of home and family; while that expectation limited their reach, it also encouraged involvement in outside activities for preserving the home and its values.[23] When a black female middle class emerged in the South during the early twentieth century, its members seemed to follow a course similar to that of their white counterparts. As clubwomen, health reformers, and educators, they sought to investigate and eradicate those conditions that tended to keep their race down. For example, Lugenia Hope established the Atlanta Neighborhood Union in 1908, and Modejeska Monteith became South Carolina's only full-time statewide black health worker in 1931; these women led two of the most effective voluntary health organizations in the South.[24]

Newly assertive black leaders, ministers, and educators also emphasized racial pride, advocating cleanliness and grooming in their crusade for social acceptance. They also called upon women to spurn bleaching of faces and straightening of hair as degrading practices that represented a denial of their racial heritage. "From our viewpoint it simply means that the women who practice it wish they had white faces and straight hair," pointed out Nannie Burroughs, a prominent African American clubwoman and head of a school for black girls in Washington, D.C.[25] Prominent beauty culturists Madame C. J. Walker and Annie Turbo Malone, founder of Poro College, refused to sell bleach and emphasized hair care, not straightening.[26]

African American periodicals, advice literature, and beauty manuals also situated cleansing and beautification within the political mission of black uplift. For example, a 1904 periodical, *Voice of the New Negro*, published the "Features of the New Negro Woman." The study presented

FLOYD'S FLOWERS, OR; DUTY AND BEAUTY
A Book for Colored Children

Designed especially for Colored children, with the purpose of giving them clean and inspiring literature, which will cultivate their minds and teach them lessons of morality.

BY

SILAS X. FLOYD, D.D.

Illustrated by

JOHN HENRY ADAMS

Over 300 pages.   80 illustrations.

Size 6 x 8¼.

Cloth, Very Attractive, - - - $1.00
Half Morocco, Library Edition,   1.50
Full Morocco, Handsome and
Durable, - - - - - - -   2.00

A HERO IN BLACK

The First and Only Race Book of the Kind Ever Written
Sets Before the Colored Boys and Girls High Ideals and Sound Advice

Stories of Slavery Days; Stories of Bravery; Stories of Faithfulness; Stories of Schooldays; Stories of Useful Lives; Stories of Great Men; Stories about Animals; Stories about Bad Boys and Girls and their Troubles; Stories of Success; Stories of Pluck; Stories of Real Fun; Stories of Jolly Times; Stories of Hardship; Funny Stories, Helpful Stories.

In all, 100 stories told as only Prof. Floyd can tell them, and nearly all teaching some important moral lesson.

SELF HELP.
How much more fortunate children are, whose parents teach them to do little things for themselves. Prof. Floyd tells of many ways little folks can be helpful and help themselves at the same time.

Agents, remember this Book has been on the market only 30 days and no territory has been worked. If you want to be first in the field, send for outfit TO-DAY.

Outfit and Complete Copy
FREE!

Send 10c. for outfit and full instructions, and with your first order for one dozen, we 'll refund the 10c. and give you One Copy Free

Hertel, Jenkins & Co.,

Austell Bldg., Atlanta, Ga.

WASHING DOLLIE'S CLOTHES

This little girl's mama was too poor to buy her a Christmas present. On Christmas eve a poor little kitten was lost in the snow. Something scared it and it ran right into her home. So she had a Christmas present after all.

"Mama, this must be the present that Santa brought.

Every Colored Home Should Have It.   Every Colored Boy and Girl Should Read It

Fig. 7.4. The conduct book *Floyd's Flowers*, advertisement, *Voice of the Negro*, July 1904.

sketches and portraits of "colored women [*sic*] today as she impresses her-self in the world as a growing factor for good and in her beauty, intelligence and character for better social recognition."[27] New literature of advice, including conduct books, etiquette books, and beauty manuals, targeted African Americans. For example, E. M. Wood's *The Negro in Etiquette* appeared in 1899; while Reverend Silas X. Floyd's conduct book *Floyd's Flowers, Or; Duty and Beauty* was promoted in 1905 as "the first, and only race book of the kind ever written," offering "the colored boys and girls high ideals and sound advice" (see Fig. 7.4). Beauty manuals also came on the scene specifically aimed at the African American market, like Hackley E. Azalia's beauty manual *The Colored Girl Beautiful*. Beauty advice, fashion news, and grooming tips also began to appear in African American periodicals on a regular basis. The *Colored American* magazine, devoted to the "higher culture," brought the fashion column of Madame Rumford to middle-class readers. Likewise, the black *Half-Century* magazine, modeled on the *Ladies' Home Journal*, ran a "Beauty Hints" column from 1916 to 1925, featuring tips on care of the hands, hair, and teeth and stressing per-sonal cleanliness. The black press also reported on women's work in clubs, churches, and other organizations, documenting their wide influence in community affairs. Photographs of beautiful performers, celebrities, and fashion models also ran in black newspapers as icons of racial pride.[28]

These messages collectively reinforced the point that an improved appearance would express self-respect, register collective progress, and expedite social acceptance. From the turn of the century until World War II, the enforced isolation of African Americans would continue to foster the same self-sufficiency that nations placed in similar situations have devel-oped, with blacks educating their young, building trade, establishing finan-cial stability, and raising their standard of living.

The Great Migration

The migration away from the South further heightened African Americans' self-consciousness about appearance. Deepening poverty, segregation, and vio-lence, combined with perceived opportunities in the North for jobs and just treatment, sparked an African American exodus from the South after 1915. Rural blacks moving to northern cities got the soap-and-water message not only from white society but also from the emerging African American middle class which preached Washington's "gospel of the toothbrush." Echoing earlier white reformers, black newspapers and social service agencies issued instructions on personal cleanliness rituals, proper appearance, and deportment.

Although southern blacks moved in great numbers to New York and Detroit, their mecca was Chicago. The Illinois Central railroad made it easy for anyone in the Deep South to reach what appeared to be the Promised Land. The Chicago *Defender*, the most popular newspaper among southern blacks, invited its readers to hop a train by telling them about job opportunities and showing them how prosperous and influential Chicago's African American community had become.[29] Yet the *Defender* also reflected Washington's notions of self-help. Frequent editorials on manners and morals, as well as Dr. A. Wilberforce Williams's weekly "Keep Healthy" columns on health and hygiene echoed the advice given to African Americans in the pages of *Southern Workman*. Williams repeatedly exhorted on topics such as cleanliness, bathing, tuberculosis, sanitary homes, spring cleaning, and summer hygiene to the newcomers struggling to make a home for themselves and to adopt a style of self-presentation suited to urban life.

In the cities, some African Americans did acquire more comfortable and pleasant housing. At their best, such houses might have had seven or eight rooms, many windows, bathrooms and water in the house, and a full assortment of furniture. By the early twentieth century, perhaps as many as 5 percent of urban black houses were of this type, occupied by the most successful professionals, craftsmen, business owners, and laborers.[30] The great majority of blacks, however, lived in gloomy, disease-ridden, and dangerous environments that lacked some of the most basic accommodations for health. Like many immigrants before them, many black southerners were naive about city ways. They knew very little about sanitation, ventilation, filtered water, the effects of overcrowding, or the use of the bathtub.

In response, groups like the Chicago Urban League initiated health campaigns and funneled an array of social services to the black community in the 1910s and 1920s, hammering away at the importance of cleanliness, particularly to halt the spread of tuberculosis. Urban League volunteers handed out leaflets and made door-to-door visits, counseling the newcomers on how to adopt modern methods of sanitation and personal hygiene. Public schools also became a principal force for educating, socializing, and sanitizing the young. For example, once poster in a series pictured a proud African American youth with this prose (see Fig. 7.5):

> No Health Crusader is content
> With just a hasty, careless rub;
> I give my neck and ears and nails
> A thorough, hearty, soapy scrub.

The message was the same in other cities where southern African Americans moved in great numbers: they were more likely to find success with scrubbed faces and clean white collars.

The predominantly rural South, which was nearly one-third black in 1910, trailed behind the public health and school reform movements of the rest of the country. Although countryside housing also gradually improved for African Americans in the half century after emancipation, many still lacked the basic accommodations necessary to health. Log cabins gave way to more spacious frame dwellings, from one-room affairs to modest three-room houses, made up of a general family room containing the family beds, a separate bedroom, and a kitchen—but no bathroom. In 1908, W. E. B. DuBois gave a vivid description of the poorer rural homes: "[T]here were either no privies or bad ones; facilities for bathing even the face and hands are poor; and there is almost no provision for washing the other parts of the body"[31]

This situation began to change when schools attended by African American youngsters began to receive sizable financial contributions. As a result of the Negro Rural School Fund, also known as the Anna T. Jeanes Foundation, created in 1907, and money from the Julius Rosenwald fund, established in 1914, African Americans and their country schools benefited from the supervision and dedication of "Jeanes teachers." The Jeanes teachers, almost all of whom were African American women, led fundraising campaigns, modernized school facilities, and fostered habits of personal hygiene.[32] The school campaigners also collaborated with other Progressive Era health reformers. Not unlike the health and school reformers in the North, a southern group of white middle-class reformers believed that environment shaped character and sought to bring about behavioral changes. Before long, country folk were gathering to learn the value of personal cleanliness in churches, schoolhouses, and makeshift clinics.

Together settlement workers and sanitarians "Americanized" southern

No Health Crusader is content
. With just a hasty, careless rub;
I give my neck and ears and nails
A thorough, hearty, soapy scrub.

Fig. 7.5. National Child Welfare Association posters, *Survey*, 1923.

African Americans much as European immigrants were, inculcating middle-class values of cleanliness as well as trying to improve living conditions. Health and hygiene programs were introduced into schools and workplaces nationwide, as state and local health departments became committed to promoting cleanliness. Settlement campaigns and other private initiatives continued. After 1910, however, the "gospel of the toothbrush" was no longer limited to the personal; it became a matter of national politics.

With the rise of new movements for racial solidarity in the 1910s and 1920s, skin color and appearance became increasingly charged issues. Marcus Garvey's United Negro Improvement Association (UNIA) proclaimed not only a new political destiny for the masses of African Americans, but also a new aesthetic for dark-skinned people. In particular, the assertion that black women were beautiful became an important assertion of cultural legitimacy. The African American press had long reported on black women's work in clubs, churches, and other organizations, documenting their wide influence in community affairs. In this period, black women represented their race in an added way—through a well-groomed and attractive appearance. Racial pride often took the guise of a beautiful woman on display. For example, the militant journal *Crusader* featured dark-skinned girls and beautiful African women with traditional hair arrangements and dress on its covers. In 1924, the radical *Messenger*, which defined the New Negro as a man demanding political and economic equality, recognized the arrival of the New Negro Woman with appealing portraits of "accomplished, beautiful, intelligent" women in each issue.[33]

The dramatic upsurge of creativity in literature, music, and art within black America reached its zenith in the second half of the 1920s, in a movement known to many scholars and critics as the Harlem Renaissance. *The New Negro* emerged as the definitive text in 1925, exuding racial pride and self-expression. The anthology, conceived and edited by Alain Locke, had its origins in the magazine *Survey* and the heavily illustrated special issue the *Survey Graphic*. This special volume featured historical essays on African American art and literature, as well as a generous sample of the fiction, poetry, and drama composed by the leading young writers. In addition, there was a section on music and on black history, including folklore as seen in cultural legacies from Africa. *When Harlem Was in Vogue*, a study of the Harlem Renaissance by David Levering Lewis, challenged Locke's central premise that the race's "more immediate hope rests in the revaluation by white and black alike of the Negro in terms of his artistic endowment and cultural contributions, past and prospective."[34] "Eurocentric to the tip of his cane," sums up Lewis. "Locke sought to graft abstractions from German, Irish, Italian, Jewish, and Slovakian nationalism to Afro-Americans."[35]

Although black culture propounded black advancement and racial pride, there were also more than enough paradoxes to go around. At issue were not only the prejudices of white Americans but also an elitist perception by black Americans of the existence of color hierarchies. For example, anthropologist Melville J. Herskovits raised this point in *The New Negro*, where he remarked that "some colored people form color lines within the color line."[36] Middle-class reformers like Nannie H. Burroughs also spoke critically of color prejudices among African Americans. "Many Negroes have colorphobia as badly as the white folk have Negrophobia," from families and churches to social circles.[37] During slavery, light-skinned African Americas received preferential treatment in work assignments, becoming household servants and sometimes getting training in skilled trades. Because they were often the offspring of plantation owners, they were more likely to be given such privileges. With emancipation, these advantages gave them greater job security, independence, and influence. By the 1890s, the "mulatto elite" were often suspected of trying to become a separate race or to pass for white.

Black leaders and journalists were also deeply ambivalent about the African American toiletries industry. Ironically, even while exploiting the desire to pass for white, the industry found itself serving as an exemplary model of black economic development. Critics denounced such newspapers as the Chicago *Defender*, the *Pittsburgh Courier*, and the Baltimore *African American* because they carried such advertisements. Ads for soaps, beauty products, and services dominated their pages. In the 1920s, toiletries and cosmetics, including bleaches and straighteners, accounted for 30 to 40 percent of black newspaper advertising, and in a few cases as much as 50 percent.[38] Others attacked periodicals like the *Crusader* and *Negro World*, which criticized skin bleaching and hair straightening as attempts to pass for white, yet advertised whitening soaps, creams, pressing oils, and similar preparations made by African Americans. Black commercial culture further complicated the picture, claimed Chandler Owens in the *Messenger*:

"Garveyites and other dark people constantly inveigh against the white man, and the Negroes imitating the white man—yet to take this very crowd away from the world would bankrupt Madame Walker, the Poro, Overton, Dr. Palmer's, the Apex, and all other skin whitening and hair straightening systems in a few weeks."[39]

BEAUTY TYPES, STEREOTYPES, AND COUNTERTYPES

The political debate over personal appearance and charges of white emulation heightened as both race-conscious and racist white companies developed toiletry products specifically for the African American market. In the process, black advertisers adopted a sales pitch similar to that of white national advertisers, offering skin- and hair-care systems that revolved around beauty appeals. As if in direct response to the devaluation of African American appearance, black-owned toiletry companies did much to promote the centrality of beauty in black women's racial identity, while white-owned companies often generated public controversy as unscrupulous exploiters of black consumers. Nevertheless, manufacturers and mass-market retailers expanded to meet the demand for personal care products developed specifically for the African American market.

The Great Migration had created the "Negro market." Both white and African American merchants, as well as black consumers, became increasingly conscious of the purchasing power of hundreds of thousands people massed in one compact community. The leading cities in terms of African American population included New York; Philadelphia; Chicago; Baltimore; Washington, D.C.; and Detroit, among others.[40] The rapid growth of African American urban communities between 1915 and 1929 was accompanied by expansion in all types of black-owned business, not the least lucrative of which was the personal care industry. For example, Chicago's black ghetto already housed 30,000 people by 1900, and the African American population increased to 250,000 in 1930.[41] By the early 1920s, over nine toiletry companies served black Chicagoans alone.[42] African Americans nationwide spent over 40 percent more on personal care from 1920 to 1930. Alert manufacturers and salespeople began to recognize and take advantage of this fact.

Focusing on racial pride and the universality of female desire to look beautiful, the commerce in personal care products took on new symbolic and political meanings in light of the politics of appearance. Personal care product manufacturers positioned their toilet soaps, hair-care products, skin preparations, and cosmetics with a race-conscious economic nationalism, by both proclaiming women's beauty as a sign of racial pride and asserting that African Americans had the same natural right as all women to be beautiful. "One must have in mind not any one Negro woman, but rather a colorful pageant of individuals, each differently endowed," wrote Elise Johnson McDougald in *The New Negro*. "Like the red and yellow of the tiger-lily, the skin of one is brilliant against the star-lit darkness of a racial sister."[43] It followed that the products of black-owned companies, specifically made with the African American woman in mind, were each endowed to promote the charm, beauty, and character of the black women. Thus, the brands cannot be thought of en masse; rather, each emerged as an icon of race pride.

As Kathy Peiss has shown, only a few of the black-owned toilet article manufacturers regularly bought full-page advertisements, while other firms ran smaller ads that dotted newspaper columns in the 1910s and 1920s.[44] Among them, Madame C. J. Walker pioneered an African American beauty culture, due in large part to innovative direct-sales techniques, which employed traveling representatives who trained others in the firm's skin- and hair-care systems. Others launched toiletry enterprises with a vision of consumer culture closer to that of the predominantly white mass market and used extensive advertising to promote demand for their goods in retail outlets. In particular, Anthony Overton paved the way with his High-Brown toiletries, followed by Claude Barnett, who helped launch the Nile Queen line. Their ads appeared everywhere in African American society from black-owned newspapers and magazines to drugstore displays.

Madame C. J. Walker, born to former slaves under the name Sarah Breedlove in 1867, went from working in the cotton fields to become the country's first female African American millionaire by developing and manufacturing her signature line of cosmetics and hair-care products for black women. In 1905, Walker moved to Denver, where she worked as a cook for a local druggist and married a former newspaper salesman, C. J. Walker. With the pharmacist's occasional assistance, she concocted hair conditioners designed to prevent women's hair from thinning and falling out, a common condition among black women, perhaps due to poor diet and use of hair straighteners. When Walker created a shampoo with an antidandruff agent and a hair oil that seemed to help, she started selling it door-to-door as the Walker system. As Walker became known, she set up an office in Pittsburgh, a factory in Indianapolis, and a salon in New York City. "Sarah Walker also began calling herself Madame, not only to identify her marital status but to give her products more appeal," notes historian A'Lelia Bundles.[45]

In the process, Walker provided dignified employment to thousands of women who would otherwise have had to make their living in domestic service, and stimulated great interest in the culture of African American beauty. She built up a sales force of two thousand mainly black women who were trained in hairdressing and in sales techniques at company-run schools. The Walker system attracted thousands of black hairdressers as well, many of whom made the transition from certified beauticians to owners of their own salons, advertised their services as "Walker system" shops, and capitalized on the Walker name and reputation. When Walker died in 1919, the Walker Manufacturing Company was generating revenues of half a million dollars a year, one of the most successful black-owned businesses of the day. But the psychological effect of Walker's achievements could hardly be overestimated. "What a boon it was," the *Messenger* reported in 1924, "for one of their own race to stand upon the pinnacle and exhort the womanhood of her own race to come forth, lift up their heads and beautify and improve their looks, even as Woman has done all through the ages."[46]

Indeed, Walker gave not only her products, but to the African American race an image of worth and beauty. The entire Walker product line, which totaled more than seventy-five items, replaced miscellaneous soaps, creams, and lotions with specialized and coordinated products along with step-by-step techniques.[47] Among Walker's beauty preparations, the product line included three soaps. A perfumed Complexion and Toilet Soap was promoted as a "preservative of beauty—mild and safe for the most tender skin," selling for twenty cents per "large bar." The Vegetable Oil Antiseptic Soap sold as a "household soap of purest vegetable oils" that would not harm a baby's skin, a "bargain" at ten cents a bar.[48] Vegetable Shampoo, one of the company's most popular offerings, promised to ease dandruff and other scalp problems.[49]

Unlike most manufacturers of black hair-care products, Walker promoted her wares with her own likeness on packages and ads, rather than using light-skinned models.[50] Walker advertised her products nationally in a number of African American newspapers and magazines, reaching into the homes of over twenty million African Americans. At the time, firms like the Inter-State Sales & Advertising Agency, headquartered in New York City, and the Southern Circulating & Publicity Bureau, based in Greensboro, North Carolina, specialized in maintaining a list of "colored papers," religious periodicals, and southern white dailies published in the United States. Among the black publications, the Walker campaign ran in papers such as the Chicago *Defender*, the *Pittsburgh Courier*, Maryland's *Afro-American*, Cleveland's *Advocate*, and the Philadelphia *Christian Banner*.[51]

The early advertisements of Madame C. J. Walker emphasized the features of her preparations, the creation of job opportunities, and the vast size and scope of her enterprise. For example, one 1919 advertisement indicated Walker's popularity with maps of the Western Hemisphere and images of arms stretching up to the rising sun and encircling Madame C. J. Walker's products. "We Belt the World," proclaimed one headline tinged with nationalist pride.[52] Photographs of Walker appeared on the package labels and in ads for her products. These images personified the entrepreneur's claims and reinforced her accountability to consumers.

What clearly set Walker's ads apart from those of white manufacturers, however, was the strong appeal to promote personal cleanliness rituals and beautification as a matter of racial pride. One ad, headlined "Glorifying Our Womanhood," made an even more direct appeal. The copy dramatically continued, "No greater force is working to glorify the womanhood of our Race than Madame C. J. Walker's Wonderful Hair and Skin Preparation" (see Fig. 7.6).[53] Achieving racial pride, the industry claimed, was a first step in achieving racial equality. Thus, "Glorifying our Womanhood" was integral to African American advancement, implied Walker's advertisements.

The company newsletter took a similar approach in addressing sales agents. Called the *Walker News*, the publication emphasized the efficacy of its preparations, new product introductions, selling techniques, window displays, and tips on hair and skin care. For example, one 1928 issue ran an article on "Soap and Water and the Skin." The column made the point that a "dab of water and quick rinse off" won't keep one's face clean. Instead, the skin should be "thoroughly mopped" with a wash cloth to free the surface of dirt; a good supply of cleansing cream was also recom-

Fig. 7.6. Madame C. J. Walker Manufacturing Company, advertisement.

mended.[54] Another column, titled "News of Walker Agents," acknowledged agents who sent in large orders for goods, and did charitable deeds, and even those who suffered misfortunes like a long-term illness or a home destroyed by a fire, among other news. These sales agents fanned out to areas otherwise isolated from the consumer market.

Yet as manufacturers increasingly turned toward media-based, marketing ways to represent African American beauty in advertising became an important question. In the early days of the industry, Anthony Overton, known as the "Merchant Prince" of the black race, paved the way with High-Brown preparations.[55] In 1898, as proprietor of an Oklahoma general store, he founded the Overton-Hygienic Company and began to manufacture baking powder and then added preserves and extracts. Within a few years Overton began to specialize in the black cosmetics market, first offering High-Brown face powder designed to harmonize with the color and skin of African American women. He later added toilet soap, perfumes, toilet waters, sachet powders, vanishing cream, face bleach, toothpaste, and deodorant to the product line. In need of expanded facilities, Overton moved his manufacturing plant to Chicago in 1911, where he set up operations as a hub for distribution, transportation, and advertising. In 1918, Overton became the first African American to have products sold at Woolworth's. Overton overcame seemingly "unsurmountable handicaps" of distribution and succeeded in convincing wholesalers and retailers to handle the High-Brown product line, according to the *Messenger*. "He blazed the way and made it easier for other toilet products to reach the retail trade through regular channels."[56]

Among Overton's extensive product line were four different soaps, each positioned for a specific purpose. High-Brown Soap was a highly perfumed toilet soap to keep the pores clean and free from impurities. The specially prepared High-Brown Bleach Soap had skin-bleaching properties to be used in connection with Roz-ol or High-Brown bleach. The antiseptic High-Brown Shampoo soap covered the need for a good soap to thoroughly cleanse the hair and scalp after using hairdressings and pomades; it was made from the finest of coconut oils. Finally, the Hygienic Vegetable Soap could be used for both toilet and bath purposes and was recommended for bathing babies as it would not injure their tender skin.

Overton also underwrote a monthly magazine, the *Half-Century*, oriented to black women; published from 1916 to 1922, the periodical ran a mix of articles, fashions, and beauty tips similar to *Ladies' Home Journal*. One continuing feature of the *Half-Century* was a column entitled "Beauty Hints," offering hints on everything from face powder as a preservative to the importance of cultivation of a pleasing disposition to make a woman

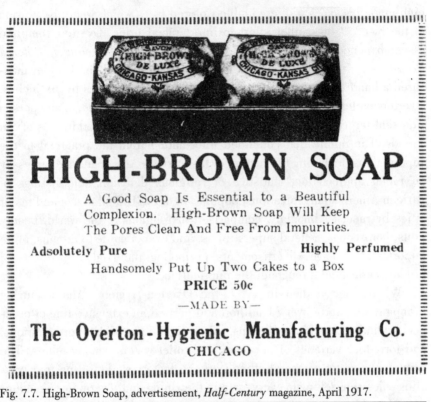

HIGH-BROWN SOAP

A Good Soap Is Essential to a Beautiful
Complexion. High-Brown Soap Will Keep
The Pores Clean And Free From Impurities.

Adsolutely Pure   **Highly Perfumed**

Handsomely Put Up Two Cakes to a Box

PRICE 50c

—MADE BY—

The Overton-Hygienic Manufacturing Co.
CHICAGO

Fig. 7.7. High-Brown Soap, advertisement, *Half-Century* magazine, April 1917.

more beautiful. One point appeared repeatedly: "Cleanliness, immaculate cleanliness, is the first essential to a healthy skin . . . never let a day go by without bathing the entire body with a good, pure Toilet Soap."[57]

Alongside the column of beauty hints ran advertisements for High-Brown products (see Fig. 7.7). One ad in the series featured High-Brown Soap, displaying two handsomely packaged cakes in a box with the words "Absolutely Pure" and "Highly Perfumed." The copy continued, "A good soap is essential to a beautiful complexion. High Brown will keep the pores clean and free from impurities."[58] High-Brown Soap sold in a two-cake package for fifty cents, thus positioning the product with better-quality toilet soaps such as Woodbury's Facial Soap and Colgate's Cashmere Bouquet.

In Overton's advertising for the High-Brown line, he pictured respectable, well-groomed girls and refined light-skinned women. According to Overton, African Americans had been "pioneers in putting out high-grade packages with creditable Colored faces which would be a pride to the race."[59] In another effort to build racial pride, Overton compiled research concerning African Americans in the *Encyclopedia of Colored People*, a 124-page compendium of useful information. The booklet measured a handy size, approximately four and one-half inches by six inches. Overton mailed a copy of the encyclopedia, a fifty-cent value, to any person who sent ten cents in stamps or coin and the names and addresses of ten friends. The publication contained information from the practical to the superstitious, including the history of the African American race, an essay on racial appreciation, statistics of religious denomination, listings of African American organizations, population of the United States and major cities by race, testimonials, comparison of religions of the world, beauty hints, horoscopes, general superstitions, and even a guide to dreams. More important, full-page advertisements promoting the High-Brown line of products appeared throughout the publication.

When Overton died in 1937, the Overton-Hygienic Manufacturing Company was worth over $1 million and carried an extensive line of products, including five kinds of soaps, thirty-eight types of toilet preparations, and forty-four varieties of perfumes and toilet waters, among others. The firm employed forty general office workers, factory workers, and four traveling salesmen, selling to every state in the Union and several foreign countries. In addition to making the products that it sold under its own name, the company also made products for other concerns.[60] Among the diverse enterprises founded by Overton in response to the needs of growing black community were the Victory Life Insurance Company; the *Chicago Bee*, a major black newspaper; and the Douglas National Bank, the first African American–owned bank to be granted a national charter.[61]

Overton's early success may have been the inspiration for another group of black Chicago investors, who formed the Kashmir Chemical Company and launched Nile Queen Cosmetics in 1918. Among them was Claude Barnett, a pioneering publicist and journalist, who appreciated modern methods of marketing. In 1916, he had set up an advertising agency and created a separate mail-order operation to sell portraits of well-known African Americans. Three years later he founded the Associated Negro Press, the first press service for black newspapers. He distributed news releases in exchange for advertising, which he sold or used to promote Nile Queen products.

Fig. 7.8. Cover for Nile Queen brochure, Kashmir Chemical, 1919.

The larger transformation of national advertising in the 1910s and 1920s became evident in Barnett's work. Barnett's savvy advertising campaign for the Nile Queen line replaced the old-fashioned patent-medicine style used by Walker and Overton with popular appeals to modernity, romance, and emulation that had proved successful in selling products in national white publications. The Nile Queen packaging, brochures, and ads were strikingly elegant and fashion conscious, reflecting Barnett's familiarity with modern design and advertising appeals (see Fig. 7.8).

Barnett, for the most part, projected black women's sensual desires. Using Egyptian images and hieroglyphic symbols, Barnett harnessed the larger cultural meaning of Cleopatra, and her ancient legacy of beauty, to the ongoing debate within black intellectual circles over the origins of Western civilization. According to one Kashmir beauty pamphlet, the hair and skin products were based upon ancient Egyptian formulas, used by "Kleopatra [sic], the dusky Nile Queen." Properly used, the products would "do as much for the maids of today as they did for Kleopatra in times gone by."[62] The name "Kashmir" further added to the rich mixture by evoking the luxuries of the Mideast, celebrating women of color as exotic. The extensive product line included the Nile Queen Shampoo or Beauty Soap. The pure soap gave a "wonderful" shampoo, it could also be used as a beauty soap, imparting a delicate oriental perfume made from a rare old Egyptian formula. Kashmir also offered the Nile Queen Whitener and Cleaner. The treatment promoted an even, smooth color as it cleared the complexion of liver spots, discoloration, and wrinkles.[63]

Claude Barnett's promotion of Kashmir beauty products played an important role in changing the look of advertising by the African American–owned toiletry manufacturers. Addressing a more urbane, upscale consumer than did Walker, Barnett's Nile Queen advertisements portrayed elaborate consumer fantasies with images of fur-clad women, glamorous automobiles, and other icons of luxury. The results were striking ads characterized by modern graphic designs and psychological appeals. The new concept of advertising beauty products for the black market attracted attention, and soon the entire field had switched to the emotional appeal approach long used by Kashmir.

By the mid-1920s, the advertisements of the Walker Company prominently featured the changed look in advertising with popular appeals to

Fig. 7.9. Madame C. J. Walker Manufacturing Company, advertisement, *Messenger*, September 1924.

modernity, romance, and emulation. In 1924, for example, the *Messenger* featured a Walker ad that was the hallmark of modern appeal—"from boudoir to beach wherever beauty's charms are shown" (see Fig. 7.9). It pictured stylish young women attending to their beauty rituals and at play in a beach scene, one wearing long hair while others sported the white flapper's bob. Such images were interchangeable with those of white women's beauty featured in mass circulation magazines. The copy continued, "Only a few women are born beautiful, but all can achieve it" if they use Madame C. J. Walker's Superfine Toilet Preparations.[64] Another ad stated, "You, too, may be a fascinating beauty" (see Fig. 7.10). Walker's ads were not much different from those for Woodbury's Facial Soap in touting a treatment that could preserve and enhance beauty while making the product user admired by men and envied by women. Although the ads had a more stylish appeal, they still continued to focus on the products themselves, with the copy explaining the benefits of the Walker system and warning of adulterated preparations.

If dark skin mattered as a symbol and instrument of racial pride and advancement, then black producers and consumers of toiletries seemed

Fig. 7.10. Madame C. J. Walker Manufacturing Company, newspaper advertisement.

innocent of the charge of white emulation. Although the women's pages of African American publications occasionally gave tips specifically for black women, much of the advice was identical to that in such mass-circulation magazines as the *Ladies' Home Journal* aimed at middle-class white women. Perhaps the most striking message that the consumer culture offered black women was an insistence on the pursuit of beauty as a universal ideal.

Americans still classified people by skin tone, a sliding scale from white to black; the ideal of brown-skinned beauty was vigorously promoted to the African American beauty trade. Photographs of beautiful female performers, celebrities, and fashion models, generally with light skin and European features, ran in black newspapers and magazines as icons of pride. According to Shane White and Graham White in *Stylin'*, the growing popularity of beauty contests and fashion shows "provided African American newspapers with a further opportunity to display attractive young black women."[65] Toiletry firms also did much to promote the New Negro Woman, but the African American consumer did not appear to spurn the black-manufactured beauty ideal, which assimilated darker skins with that of a mass-market, light-brown-skinned model.

Despite the growing consciousness of black Americans' heritage, African American firms found that consumers seemingly approved their representations of women of color. In a rare study of black consumers' responses to advertising in 1932, Paul Edwards found that African Americans detested images like Aunt Jemima, who "looks too much like old-time mammy," but approved of the well-groomed, brown-skinned woman depicted in cosmetic advertisements for Madame Walker's face powder. "Here the Negro was dignified and made to look as he [*sic*] is striving to look and not as he looked in antebellum days . . . here was the New Negro."[66] As they left behind the world of servility, black consumers adopted personal cleanliness rituals and beautification as an essential aspect of becoming a confident, modern African American woman. Still, the beauty ideal they favored remained a restrictive one.

THE WHITE TRADE IN BLACK BEAUTY

Whatever questions African Americans may have had about goods produced by their own companies, public controversy erupted over the activities of white-owned companies. White businesses had the tendency to look upon large segments of African Americans as "appendages to the white market," observed market researcher Paul K. Edwards in 1932. Their demands corresponded to those of the white working class, and therefore, the purchases made by African Americans were mostly of the cheapest types of necessities.

Yet Edwards argued that distinctly different social classes persisted within this economic class, ranging from the domestic employed by a prominent or wealthy white family with greater social obligations to the domestic cook working in the average white home. At the opposite extreme was the successful black merchant, who was really in a much more important position socially and otherwise than a white merchant doing the same volume of business. As far as his race was concerned, the merchant was expected to assume civic and social responsibilities because of the smaller number of community leaders in the group, as well as to own luxuries far above the requirements of his economic level. Thus, Edwards concluded, "although price is of major importance as an appeal in selling to the Negro, it by no means stands alone as an influence."[67]

With the tremendous growth of the African American personal-care product market, white-owned companies eyed the field with great interest. Increasingly aware of black purchasing power, some mass-market firms that had sold primarily to white consumers began to solicit black patronage. Such long-established firms as American Products, a mail-order firm, and J. E. McBrady, a Chicago wholesale supplier, also courted African American consumers. American Products included Overton's popular High Brown line of face powders made especially for dark-complexioned people. As Chicago's African American population grew after World War I, J. E. McBrady created a complete toiletry line, called "Specialties for Brown Skin People." White start-up entrepreneurs also built up huge businesses manufacturing hair and skin preparations for African Americans. Relying heavily on newspaper advertising, they made such brand names as Golden Brown, Nadinola, and Golden Peacock familiar to black women.

Of these white companies, Plough Chemical proved the most aggressive and successful. In 1908, Abe Plough started to produce medicinal products in Memphis, Tennessee, a center for pharmaceutical manufacturing in the South. Six years later Plough opened a drugstore, where he promoted the Black and White cosmetics line through drugstores, not agents, and priced them below those of the Walker brands. A specially prepared Black and White Skin Soap had skin-bleaching properties to be used in connection with Black and White Ointment, a complete treatment for skin diseases, blemishes, blotches, and discolorations. By World War I, Plough had become the largest advertiser in the black newspapers, able to pressure publishers for reduced rates.[68]

In the 1920s, however, Plough began advertising Black and White beauty preparations to white women in national publications.[69] Perhaps feeling the heat of black public opinion, Plough also rewrote the company's advertising to black consumers in less explicitly racist language, with a general promise of light, clear skin like other mass-market advertisers. For example, one 1928 ad for the Black and White Skin Soap treatment in the *Pittsburgh Courier* simply promised, "Rough, dark skin quickly becomes smooth and bright." (see Fig. 7.11)[70] This use of the word "bright" in a sense implied improving the reflectivity of skin, but among African Americans the term had a distinct connotation, that of lightening darker skin. In 1929, Plough did about $12 million in business, and of this amount, an estimated $5 million was in the African American market.[71]

Despite tirades against bleaching and white emulation, many of Plough's Black and White Skin Soap treatments were sold. Like their white counterparts, black women were buying and using a wide range of facial cleansers and cosmetics in their beauty rituals. White emulation was hardly the issue in this practice. While race leaders and beauty leaders interpreted toiletries in symbolic and political terms, consumers stressed cleansing and beautification more in light of their own physical condition and social circumstance. Some consumers indeed may have wished for the Black and White Soap to bleach their skin, as the most extreme advertisements promised and as critics charged. But women used this product and other formulas for different purposes. Some dotted them on spots or blemishes to even the complexion tone; others used them across their entire face, hands, and arms to fade their skin. For those women, their very ability

Fig. 7.11. Black and White Skin Ointment and Skin Soap, newspaper advertisement, *Pittsburgh Courier*, August 4, 1928.

to be looked upon as respectable, to be sociable, depended on the magic of the advertised products.

White businessmen such as Plough gave drug and chain stores special deals, lowered prices, and effectively undercut African American firms. African Americans remember the story of how Plough built one of the largest pharmaceutical houses in the United States. Alsom Holsey, the secretary for the National Business League, recalls, "Plough made a fortune in Negro newspapers and selling his products." Other business leaders made the same point, but more explicitly. "Many Negroes like to think that the Plough fortune is founded upon the generous support which colored people gave to his early efforts," sardonically reported the Associated Negro Press in 1951. "Plough used to go about driving an old white crippled horse to a buggy selling straightener, pomades, perfume etc."[72]

To counter this competition, African American cosmetic manufacturers tried to form a trade association, which over the next decade discussed how to force "Plough's Chemical Company and other unscrupulous white concerns off the market."[73] Cooperation proved difficult. Although the call for racial solidarity had proved an effective commercial strategy, the African American press depended on advertising revenue and resisted the pressure to reject business from white-owned companies. Like Plough, Lever, Gillette, and other white businesses began to advertise in black periodicals. They recognized that African Americans were buying everything from necessities to luxuries just like white consumers, both for their own consumption and, in many cases, for the households of their employers. Toiletries manufacturers like Plough, Walker Manufacturing, Overton-Hygienic, and Kashmir Chemical had proven that the black press was an effective medium for national advertising. Thus, cosmetics and toiletries accounted for 30 to 40 percent of black newspaper advertising in the 1920s, and in some cases, 50 percent.[74]

Not surprisingly, African Americans fervently supported these papers. In the black press, they read about themselves, including news, announcements, sport activities, and editorial opinions. Their "race news," features, and assertive editorials epitomized issues of freedom and modernity. At the time, such news was of little interest to the readers of the white daily newspapers. "But to the Negroes, it is LIVE NEWS—as vital to their lives as the news in the metropolitan dailies is to their white readers," explained the W. B. Ziff Company, a white agency based in Chicago that represented the media reaching the African American market.[75]

In 1932, Ziff published *The Negro Market: Published in the Interest of the Negro Press* to sell white businesses on advertising their products and services in the black press. In the merchandising booklet, Ziff made the point that "Colored people" have the same lifestyle as whites, only separate; but they both had the same needs for food, clothing, transportation, homes, and so on. In the promotional piece, Ziff wrote that "the home life of the Negro is a duplicate of the white man's—but in different neighborhoods." The booklet then pictured African Americans at school, at play, and at business. Then again, "Negro society with its varied activities, class distinctions," and so on, were "as complex and as rigid as white society."[76] To reach this lucrative audience, Ziff urged advertisers to employ the "proper appeals and illustrations" in their ads. The agency put it this way:

> Negroes have a certain amount of Race pride, which asserts itself in rebellion against advertisements which make comedy at their expense. Copy should be written in a natural vein. No attempt should be made to "talk down" to them and extreme caution should be exercised in the use of Colored slang. Negroes are quick to respond to advertising which captures their fancy, and a trial campaign in any of the leading Race papers will readily provide this.[77]

Yet white manufacturers were slow to recognize and take advantage of the opportunities presented by the rapid growth in the African American urban markets.

SEXUALIZING THE SELL

Throughout the 1930s, black women hard hit by the Depression continued to purchase toilet soap, cosmetics, and beauty services, while black toiletry firms struggled to stay in business. "Beautification continued to be a central economic and cultural activity, the message of female dignity and racial advancement allied with it became more subdued as the decade wore on," observed Kathy Peiss. This trend became evident in commercial messages. Peiss continues, "beauty columns that ran alongside stories on politics and notable African Americans; by the mid-thirties, these had begun to disappear replaced by articles on romance, marriage, and the psychological effects of beautification."[78]

During the troubled times, newer companies like Valmor and Snow White came out with cheaper products, but the commercial images projected by the beauty business were increasingly depoliticized. Valmor, a mail-order firm selling Sweet Georgia Brown preparations, went even further, explicitly sexualizing the sale of beauty products. Illustrations of steamy embraces, passionate kisses, and women in negligees, along with old-fashioned before-and-after pictures and lighten-your-skin copy, appeared throughout its catalogs (see Fig. 7.12). Here black women's identity was centered on achieving beauty to attract a man, rather than female

Fig. 7.12. Valmor catalog cover, 1936.

dignity and racial advancement. Sweet Georgia Brown became a leading brand in the African American market in the 1930s and 1940s, and according to New York retailers, aggressive promotion explained its success.

Thematically, at the heart of most, if not all, of Valmor's advertising was the romantic love myth—perhaps the most common central narrative strategy evident in the advertising of white-manufactured toilet soap, cosmetics, and other toiletries. Like Woodbury and Palmolive, Valmor's advertising suggested that the continued use of the advertised product would not only bring romance but, once found, the perfect partner would make life complete. Thus, Valmor also successfully repackaged Anglo-Saxon nineteenth-century ideals and gender roles.

More importantly, the introduction of the sensational Sweet Georgia Brown brand paralleled a similar shift in white newspapers, magazines, and advertising in the 1920s and 1930s. The new mass media—movies, radio, glossy magazines, and tabloid newspapers—were shaping the values of a younger generation not only of white Americans, but also of African Americans. African American women spared little effort or expense trying to make their appearance over to the new ideals set forth in national media. Valmor's rise signaled the end of an era, promoting beauty as a means of racial pride and advancement. In the 1960s, however, African Americans would again reexamine their heritage and search for a connection to their African past. They would reject white standards of beauty, and "Black is beautiful" would again become a common theme, as would "Be Black. Buy Black."

Outside the black publications, however, national advertising continued to limit the role of African Americans. Instead of portraying blacks in a range of normal occupations and tasks, white advertisers continued to present blacks in demeaning, stereotypical images—as shuffling servants, polite porters, and cheerful cooks—reinforcing the popular conception that they were suitable only for menial jobs. Overall, however, the extent to which advertisers cultivated the African American consumer remained relatively small in relation to the efforts to influence the white consumer. Not until the 1970s would white manufacturers recognize the "black market" as a lucrative audience.

Afterword

ationally advertised, brand-name soap, toiletries, and even bathrooms made their way from seldom-used luxuries to necessities of American life in a remarkably short period of time—less than sixty-five years spanning the period between 1875 and 1940. For nineteenth- and twentieth-century Americans, the presence or absence of soap marked the divide between the clean and unclean, the civilized and uncivilized world. Although the manufacture of soap has played an ever-larger role in our economy, soap advertising has also been a large part of the American cultural landscape since Babbitt enticed people to buy consumer-sized packages before the Civil War. "For in the soap industry it does not merely pay to advertise; it is death not to advertise," explained the *Soap Gazette and Perfumer* in 1939.[1]

By 1939, manufactured soap formed a major sector of the American economy. The combined revenues of the three major soapmakers totaled more than $35 billion annually, and the American people consumed three billion pounds of soap each year. Of this amount, Procter & Gamble supplied nearly 40 percent, Colgate-Palmolive-Peet Co. accounted for around 20 percent, and Lever Bros., the American subsidiary of the huge British firm of Unilever, perhaps 20 percent. The remainder of the business was divided among Fels & Co., Swift & Co., Armour & Co., and several hundred smaller firms that operated mainly on a local or regional scale.[2]

Yet for all the talk of the new mass-market soap industry, the firms had to sell it in vast amounts to make money out of a universal commodity. Soap had become more widely available as new techniques of mass production had made it cheaper to produce it. Soapmakers passed these savings on to the consumer. In 1890, for example, the average retail price of a medium cake of Ivory Soap was 4.75 cents; and fifty years later, the average price had increased only about 16 percent to 5.5 cents.[3] While the selling price remained relatively low, costs of raw materials and labor continued to increase. For this reason, firms continually had to find new ways to sell a lot of soap.

Today American soapmakers advertise around the globe, spending millions of dollars every year to stimulate demand for their brands and to support the retailers who carry it. The leading soapmakers of a century ago are still among the leading national advertisers: Procter & Gamble, Colgate-Palmolive, and UniLever. The manufacturers pioneered new innovations in media use, market research, and advertising strategy, copy, and art. Spanning more than 180 years, their relationship not only parallels the history of modern advertising but has literally *made* advertising history.

ADVERTISING AND THE CONSUMER CULTURE

Advertising had gathered power early in this century and reached deeply into consumer culture by the 1920s. Ads targeted the newly emancipated women, selling them everything from toilet soap to toilets. Ads introduced new modern-art styles to readers who never had been in museums. Ads promoted bathrooms as shrines of cleanliness and shaped such daily rituals as hand washing before meals, jumping into the shower each morning, and even rinsing with mouthwash. Americans also had come to inhabit a society in which to some extent individuals were defined by the sum of their purchases—what Stuart Ewen labeled "the commodity self," the personage created through the purchase and use of products. Ewen was specifically thinking about physical appearance, about how lips, eyes, nails, breasts, and legs became defined through the commodities bought to alter them; the "ads intimated that anything natural about the consumer was worthless or deplorable."[4] Such commodity fixation offered up potential meanings and so helped signal an identity to oneself as well as to others.

Since the 1930s, however, the institution of advertising has been constrained by government regulations and a more sophisticated and skeptical public. The advertising system came under fire from both ends of the spectrum, from consumers and federal agencies, which led to an unprecedented amount of social criticism and legal regulation.[5] As always, critics suggested that advertisers knew too much about Americans as a result of the vast amount of time, money, and effort they spent counting, categorizing, and analyzing the public's buying habits. Perhaps one of the most common and stinging criticisms was that advertising techniques were responsible for convincing consumers that they "needed" material things and that they would be unhappy and somehow inferior people if they did not obtain these "necessities." Did advertising tell people what they wanted, or did it tell people what they should have wanted?

This issue was and is a complex one, and has led to fiery debates that continue today. The basic assumption in any justification of the advertising system is that the ads respond to a demand that only a specific product can satisfy. A need is a basic biological motive; a want represents one way society has told us that the need can be satisfied. For example, thirst is biologically based; but we are taught to want a certain brand of soft drink, rather than, say, water, to satisfy the thirst. The need is already there; advertisers simply recommend ways to satisfy it. Products like coffee, tea, and soft drinks were designed to meet existing needs, and advertising only helped to communicate their availability. In this view, advertising emerged as an important source of consumer information, reducing the time consumers spent searching for products. Advertising also stimulated competition that generally resulted in more and better products at similar or lower prices.

In the case of soap, it can be argued that the need for personal cleanliness had some basis in health, as evidenced in hygienic practices dating back to ancient times. Thus, avoiding unclean food, washing one's hands before eating, and bathing frequently prevented the spread of germs and allowed people to live longer, healthier lives. When advertising began to link the soap-and-water ritual to desirable social attributes—virtues like character, discipline, beauty, and success—it also fostered a materialistic society in which we are measured not only by what we own but also by physical appearance. Advertisements began to focus on the irrational value of the goods for what they symbolized. In this view, soap would have been good enough for us, without the additional promise that it would also make us more attractive, better workers and disease-free. Many consumers had even become socialized to consider natural body odors repulsive and were motivated to protect their self-image by using deodorant soaps. This explains the success of Lifebuoy's B.O. campaign.

One can conclude that while advertising legitimately may be criticized for sometimes offering less than perfect information and, in some instances, for creating unwanted externalities, it should also be praised for its contribution to the principles of free enterprise, which are a defining characteristic of the American way. In the case of the African American community, soap advertising and the subsequent embrace of personal cleanliness rituals also met criticism for promoting politics of appearance; but it also offered unprecedented opportunities for a new breed of entrepreneurs.

From the standpoint of business evolution, however, the decade of the 1930s may well be the single most significant transitional phase of the distribution era. American manufacturers had learned how to make consumers want the products of the production machine, and they had learned how to bring these goods to the consumer at low cost. However, they hadn't yet learned how to make prospects not only want products but force customers to buy whatever the companies produced. The future of business lay in its ability to create consumer demand as well to determine in advance what customers want and then develop goods to meet customer needs. In the last half of the twentieth century, companies steered by the marketing concept would become interested in the consumer's point of view, establish products definitely in the public mind with an identity apart from the competition, and use educational advertising to sweep aside self-consciousness and prudery regarding intimate bodily functions.

Advertisers had the means to transmit notice about their brand-name products to customers right into their homes. Each medium in the historical sequence of newspapers, magazines, radio, television, and the Internet found its purpose as a purer and more perfected advertising vehicle, thereby powering the economy and the culture of consumption. Each new medium lent advertisers a greater communication repertoire, from text alone, to text plus pictures, to the immediacy of sound, to moving pictures with compelling imagery, to the interactive format of the Internet. As more and more advertisements were sent and received, individual advertisements lost much of their singularity to the surrounding environment of advertising in general.

The acknowledgment of strongly held consumer sentiments had also become a guiding principle of advertising communication. There were many ways to sell products, but advertisers then recognized that in order to sell products to women they had to invoke strongly held feelings. Three common emotive advertising messages are detailed in this work: (1) the *first-impression formula*, in which the central story was of the hero or heroine overcoming the obstacles and dangers of a personal or domestic disaster by simply using the friendly advertiser's product; (2) the *romance formula*, in which the crucial defining characteristic of the form was not that it starred a female, but that the advertised product brings two potential lovers together and to a deeper, more secure relationship; and (3) the *emulation formula*, in which advertising presented its messages through people to whom the public would listen with interest and respect. Prominent people, professional experts, and Hollywood stars told consumers how to be socially acceptable, what their household should like, what a homemaker looked like, and even what a successful husband looked like.

What was significant was that these new emotive advertisements, so little in evidence before 1910 and so conventional after 1920, were difficult to avoid in the popular advertising of the day. Like popular literature, movies, and other well-attended amusements, the concept of formula was implicit in the nature of advertising. Both were repetitive and imitative in their attempt to ensure commercial success. There may be other important formulaic selling arguments and stereotypes characteristic of the period, but to treat with some complexity the other formulas of the age would exceed reasonable limits of this work. Therefore, the study concentrated on the first-impression, romance, and emulation formulas and certain archetypal stereotypes that emerged during this period that are characteristic of modern advertising.

The wide array of soap advertisements from this period certainly illustrated this vital function of formula: predictable sameness. As copy began to deal with the consumer experience with appeals to fear, sex, and emulation, familiar conventions appeared fully developed in the campaigns of Lifebuoy, Woodbury's Facial, and Lux Toilet soaps. Advertisements featured authority figures giving directions on the most mundane aspects of everyday life; other ads implied that domestic disasters could be averted simply by using the friendly advertiser's products; and some simply told the consumers what they could do with the product. Still other ads provided a foundation of security within which people could safely give themselves over to the exciting, titillating symbols of romance with the assurance that they would ultimately find enduring love.

These popular advertising formulas, however, were not merely a projection of beliefs and values onto society; rather, they drew legitimacy from dominant cultural myths, beliefs, and values in America. For example, bodies and hygiene formed a major part of class differentiation in American society during the late nineteenth and early twentieth centuries. Smell, appearance, and cleanliness were habitually cited as markers of a society's relative cultural "elevation" and character, while "dirty" races and their practices were frequently cited as one of the primary sources of grime, disease, and pollution. America's "unwashed" were the millions of immigrants from southern and eastern Europe who had recently arrived from peasant lands, especially those who passed a season without a bath. Messages in advertisements, however, implicitly invoked middle-class whites as living examples of true cleanliness to be observed and imitated.

Yet, do people sneer at a woman who wears a faded frock? If our hostess has a blackhead on her nose, do we gain pleasure by drawing attention to it? Do people delight in making others feel self-conscious and out of it? So prevalent was a "class atmosphere" in these social scenes that a historian relying exclusively on the advertisements could only conclude that most Americans of the 1920s were white, upper-middle-class people who enjoyed an exceedingly affluent, leisured mode of life. Clearly the scenarios were exaggerated, yet they drew much of their persuasive power from constructing the perception that first impressions made a crucial difference.

What was key here is that the first-impression, romance, and emulation formulaic approaches refer to scenes sufficiently stereotypical to evoke immediate audience recognition—what has been called a contemporary "slice-of-life" setting rather than a work of art or legendary scene. Interestingly, these social scenes were not entirely unrepresentative of the period. Although the ads reflected only a very narrow stratum of society, they also presented an idealized modern life, one to which young working girls and members of the upper middle class both presumably aspired; but also one specifically defined through the eyes of the creative elite. One of the most important effects of using the advertised products, many ads suggested, was the self-confidence it created in the consumer, a value that had become popular in the early twentieth century.

People had defined success as largely the consequence of appearance, sociability, and material goods in the mobile, urban society. By the 1920s, however, people increasingly conceived of the details of their personal grooming and that of their home as an index of their true character. In *The Lonely Crowd,* social critics David Riesman, Reuel Denney, and Nathan Glazer explained this phenomenon as a shift from "inner" to "other-direction" as Americans participated in the age of consumption by making the approval of others the end-all of their existence.[6] In another classic critical study, Warren Susman demarked the emergence of this twentieth-century character type that emphasized pleasing others as a "culture of personality."[7] One means of communicating these values became national advertising, which stressed the importance of appearance and pleasing others. In classrooms and in advertising copy, people were taught that good grooming and sociability were important in the business world. Moreover, the burden of the day-to-day responsibilities associated with a clean and comfortable home fell on the housewives. To neglect cleanliness was to court disaster.

The point for our purposes was that these formulaic advertisements also served as prescriptions of how men and women should perceive themselves and thereby fulfill their proper social roles. Thus, the decade of the 1920s not only served as the formative stage for advertising, it may also have served as the consolidation stage for the development of a culture of cleanliness. Advertisements for soap in mass-circulation magazines showed people how to cleanse themselves in order to become part of the sweatless, odorless, and successful middle class. Ad makers had made washing, bathing, and laundering seem easy and rewarding, while promoting cleanliness as value for everyone.

The advertising and popular culture that admakers produced had to be, in large part, the symbolic material that would be readily accepted in the minds of the public. It had to speak to audience members in a most attractive way, articulating their desires and satisfying their needs, or it would not be attended to and the advertised product would not sell. The distinguishing feature of modern audience members has been the extent to which each was viewed as an individual. Attention to the symbol worlds of advertising and popular culture allows the modern individual to participate knowingly in the manifest world of consumer goods.

According to anthropologist Grant McCracken, through consumer rituals old and new goods take on new meanings as consumers actively participate in the process.[8] At the same time, advertising and the fashion system give consumer goods new meaning through the media of communication and opinion leaders, who help shape and refine existing cultural meanings, which then trickle down to subordinate parties, who imitate them. Yet the fashion system may also engage in radical reformation of cultural meaning, overturning established order, as evidenced in the African American consumer culture, which linked consumption and beautification with racial pride and advancement.

Whatever the race, however, grooming rituals transform an individual from the private self to the public persona, from the natural to the social world, giving the person a new sense of confidence. In the newly industrial America, people's status changed from farmers and craftsman to workers, citizens, consumers, and eventually pleasure seekers. For people experiencing these social changes, cleanliness denoted far more than that one was clean; it also provided a system of meaning that helped men and women navigate the changing conditions of modern social experience. As cleanliness rituals changed, so did interpretive communities. Thus, the issue of what it meant to be clean in a society dominated by whites emerges as the most striking and constant theme of the *Stronger Than Dirt* story.

Advertising was just one of the cultural institutions that shaped personal cleanliness rituals. The powerful institutions of church, school, mass media, and fashion certainly influenced Americans' notion of what it was to be clean. Other cultural factors also paralleled changes in American attitudes toward personal cleanliness. There was the production of domesticity along with sweeping changes in domestic architecture that created the bathroom, a sacred space devoted to personal cleansing rituals. The work of women's clubs, the settlement movement, health education in schools and the workplace, and a proliferation of literature of advice all focused attention on middle-class habits of personal cleanliness. Together with advertising, these cultural factors promoted the idea that soap was stronger than dirt; keeping clean was not only healthy, it ensured romance, material abundance, and acceptance into the sweatless, odorless, and successful middle class.

This transformation actually involved two powerful motives. One motive corresponded to the need to form a "labor force" and ensure good health as the United States became more industrial, urban, and ethnically diverse. Cleanliness had become an indicator that some individuals were morally superior, of better character, or more civilized than others. It also served to differentiate larger numbers of Americans, especially as society increasingly became more middle-class and white-collar. The other motive involved the need to produce more customers for the mass-manufactured toiletries produced in the emerging consumer society. Indeed, cleanliness had become big business. Important to the country's standard of living, health, and social welfare, the personal care industry was also a potential source of big profits. Ultimately, Americans came clean. By the 1920s, it became not merely fashionable, but also normative, for Americans to wash their hands, bathe every day, and generally use large quantities of soap.

NEW SHRINES OF CLEANLINESS

The foregoing discussion of the soap industry's efforts to promote personal cleanliness over the period between 1875 and 1940 offers a useful window on the evolution of mass consumption in the United States. In particular, the development of both a consumer culture and a culture of cleanliness also highlights the diverse roles that women played in the phenomenon. In this context, women did not emerge merely as the passive pawns of consumer product advertisers. Sanitarians, reformers, home economists, educators, and advertising career women all actively participated in creating a consumer culture as they urged Americans to adopt middle-class habits of personal cleanliness. More important, however, was that the women readers and radio listeners were also active in the process. They controlled the magazines they read and the radio programs that they listened to; and by responding to mail hooks and promotional offers, they consciously (or unconsciously) determined which advertisements and daytime radio programs would continue and which promotional messages they would acknowledge.

Historians believed that the circumstances specific to a given era affect the phenomena associated with it. As a consequence, the insights gained from an analysis of the development of mass consumption in the period 1875 to 1940 cannot be used directly to understand consumption attitudes and behaviors in a later period. To identify the implications of the advertiser's efforts for the present, it is necessary, instead, to examine the ways in which the contemporary situation is similar to and dissimilar from that of the 1920s.

What has changed, for example, is the abundance of brands and kinds of soap. Where once an all-purpose soap was all one needed to wash the body, clothes, and even floors, today there is a virtual cornucopia of soap products—moisturizing, deodorant, and antibacterial bar soaps; liquid soaps; gel soaps; body washes; beauty cleansers; and even "soapless" soaps. This is a marked contrast to only a century ago, when one all-purpose soap seemed sufficient, and less than two centuries ago, when it was considered nonessential.

In this earlier era, newspapers, magazines, and radio were basic instruments for the national, day-to-day dissemination of a single consumption ideology. By contrast, at present, the role of broadcast media in sustaining consumer culture is more complex. National and international networks continue to provide common experiences that exert a homogenizing influence not only on consumers in the United States, but also on those in many other parts of the world. But, within this nation, a growing number of cable stations, including Black Entertainment Television, Spanish-language networks, and even MTV, have emerged as countervailing forces. Those vehicles work against a unifying trend by serving the particular needs and reinforcing separate identities and distinct consumer tastes of African Americans, Hispanics, and other subgroups.

Advertising has long been criticized for its insensitivity to minorities, women, immigrants, and myriad other groups, who, it is argued, are not being favorably portrayed in ads. By the 1920s, a number of universal archetypes had emerged fully developed, and the images remain part of today's advertising scene. In this study, we identified six female stereotypes that emerged fully developed by the 1920s; they include the homemaker, the temptress, the tutor, the modern woman, the independent woman, and the superwoman. Of course, there was also Mr. Everyman. Although contemporary audiences might reject such stereotyped gender roles as one-dimensional, the images portrayed, in many ways, a sizable market of consumers.

The congruency between emotive selling formulas and stereotypes, which served both the female audience and soap manufacturers so well in the 1920s and 1930, continued to be important at the end of the twentieth century. In the present day, however, single-target markets proportionately as large as the "captive" housewife market for the soap operas of the 1920s and 1930s no longer exist. Today millions of people tune into at least one network soap opera each week, but that audience is a diverse one, including not only traditional housewives but also men and even college students. For this reason, advertisers monitor audience demographics carefully to match the interests of subsets of viewers with program and reading content. Their efforts have resulted in distinct varieties of broadcast programs designed to appeal to the highly diverse audience; likewise beauty guides, health books, and magazines aimed at women have proliferated.

In addition to changes in advertising content and media, this study also highlighted the important role that women historically have played in affecting consumer attitudes and behaviors. In contrast, contemporary women have a more prominent place in the paid labor force than their mothers and grandmothers had, and they share more household duties with their spouses. Nevertheless, today's women still have primary responsibility for many aspects of consumer activity. Women, in their role of consumer, had played an important part in the development of our industrial society. Behavior that was essential for economic reasons was transformed into a social virtue. Thus, women's primary social value can no longer be defined as the attainment of virtuous domesticity; the industrial revolution had redefined it as the attainment of virtuous consumption. With the rise of a consumer society, women's role also shifted from primary agents in the production of cleanliness to consumers of commodified cleanliness rituals.

Over the century women and social values may have changed, but soap advertising, with its appeals to health and beauty, has not changed. Standards of modesty have relaxed, and the public is far more receptive to ads for body-care products than in the 1920s. Ads for deodorant soaps still promise to protect people from what Lifebuoy then called "B.O." In the 1960s, people heard, "Aren't you glad you use Dial? Don't you wish everybody did!" As for revealing more skin, the 1991 introduction of Lever 2000 bar soap creatively presented some of the two thousand body parts one could clean with this specially designed skin-care product. One could use it everywhere: "On hard parts. Soft parts. Tough parts. And pretty parts. All your 2000 parts." Just six months after its introduction, the strong positioning of the product as a deodorant soap that's better for one's skin took the soap to number two in deodorant soap in sales revenues.[9]

Other ads also continue to reaffirm the value placed by the culture on personal cleanliness, beauty, and the quest for eternal youth, as did Woodbury, Lux, and Palmolive soaps. This focus is obvious in ads for Oil of Olay Beauty Cleanser: "And so your day begins, the Ritual of Oil of Olay."[10] Still, the cachet of a beauty product allows manufacturers to charge more too. According to advertising executive Jane Trachtenberg, "Women would pay 25 cents for a bar of soap that made their hands clean, but $2.50 for a bar of soap that promised to make them beautiful."[11]

Just as in the past, ads continue to show people how to cleanse themselves in order to be attractive, well-liked, and part of the successful middle class. At the same time, the bathroom has become one of the most important rooms in American homes. In the 1920s the bathroom had transformed from a utility to a shrine of cleanliness; and in the 1990s, the room since has been touted as a sanctuary. Every week, the average American adult takes at least seven baths or showers. While getting clean was the main objective for many people, nearly half of the cleansings were for "refreshment as well as cleansing," reported one study. Some people even take two or three showers a day, often after a gym workout or before a social engagement at night.[12] When people have plenty of time to truly relax, they would prefer a hot soaking bath to a shower revealed a 1999 bathroom habits survey. In addition to hot baths, other favorite bathroom activities among Americans include dressing, applying makeup, reading a newspaper or catalog, and singing; while others enjoy having telephone conversations with the rise of cordless phones. "Americans have unique relationship with their bathroom," says Jeanette Long, American Standard's senior marketing executive.

"With today's highly stressful lifestyles, the bathroom has truly become a sanctuary; a place where people can unwind and refresh themselves."[13]

Thus, women's continuous association with consumption calls attention to the fact that important evidence of changes in consumer behaviors and attitudes occurring throughout the twentieth century is likely to be found in sources relating to women's everyday lives. And perhaps this is most notable in materials associated with popular culture. Those sources need to be examined more closely by all researchers who are interested in the role of consumption in American life.

In addition, further research could consider documenting personal cleanliness rituals and advertising for body-care products in other cultures, particularly Asian soap advertising. Japan has long been a nation of fastidious bathers and groomers, a legacy of the ancient Shinto religion's emphasis on ritual purification. But over the last decade, the Japanese have become exceptionally hygiene-conscious and intolerant of anyone who is not. The Japanese consumer is inundated with new products that promise to kill germs, inhibit their growth, or banish unpleasant odors from the body, home, factory, or office. The items range from mundane antibacterial soaps, wet tissues, and towels to tongue scrapers for removing bacteria from the mouth. For the truly hygiene-obsessed, there are antibacterial toothbrushes, hairbrushes, and towels; showerheads that clean and ionize water; and even pills that claim to prevent human waste from smelling. Many Japanese also have toilets equipped with built-in bidets and blow dryers— the devices are known as "bottom-washers."[14] That is very different from the American dynamic. Research of Japanese cleanliness habits should suggest new conceptions of consumers and consumer needs, as well as a new conception of soap advertising.

Today advertising continues to play an ever-greater role in creating and fueling desires that both reflect and shape life around the world—desires that are a driving force in a capitalist economy. If everyday media images and words pitch desire, advertisements may well be the closest representation of the desires of our time. Future study of cultural history might well take the observation of formulaic elements common in popular culture studies as a flexible and useful framework to interpret the content of advertisements as revelatory of not only our past but contemporary beliefs and needs. The process of studying advertising as a popular art form thus opens up realms of thought about how the culture within these advertisements and their advertised products were positioned. Advertising invites this kind of aesthetic interpretation. Perhaps only then will advertising achieve the respectability as both a historical and artistic artifact that it so clearly deserves.

A Word about Sources

7 his work is based mainly on primary sources and advertisements. In order to obtain consumer advertising for the major soap manufacturers, I focused primarily on material from the top three agencies responsible for the content of national advertising over the period of 1875 to 1940. In this group, J. Walter Thompson Agency ranked first in 1927, Lord & Thomas (later Foote Cone & Belding) second, and N. W. Ayer & Son third, based on billings. By far the most important repository of agency material is the Hartman Center at Duke University. The library's J. Walter Thompson Collection provides the most in-depth material on the agency's operations. In addition to the domestic ad collection, the Hartman Center also has account files, status reports, staff minutes, marketing research studies, and house organs such as company newsletters. These materials reveal the conscious strategies and creative processes that underlay the finished advertising campaigns for such clients as Lever Brothers and Jergens Company. Also, the center holds the archives of the Outdoor Advertising Association; D'Arcy, Masius, Benton, & Bowles; and a wide range of early advertising textbooks.

Though not as extensive as the Hartman Center archives, two other collections are important. The Foote Cone & Belding collection at the State Historical Society of Wisconsin contains tearsheets of Palmolive soap advertisements—the printed ads cut out and sent by the publisher to the advertiser as proof they were published. Likewise, the Smithsonian's N. W. Ayer collection catalogs only tearsheets of the agency's advertisements without supporting account histories or marketing research studies. As for printed advertising ephemera, the Hagley, Winterthur, Smithsonian, and New York Public Library furnish extensive collections of trade cards, postcards, and broadsides from the nineteenth to the early twentieth century.

In addition to agency archives, trade journals provide a copious record of the industry. For advertising, the business branch of the New York Public Library offers bound volumes of the early editions of *Judicious Selling* (later *Advertising & Selling*) dating from 1885 to 1910. The combined holdings of University of Wisconsin Library and Duke University provide *Printers' Ink* for the years 1890 to 1940. For the soap industry, the Hagley Library holds from 1890 to 1940 the *Soap Gazette and Perfumer*, the only continuous trade magazine for the soap industry. The Hagley also provides the most extensive collection of trade catalogs, providing samples of nineteenth-century druggist price lists to a cross section of issues for the three major plumbingware manufacturers, Standard Manufacturing, Kohler, and Crane, from the 1890s.

Two collections are important sources for late-nineteenth- and early-twentieth-century domestic architecture and American material culture. Winterthur Library offers materials from the seventeenth to twentieth century, including recipe books, household encyclopedias, health and beauty guides, and conduct and etiquette books. These publications chronicle the change of societal standards in personal cleanliness. Also, the Winterthur Library provides a cross section of more general sources on nineteenth- and early-twentieth-century domestic architecture and material culture. Smithsonian's Warshaw Collection provides some notable examples for several of the narrative vignettes.

The University of Delaware's Accessible Archives provide online access to the nineteenth-century black press such as the *North Star* and the *Colored American*. For consumer advertising targeting African Americans in the twentieth century, commercial development can best be seen among the newspapers published in the North, among them the *New York Age,* the

Pittsburgh Courier, the *Washington Bee,* the *Chicago Broad Ax,* and the *Freemen.* However, the *Chicago Defender* epitomized the commercial development of the black press.[1] Most of the consumer magazine advertising and articles on personal care directed to African Americans appear in the *Colored American* magazine, the *Half-Century* magazine, *Voice of the Negro,* and the *Messenger,* bound volumes of which are found at the University of Delaware. The Hagley Library also provides texts on early black enterprise and market studies. As for black entrepreneurs, the Chicago Historical Society offers material on Overton Manufacturing and Claude Barnett's Kashmir Chemical Company based in Chicago, while the Indiana Historical Society holds the papers of Madame C. J. Walker.

A few secondary works deserve mention here, because they provide a detailed chronicle of the companies since their inception. The company publication Alfred Lief's *It Floats: The Story of Procter & Gamble,* Oscar Schisgall's *Eyes on Tomorrow,* and Advertising Age's *Procter & Gamble: The House That Ivory Built* present the history of Procter & Gamble. William Lee Sims's *150 Years—and the Future!* chronicles the development of Colgate-Palmolive from 1806 to 1956. David K. Fieldhouse's *Unilever Overseas* and W. J. Reader's *Fifty Years of Lever, 1930–1980* contains important insights on Unilever, and Paul F. Erwin's *With Lotions of Love* provides background on Jergens.

Notes

CHAPTER I: A CULTURE OF CLEANLINESS

1. "For the first time in history soap is part of a soldier's equipment": Lifebuoy, advertisement (1919), Research Reports, reel 16, J. Walter Thompson Company Archives, Hartman Center for Advertising History, Duke University Library. In 1775, the first army ration included .1830 oz. soap for one person for one day. By the Civil War, the ration for soap more than tripled, from .1830 oz. to .64 oz., and the amount remained the same for World War I. See "Rations," in Conference Notes Prepared by the Quartermaster School for the Quartermaster General, January 1949, Military History Institute Archives [www.qmf/historyof rations.htm].

2. Roland Marchand, *Advertising the American Dream: Making Way for Modernity* (Berkeley: University of California Press, 1985), p. 337.

3. Melville J. Herskovits, *Cultural Anthropology* (New York: Knopf, 1963), p. 119. On material culture studies, see also Thomas J. Schlereth, ed., *Material Culture Studies* (Nashville, Tenn.: AASHL Press, 1982).

4. Unquestionably, cadres of social workers, sanitarians, teachers, and advertisers encouraged a surveillance of the dirty, germ-

laden civil body in order to foster cleanliness—and sell soap. While the situation admits to a now classic Foucaultian interpretation of surveillance and any number of postmodern theoretic interpretations, the vision of the present work is to document and piece together the artifacts and activities involved in the social dynamic concerning cleanliness in North American from 1875 to 1940, not to theorize about it. That is a different project and will be left to others.

5. Marchand, *Advertising the American Dream*, pp. 206–36.

6. Carl B. Holmberg, *Sexualities and Popular Culture* (Thousand Oaks, Calif.: Sage, 1998), p. 32.

7. Harold M. Miner, "Body Ritual Among the Nacirema," *American Anthropologist* (June 1956): 118–21.

CHAPTER 2: CLEANLINESS, NOT ALWAYS A VIRTUE

1. *Printers' Ink* (April 10, 1913): 37.

2. *Soap Gazette and Perfumer* (September 1925): 9.

3. "Strong" and "weak" lye: Book of receipts, Lydia G. Jarvis (*circa* 1840s), printed ephemera no. 79 x 117, Winterthur Library, Wilmington, Delaware. "Sufficiently to bear up an egg": Book of receipts, Andrew S. Rappe (*circa* early 1800s), printed ephemera no. 74 x 116, Winterthur Library, Wilmington, Delaware.

4. Susan Strasser, *Never Done: A History of American Housework* (New York: Pantheon Books, 1982), pp. 85–89.

5. Jacqueline S. Wilkie, "Submerged Sensuality: Technology and Perceptions of Bathing," *Journal of Social History* (summer 1986): 651.

6. Richard L. and Claudia L. Bushman, "The Early History of Cleanliness in America," *Journal of American History* (March 1988): 1225.

7. *Soap and Detergents*, 2d ed. (New York: Soap and Detergent Association, 1994), pp. 3–4.

8. "Putrid urine" and "abrasives": "Soap and Other Detergents of Antiquity," *Scientific American* (June 26, 1909): 482. Personal standards of hygiene varied considerably from one class to another among ancient people, depending on the scarcity of water. For the Romans, bathing was a social event, while only wealthy Greeks were able to immerse themselves in a full bath. See Garret G. Fagan, *Bathing in Public in the Roman World* (Ann Arbor: University of Michigan Press, 1999); and Robert Garland, *Daily Life of the Ancient Greeks* (Westport, Conn.: Greenwood Press, 1998), pp. 86–87.

9. Mary Douglas, *Purity and Danger: An Analysis of Concepts of Pollution and Taboo* (New York: Praeger, 1966).

10. See Fagan, *Bathing in Public*, pp. 2–5.

11. Quoted in "From the Outhouse to Your House: How the Bathroom Sink

Became a Fixture in Our Lives," *Chicago Tribune*, November 23, 1986, Home section, 1, Zone C.

12. On "stews," see "Historical and Popular Exhibits at the International Hygienic Exposition in Dresden," *Scientific American* (August 5, 1911): 121. On hygiene, see George Vigarello, *Concepts of Cleanliness: Changing Attitudes in France since the Middle Ages* (Cambridge/New York: Cambridge University Press, 1988). On everyday life in medieval times, see Hans Werther, *Life in the Middle Ages: From the Seventh to the Thirteenth Century* (Notre Dame, Ind.: University of Notre Dame Press, 1993).

13. Wilkie, "Submerged Sensuality: Technology and Perceptions of Bathing."

14. On hygiene in England, see Kirstin Olsen, *Daily Life in 18th-Century England* (Westport, Conn.: Greenwood Press, 1999). On soap tax, see "Soap and Detergent Association," *Soap and Detergents*, pp. 5–6.

15. On hygiene in medieval Europe, see Jeffery L. Singman, *Daily Life in Medieval Europe* (Westport, Conn.: Greenwood Press, 1999), pp. 48–50.

16. "Eccrine sweat glands": *The New Encyclopedia of Britannica*, 11 (Chicago: Encyclopedia, Inc., 1997): 435.

17. "Aprocine sweat glands": *Britannica*, 11: 435; and "pheromones": *Britannica*, 9: 362

18. Susan Goodman, "Simple Story of Personal Hygiene," *Current Health* (January 1992): 1.

19. Quoted in "Cleanliness Is Only Recently a Virtue," *Smithsonian* (February 1991): 127.

20. John A. Hunt, "A Short History of Soap," *Pharmaceutical Journal* 263, no. 7076 (1999): 985–89.

21. The first printing of Sir Hugh Platt's *Delightes for Ladies*, in 1602, contained 107 pages, size 2 1/2 inches by 4 1/2 inches. (4th ed., 1609; reprint, Herrin, Ill.: Trovillion Press, 1939), xiii (page citations are to the reprint edition).

22. Christopher Nyerges, "Naturally Clean: How to Find and Use Some of Nature's Most Common Soaps; Herbal Remedies," *Mother Earth News* (August 18, 1997): 18.

23. *Soap and Detergents*, pp. 4–5. See also "The Basics of Making Soap," *Countryside & Small Stock Journal* (March 1995): 38.

24. "From the Outhouse to Your House."

25. Richard L. Bushman, *Refinement of American Persons, Houses, Cities* (New York: Knopf, 1992), pp. 63, 64.

26. The acquisition of gentility required attention to hundreds of details of conduct by which courtesy book writers summed up their rules. Among the aims of the courtesy books was the creation of the immaculate body through careful discipline. Clean hands and greaseless clothes were but one aspect; regulation of the mouth also received particular attention. Rules forbade people from talking with their mouths full, rinsing their mouths in the presence of others, biting their lips, or sticking out their tongue, among others. Other limits on bodily actions

included bodily posture, motion, and dress. Typical were Francis Hawkin, *Youth's Behaviour, or Decency in Conversation Among Men* (1640), Eleazar Moody, *The School of Good Manners* (1715), and Samuel Richardson, *Sir Charles Grandison* (circa 1753–54).

27. Quoted in Bushman, *Refinement*, p. 31.

28. Ibid.

29. N. Lémery, *New Curiosities in Art and Nature: or, A Collection of the Most Valuable Secrets in All Arts and Sciences* (London: Printed for John King, 1711), pp. 274–75; and *Valuable Secrets in Arts and Trades: Or, Approved Directions from the Best Artists, Containing Upward of One Thousand Approved Receipts* (London: Printed for J. Barker and J. Scatcherd, *circa* 1797), Winterthur Library, Wilmington, Delaware.

30. Bushman and Bushman, "The Early History of Cleanliness," p. 1222.

31. Ibid., p. 1223.

32. John Wesley, "Sermon XCII—On Dress," in *Sermons on Several Occasions*, vol. 2 (1788; reprint, New York, 1829), p. 259 (page citations are to the reprint edition), Winterthur Library, Wilmington, Delaware. See also Bushman, "The Early History of Cleanliness," pp. 1219, 1222.

33. On urban and rural sanitation practices, see Jack Larkin, *The Reshaping of Everyday Life, 1790–1840* (New York: Harper & Row, 1988), pp. 157–66; Suellen Hoy, *Chasing Dirt: The American Pursuit of Cleanliness* (New York: Oxford University Press, 1995), pp. 3–15; and Ellis L. Armstrong, Michael Robinson, and Suellen M. Hoy, eds. *The History of Public Works in the United States, 1776–1976* (Chicago: American Public Works Association, 1976).

34. Between 1860 and 1910, Chicago's population increased from 109,000 to more than 2 million; Philadelphia's tripled, to 1.5 million; and New York City grew fourfold, to nearly 5 million. Herbert J. Bass, George A. Billias, and Emma Jones Lapsansky, *America and Americans*, vol. 2 (Morristown, N.J.: Silver Burdett Company, 1983), p. 241.

35. "On the Female Form," *Lady's Book* (December 1831): 350, Accessible Archives, University of Delaware.

36. J. Thomas, *The Book of Health & Beauty, or the Toiletries of Rank and Fashion* (London, 1837), pp. 31–32, Winterthur Library, Wilmington, Delaware.

37. Dozens of encyclopedias and ladies' guides were published in the mid–nineteenth century. Typical were *Etiquette for Ladies* (Philadelphia: Lea & Blanchard, 1839); John Gunn, *Gunn's Domestic Medicine* (1830; reprint, Knoxville: University of Tennessee Press, 1986); Sir James Clark, *The Ladies Guide to Beauty* (New York: Dick & Fitzgerald, 1858); Thomas Webster and Mrs. Parkes, *The American Family Encyclopedia of Useful Knowledge* (New York: Derby & Jackson, 1859). See also Eleanor Lowenstein, *Bibliography of American Cookery Books, 1742–1860* (Worcester, Mass.: American Antiquarian Society, 1972).

38. Marion Harland, *Common Sense in the Household: A Manual of Practical Housewifery* (New York: Charles Scribner's Sons, 1871), Winterthur Library, Wilmington, Delaware.

39. S. Pancoast, M.D., *The Ladies Medical Guide* (Philadelphia: John E. Potter & Co., 1859), p. 541, Winterthur Library, Wilmington, Delaware.

40. Estelle Woods Wilcox, *Practical Housekeeping: A Careful Compilation of Tried and True Recipes* (Minneapolis: Buckeye Publishing Co., 1883), pp. 579–80, Winterthur Library, Wilmington, Delaware.

41. Owsei Temkin, *Galenism: Rise and Decline of a Medical Philosophy* (Ithaca: Cornell University Press, 1973), pp. 17, 164–79.

42. Kathy Peiss, *Hope in a Jar: The Making of American's Beauty Culture* (New York: Owl Books, 1999), p. 16.

43. *The Mischief of Bad Air: Or What 'Bad Air' Really Is*, booklet (1850), Hagley Library, Wilmington, Delaware.

44. Harvey Green, *Fit for America: Health, Fitness, Sport, and American Society* (New York: Pantheon, 1986), pp. 46–49.

45. Kathryn Kish Sklar, *Catherine Beecher: A Study in American Domesticity* (New York: Norton, 1975), p. 5.

46. James Baird, *The Management of Health: A Manual of Home and Personal Hygiene* (London: Virtue & Co, 1867), p. 73, Winterthur Library, Wilmington, Delaware.

47. Robert Tomes, *The Bazar Book of Decorum: The Care of the Person, Manners, Etiquette and Ceremonials* (New York, 1871), pp. 27–28, Winterthur Library, Wilmington, Delaware.

48. Marion Holland, *Eve's Daughters or Common Sense for Maid, Wife and Mother* (New York: J. R. Anderson & Henry S. Allen, 1882), p. 106, Winterthur Library, Wilmington, Delaware.

49. Charles Goodrum and Helen Dalrymple, *Advertising in America: The First 200 Years* (New York: Abrams, 1990), p. 50.

50. "Fifteen Rules for the Preservation of Health," *Godey's Lady's Book* (October 1860): 364.

51. Hoy, *Chasing Dirt*, p. 23.

52. For the idea that two ideals co-existed for women during mid–nineteenth century, the Cult of True Womanhood (the fragile maiden) and the Cult of Real Womanhood (emphasis on self-reliance and self-support), see Frances B. Cogan, *All-American Girl: The Ideal of Real Womanhood in Mid–Nineteenth Century America* (Athens: University of Georgia Press, 1989), chap. 1.

53. Hoy, *Chasing Dirt*, p. 47.

54. *Revised United States Army Regulations of 1861. With an Appendix Containing the Changes and Laws Affecting Army Regulations and Articles of War to June 25, 1863* (Washington: Government Printing Office, 1863).

55. C. L. Kilburn, *Notes on Preparing Stores for the United States Army; and on the Care of the Same, etc., with few rules for detecting adulteration*, 2d ed. (Cincinnati: Steam Printer and Stationer, 1963).

56. George Campbell, "Personal Reminiscences of the War," Minnesota Historical Society.

57. Catherine E. Beecher, *A Treatise on Domestic Economy* (Boston: Marsh, Capen, Lyon, and Webb, 1841).

58. May Brawley Hill, "Making a Virtue of Necessity: Decorative American Privies," *The Magazine Antiques* (August 1998): 182. See also Dottie Booth, *Nature Calls: The History, Lore, and Charm of Outhouse* (Berkeley: Ten Speed Press, 1998), p. 3.

59. Booth, *Nature Calls*, p. 26.

60. Joseph N. Kane, *Famous First Facts* (New York: Wilson, 1950), p. 329.

61. Carl B. Holmberg, *Sexualities and Popular Culture* (Thousand Oaks, Calif.: Sage, 1998), pp. 156–58.

62. *Soaps and Detergents*, p. 6.

63. Robert Jones, "The Basics of Making Soap," *Countryside and Small Stock Journal* (March 1995): 38.

64. *Soap Gazette and Perfumer* (June 1, 1938): 9.

65. "The Story of Soap-Making Is Told," *Soap Gazette and Perfumer* (June 1, 1938): 9; "The House of Colgate," *Profitable Advertising* (June 1910): 53.

66. "Something About Soap," company publication, Procter & Gamble (1881), Chicago Historical Society. See also *Soap Gazette and Perfumer* (June 1, 1938): 9.

67. *Profitable Advertising* (June 1910): 53.

68. Oscar Schisgall, *Eyes on Tomorrow: The Evolution of Procter & Gamble* (Chicago: J. G. Ferguson Publishing Co., 1981), p. 24.

69. "Merger of Colgate with Palmolive-Peet," *Soap Gazette and Perfumer* (August 1, 1928): 235.

70. David R. Foster, *The Story of Colgate-Palmolive: One Hundred and Sixty-Nine Years of Progress* (New York: Newcomen Society, 1975), p. 9.

71. Colgate & Co., *Spring Price List of Toilet Soaps, Perfumery, and Vaseline Preparations*, trade catalog (1877), Hagley Library, Wilmington, Delaware.

72. Schisgall, *Eyes on Tomorrow*, p. 1.

73. Procter & Gamble, *Something About Soap*, booklet (1881), p. 4.

74. Schisgall, *Eyes on Tomorrow*, p. 11.

75. Procter & Gamble, *Memorable Years in P & G History*, booklet (1978), pp. 8–9, Hagley Library, Wilmington, Delaware.

76. B. T. Babbitt Best Soap, *Washing Made Easy*, booklet (1870), Advertising Ephemera Collection, Toiletries, box 52, J. Walter Thompson Company Archives, Hartman Center for Advertising History, Duke University Library.

77. *Printer's Ink* (April 10, 1913): 37.

78. "Free Premiums," B.T. Babbitt, advertisement (n.d.), 60: Soap, box 1, folder: Babbitt. Warshaw Collection of Business Americana, Archives Center, National Museum of American History, Smithsonian Institution.

79. *Soap Gazette and Perfumer* (October 1, 1900): 200–201.

80. Bass, Billias, and Lapansky, *America and Americans*, p. 325.

81. Goodrum and Dalrymple, *Advertising in America*, p. 22.

82. On retailing history, see Gerald Carson, *The Old Country Store* (New York:

Oxford University Press, 1954); James M. Mayo, *The American Grocery Store: The Business Evolution of an Architectural Space* (Westport, Conn.: Greenwood Press, 1993); and William Leach, *Land of Desire: Merchants, Power, and the Rise of a New American Culture* (New York: Pantheon, 1993).

CHAPTER 3: RISE OF THE MASS MARKET, 1875 TO 1900

1. *The Household* (March–June 1889).

2. "Air Famine," *Good Housekeeping* (August 1889): 150.

3. Phyllis Ann Richmond, "American Attitudes Toward the Germ Theory of Disease (1860–1880)," *Theory and Practice in American Medicine: Historical Studies from the Journal of the History of Medicine & Allied Sciences*, ed. Gert H. Brieger (New York: Science History Publications, 1976).

4. Jacqueline S. Wilkie, "Submerged Sensuality: Technological and Perceptions of Bathing," *Journal of Social History* (summer 1986): p. 651.

5. On consumer culture, see Thorstein Veblen, *The Theory of the Leisure Class* (1899; reprint, New York: Vanguard, 1926). See also Warren Susman, *Culture as History: The Transformation of American Society in the Twentieth Century* (New York: Pantheon, 1984), p. 281; and Richard Wightman and T. J. Jackson Lears, eds. *The Culture of Consumption: Critical Essays in American History, 1880–1980* (New York: Pantheon Books, 1983).

6. On domesticity as sphere see Harvey Green, *Light of the Home: An Intimate View of the Lives of Women in Victorian America* (New York: Pantheon, 1983), pp. 10–28. On rhetoric of domestic ideologies in literature of domesticity, see Jackson Lears, *Fables of Abundance: A Cultural History of Advertising in America* (New York: Basic Books, 1994), pp. 75–78.

7. *Ladies' Home Journal* (November 1896): 14.

8. Ibid.

9. Joseph A. Banks, *Prosperity and Parenthood: A Study of Family Planning among the Victorian Middle Classes* (London: Routledge & Paul, 1954).

10. *Ladies' Home Journal* (November 1896): 14.

11. For a history of women's clubs, see Karen J. Blair, *The Clubwoman As Feminist: True Womanhood Redefined, 1868–1914* (New York: Holmes & Meier, 1980); Ann Ruggles Gere, *Intimate Practices: Literacy and Cultural Work in U.S. Women's Clubs, 1880–1920* (Urbana, Ill.: University of Illinois Press, 1997); and Theodora Penny Martin, *The Sound of Our Own Voice: Women's Study Clubs, 1880–1910* (Boston: Beacon, 1987). On African American women's groups, see Cynthia Neverdon-Morton, "Self-Help Programs as Educative Activities of Black Women in the South, 1895–1925: Focus on Four Areas," *Journal of Negro Education* (summer 1982), as well as her monograph, *African-American Women of the*

South and Advancement of the Race, 1895–1925 (Knoxville: University of Tennessee Press, 1989); and Gerda Lerner, "Early Community Work of Black Club Women," *Journal of Negro Education* [April 1974]).

12. Martha E. D. White, "The Work of the Woman's Club," *Atlantic Monthly* (May 1904): 614–15.

13. Suellen Hoy, *Chasing Dirt: The American Pursuit of Cleanliness* (New York: Basic Books, 1995), pp. 74–75.

14. Charles H. Starring, "Caroline Julia Bartlett Crane," in *Notable Women, 1607–1950*, ed. Edward T. James, Janet Wilson James, and Paul S. Boyers (Cambridge: Harvard University Press, 1971), vol. 1, p. 15. See also Helen Christine Bennett, *American Women in Civic Work* (New York: Dodd, Mead, 1915), pp. 41–42.

15. "Be Always Neat," *Householder* (January 1874): 2.

16. "A bath in a china dish," Standard Manufacturing Co., advertisement, 1892.

17. "Standard Manufacturing Co., *Roll Rim Baths,* trade catalog (Pittsburgh, 1892), pp. 5, 17, Hagley Library, Wilmington, Delaware.

18. J. L. Mott Iron Works, *Modern Plumbing*, trade catalog (New York, 1898), inside back cover, Baths and Bathing, box 1, folder 26. Warshaw Collection of Business Americana, Archives Center, National Museum of American History, Smithsonian Institution.

19. Ibid.

20. Up until 1920, the leading women's magazines refused advertising of any toilet tissue; it was an unmentionable subject. Typical Scott advertisements prior to 1927 suggested the proper thing to say: "don't ask for toilet paper—ask for Scot-Tissue"; *Ladies' Home Journal* (October 1920, April 1924, and February 1925). See also "Short History of the Scott Paper Company," Account Files, folder: Scott Paper Company, J. Walter Thompson Company Archives, Hartman Center for Advertising History, Duke University Library. See also Frank Muir, *An Irreverent and Almost Complete Social History of the Bathroom* (Briarcliff Manor, N.Y.: Stein and Day, 1982), pp. 85–86.

21. With the rise of national advertisers and the advent of new media, advertising agencies changed to meet the demands of American businesses. Agencies expanded beyond their initial role as sellers of newspaper space. Some agents formed billposting companies, which erected their own boards and leased space. Others organized streetcar and magazine advertising, selling the media on a national basis. Agencies also learned how to create advertising campaigns and plan marketing strategies. For the development of national, and sometimes global, advertising organizations, see Stephen Fox, *The Mirror Makers: A History of Advertising and Its Creators* (New York: Vintage, 1983). See also Daniel Pope, *The Making of Modern Advertising* (New York: Basic Books, 1983).

22. Frank Presbrey, *The History and Development of Advertising* (Garden City, N.Y.: Doubleday, Doran & Co., 1929), p. 394.

23. Richard Tedlow, *New and Improved: The Story of Mass Marketing in America* (New York: Basic Books, 1976), p. 10.

24. *Advertising and Selling* (August 1911): 49.

25. Potter Drug & Chemical Corporation, *Fifty Years of Cuticura, 1878–1928,* trade catalogue (Malden, Mass., 1928): 17–19.

26. *Soap Gazette and Perfumer* (October 1, 1900): 223.

27. Dennis Sillings and Nancy Roth coined this term in "When Electroquackery Thrived," *IEEE Spectrum* (November 1978): 56–61.

28. Pamela Laird, *Advertising and Progress: American Business and the Rise of Consumer Marketing* (Baltimore: Johns Hopkins University Press: 1998), p. 54.

29. *Soap Gazette and Perfumer* (October 1, 1900): 200.

30. Olive Tardiff and Marcia Ray, "The Larkin Idea," *Spinning Wheel* (March 1975).

31. William F. Aarens, *Contemporary Advertising*, 7th ed. (Burr Ridge, Ill.: Irwin McGraw-Hill, 1999), p. 555.

32. In 1893, the Larkin catalog listed twenty-seven premium items, including silk handkerchiefs, pocket watches, butter dishes, piano lamps, and Chautauqua desk. By 1908, the premium list expanded to hundreds of items, including stoves, kitchen cabinets, sewing machines, steel beds, and even upright pianos. Larkin Manufacturing, *The Larkin Soap Mftg. Company Premium List* (Buffalo, N.Y., 1893; 1908), 60: Soap, box 4, folder: Larkin. Warshaw Collection of Business Americana, Archives Center, National Museum of American History, Smithsonian Institution.

33. Larkin Manufacturing, *The Larkin Soap Mftg. Company Premium List 1893*, company publication (Buffalo, N.Y,, 1893), 60: Soap, box 4, folder: Larkin. Warshaw Collection of Business Americana, Archives Center, National Museum of American History, Smithsonian Institution.

34. Tardiff and Ray, "The Larkin Idea."

35. Laird, *Advertising and Progress,* p. 90. See also Ellen Gruber Garvey, *The Adman in the Parlor: Magazines and the Gendering of Consumer Culture, 1880s to 1890s* (New York: Oxford University Press, 1996), pp. 16–50.

36. William Pierce Randel, *The Evolution of American Taste* (New York: Routledge, 1976), pp.146–47.

37. J. Tebbel, *The American Magazine: A Compact History* (New York: Hawthorn Books, Inc., 1969). On the "modern advice column," see Amy Janello and Brennon Jones, *The American Magazine* (New York: Harry N. Abrams, 1991), p. 20.

38. On women's magazines, see Helen Woodward, *The Lady Persuaders* (New York: Ivan Obolensky, 1960); Mary Ellen Zuckerman, *A History of Popular Women's Magazines in the United States, 1792–1995* (Westport, Conn.: Greenwood Press, 1998); Jennifer Scanlon, *Inarticulate Longings: The Ladies' Home Journal, Gender, and Promises of Consumer Culture* (New York: Routledge, 1995); Garvey, *The Adman in the Parlor*.

39. On *Saturday Evening Post,* see Janello, *The American Magazine,* p. 62.

40. Juliann Sivulka, *Soap, Sex, and Cigarettes: A Cultural History of American Advertising* (Belmont, Calif.: Wadsworth, 1998), p. 69.

41. Babbitt: "Will Spend a Fortune in Advertising Soap," *Soap Gazette and Perfumer* (September 1, 1900): 201. Procter & Gamble: Robert Sobel and David B. Sicilia, *The Entrepreneurs: An American Adventure* (Boston: Houghton Mifflin Co., 1986), p. 214.

42. Procter & Gamble, *Ivory 75,*company publication (1954), p. 17.

43. Green, *The Light of the Home*, p. 47.

44. Giles D'Souza and Ram C. Rao, "Can Repeating an Advertisement More Frequently Than the Competition Affect Brand Performance in a Mature Market?" *Journal of Marketing* (April 1995): 32–42.

45. Green, *The Light of the Home*, p. 47

46. "Hand Sapolio, A New Toilet Soap," Sapolio, advertisement (*circa* 1870s) and "Dainty Women's Friend": Sapolio, advertisement in *The District School of Spotless Town*, booklet (ca 1900), 60: Soap, box 6, folder: Enoch Morgan & Sons. Warshaw Collection of Business Americana, Archives Center, National Museum of American History, Smithsonian Institution.

47. On Sapolio as a household word, see *Printers' Ink* (March 18, 1903).

48. Mike Dempsey, ed., *Bubbles: Early Advertising Art from A. & F. Pears Ltd,* (London: Fontana, 1978).

49. Pears' Soap, advertisement, *Godey's Lady's Book* (February 1889).

50. Dempsey, *Bubbles.*

51. James Playsted Wood, *The Story of Advertising* (New York: Ronald Press, 1958).

52. Dempsey, *Bubbles.*

53. Presbrey, *The History and Development of Advertising*, p. 95 Wood, *Story of Advertising,* p. 225.

54. Stanley Fish argues that a culture as a community may be identified not just by geography, ethnicity, race, family, class, or other physical characteristics, but for its interpretive strategies of what is popular and how the sharing occurs. *Is There a Text in This Class? The Authority of Interpretive Communities* (Cambridge, Mass.: Harvard University Press, 1980), p. 14. Earlier, Daniel J. Boorstin observed that people share meanings from the commodification process: "Nearly all objects from the hats and suits and shoes men wore to the food they ate became symbols and instruments of novel communities," or "consumption communities." *The Americans: The Democratic Experience* (New York: Vintage, 1973), pp. 89–90. For a brief critique of consumption communities, see Michael Schudson, *Advertising: The Uneasy Persuasion* (New York: Basic Books, 1984), pp. 159–60.

55. R. W. Bell, *Bell's Buffalo Soap*, storybook (Buffalo, N.Y.), 60: Soap, box 3, folder: R. W. Bell. Warshaw Collection of Business Americana, Archives Center, National Museum of American History, Smithsonian Institution.

56. Larkin Soap Mftg. Co., "A Tale of the Larkin Soaps," trade card, (Buffalo, N.Y.), 60: Soap, box 4, folder: Larkin, J & I. Warshaw Collection.

57. The term *headline* refers to the words in the leading position of the advertisement, which usually appear in larger type than other parts of the ad to attract attention. The *text*, or body copy, goes on to tell the complete story and usually appears in a smaller type size than the headlines.

58. "The White Man's Burden," Pears', advertisement, *McClure's* magazine (October 1899).

59. David Starr Jordan, "The White Man's Burden," from "A Blind Man's Holiday," *Imperial Democracy* (New York: D. Appleton and Co., 1899).

60. Editorial from the *Washington Bee*, March 11, 1899.

CHAPTER 4: SOAP, SEX, AND SCIENCE, 1900 TO 1920

1. After the Spotless Town campaign had run for six years, Ward deliberately wound up the promotion rather than let it fall out of fashion. On Sapolio, see *Printers' Ink* (March 18, 1903). See also Enoch Morgan's Sons Company, *Ye Booke of Spotless Town,* booklet, 2nd edition (New York, 1909), 60, Soap, box 6, folder: Morgan's Enoch Sons Company. Warshaw Collection of Business Americana, Archives Center, National Museum of American History, Smithsonian Institution.

2. "The World's Progress and Soap," *Soap Gazette and Perfumer* (November 1, 1908): 345.

3. Richard L. Scheffel, ed. *Discovering America's Past: Customs, Legends, History and Lore of Our Great Nation* (Pleasantville, N.Y.: Reader's Digest, 1993), p. 136. See also Marilyn T. Williams, *Washing the "Great Unwashed": Public Baths in Urban America, 1840–1920* (Columbus: Ohio State University Press, 1991).

4. Suellen Hoy, *Chasing Dirt: The American Pursuit of Cleanliness* (New York: Basic Books, 1995), pp. 70–72.

5. On the settlement house movement see Mina Carson, *Settlement Folk: Social Thought and the American Settlement Movement, 1885–1930* (Chicago: University of Chicago Press, 1990); Ruth Hutchinson Crocker, *Social Work and Social Order: The Settlement Movement in Two Industrial Cities, 1889–1930* (Urbana, Ill.: University of Illinois Press, 1992); and Rivka Shipak Lissak, *Pluralism & Progressives: Hull House and the New Immigrants, 1890–1919* (Chicago: University of Chicago Press, 1989).

6. Crocker, *Social Work and Social Order*, p. 154.

7. Hoy, *Chasing Dirt*, pp. 110–13.

8. Ibid., pp. 134–35.

9. Richard L. Bushman and Claudia L. Bushman, "The Early History of Cleanliness in America," *Journal of American History* (March 1988): 1219, 1222.

10. George Stanley, "Kohler on Kohler," *Milwaukee Sentinel*, October 24, 1994, p. 15D.

11. As it turned out, the superpatriotism and nationalism that fueled the Americanization programs had diminished by the end of the 1920s, and most of these industrial efforts had been terminated. The few company programs that did survive finally ended in the Depression years.

12. Bushman and Bushman, "Early History of Cleanliness," p. 1013.

13. Mary Wood Allen, *What a Young Woman Ought to Know* (Philadelphia: Vir Publishing, 1905), pp. 80–81.

14. Harvey Green, *Light of the Home: An Intimate View of the Lives of Women in Victorian American* (New York: Pantheon, 1983), p. 105; Helen Churchil Candee, "House Building" in *The House and Home*, ed. Abbott Lyman (New York: C. Scribner Sons, 1896), p. 156.

15. Standard Sanitary Mfg. Co.,"Design Number P38," *Modern Bathrooms*, trade catalog (1906), p. 40, Hagley Library, Wilmington, Delaware.

16. Standard Sanitary Mfg. Co., *Modern Bathrooms*, trade catalog (1906), p. 66, Hagley Library, Wilmington, Delaware.

17. "Kohler manufacturers but one quality of enameled plumbing ware" and "Kohler of Kohler": Kohler, advertisements, *Kohler Sales Help*, trade catalog (1915), pp. 7–8, Kohler Company, Corporate Archives, Sheboygan, Wisconsin.

18. *Printers' Ink* (April 11, 1918): 17.

19. Ibid.

20. Ibid., pp. 17–20.

21. Richard S. Tedlow, *New and Improved: The Story of Mass Marketing in America* (New York: Basic Books, 1990), p. 192.

22. Ibid., p. 191.

23. Larkin Club-of-Ten Organizers were frequently called Larkin Secretaries in the monthly employee magazine *The Larkin Idea*; one of their duties was to keep a record of the orders, payments, and deliveries to each member of the club.

24. "The Larkin Plan": Larkin Manufacturing, *The Larkin Soap Mftg. Company Premium*, spring/summer 1905 and 1918 (Buffalo, N.Y.), 60, Soap, box 5, folder: Larkin. Warshaw Collection of Business Americana, Archives Center, National Museum of American History, Smithsonian Institution.

25. On "Larkin Pantries," a home could be stocked with Larkin products such as soaps, foodstuffs, and other sundries. Menus, entertainment ideas, and recipes appear in *The Larkin Idea*, in regular columns like "Domestic Science." On the "Larkin Look," a series of essays on furnishing a home with Larkin Premiums appears in *The Larkin Idea*. Typical was the Larkin Kitchen that could be designed with furnishings, appliances, and utensils, *The Larkin Idea* (April 1906), 60, Soap, box 4, folder: J. R. Larkin & Co. Warshaw Collection of Business Americana, Archives Center, National Museum of American History, Smithsonian Institution.

The premium catalogs also pictured rooms furnished through running Larkin clubs; for a living room, see *The Larkin Plan* (spring/summer, 1918): 4–5.

26. On employee benefit programs, see issues of *The Larkin Idea*. For listing of classes, see "Once upon a time there was a girl," pamphlet, Larkin Company (1919), Hagley Library, Wilmington, Delaware.

27. Ernestine G. Miller, *The Art of Advertising* (New York: St. Martin's Press, 1982), introduction.

28. *Profitable Advertising* (November 1902): 418.

29. By the 1920s, the average salary of "name" illustrators exceeded $60,000 to $75,000 a year (in their dollars, not ours). See Charles Goodrum and Helen Dalrymple, *Advertising in America: The First 200 Years* (New York: Vintage, 1983), p. 157.

30. There are records of women in advertising as far back as 1867, when Mathilde C. Weil ran her own advertising agency. Others were hired as freelance writers or illustrators by ad agencies such as J. Walter Thompson Company. By 1903, the advertising field had become known as a place for women of ability. There were a few well-known women, but most were hidden in support roles and not credited for their creative contribution. See Stephen Fox, *The Mirror Makers: A History of Advertising and Its Creators* (New York: Vintage, 1983), p. 285; Advertising Age, eds. *How It Was in Advertising: 1776–1976* (Chicago: Crain Books, 1976), p. 31.

31. Goodrum and Dalrymple, *Advertising in America*, p. 24.

32. Ibid., p. 45.

33. *Advertising & Selling* (February 1912): 114–20.

34. Ibid., p. 120.

35. Ibid.

36. *Printers' Ink* (June 30, 1910): 35.

37. Packer's Tar Soap, booklet (n.d.), 60, Soap, box 6, folder: Packer Manufacturing Co. Warshaw Collection of Business Americana, Archives Center, National Museum of American History, Smithsonian Institution Collection.

38. *Profitable Advertising* (January 1903): 648–49.

39. Frank Presbrey, *History and Development of Advertising* (Garden City, N.Y.: Doubleday, Doran & Co., 1929), p. 397.

40. *Profitable Advertising* (October 1901): 394.

41. *Advertising and Selling* (January 1912): 52–57.

42. Although the two alternatives of advertising communication, logical and emotional, seemed novel at the turn of the twentieth century, this persuasive strategy was described by two thousand years ago in Aristotle's *The Art of Rhetoric*. Based on his observations of speakers delivering speeches to audiences at assembly and court, Aristotle categorized three forms of persuasive arguments: (1) *ethos*, (2) *logos*, or (3) *pathos*. In other words, the messages took the form of ethical or integrity, logical, and emotional arguments. Together the three forms offered up different approaches to lead the reader or listener to draw a conclusion favorable

to the speaker or initiating communicators. Late-nineteenth- and early-twentieth-century advertising, particularly soap ads, illustrate Aristotle's three forms of persuasive arguments. See John Henry Freese, *Aristotle, with an English Translation: The Art of Rhetoric* (London: W. Heinemann; Cambridge, Mass.: Harvard University Press, 1926).

43. Stephen Mitchell, *Freud and Beyond: A History of Modern Psychoanalytic Thought* (New York: Basic Books, 1995). See also Anthony Storr, *Freud* (Oxford; New York: Oxford University Press, 1989).

44. Juliann Sivulka, *Soap, Sex, and Cigarettes: Cultural History of American Advertising* (Belmont, Calif.: Wadsworth, 1998), pp. 107–10. See also Fox, *Mirror Makers*, p. 50.

45. Scott: Edmund C. Lynch, "Walter Dill Scott: Pioneer Industrial Psychologist," *Business History Review* (summer 1968): 149–70.

46. *Printers' Ink* (April 13, 1911): 56.

47. *Printers' Ink* (July 25, 1912): 64.

48. *Profitable Advertising* (November 1901): 474.

49. "Why a Lifesaver?": Lifebuoy, advertisement, Domestic Advertisements Collection, Lever Bros., box 1, J. Walter Thompson Company Archives, Hartman Center for Advertising History, Duke University Library.

50. Lifebuoy Sanitary cleaner and disinfectant, advertisement (n.d.). Lever Bros., Domestic Advertisements, box 1.

51. *Profitable Advertising* (February 1903): 654.

52. Memorandum to Walter Scott (February 27, 1945), Information Center Records, box 3, Lever Brothers, 1916–1959, J. Walter Thompson Company Archives, Hartman Center for Advertising History, Duke University Library.

53. Lifebuoy, advertisement, *Saturday Evening Post*, July 5, 1915, p. 37.

54. Lifebuoy, advertisement, *Saturday Evening Post*, September 13, 1913, p. 57.

55. *J. Walter Thompson News Bulletin*, September 23, 1918, p. 4. Newsletter Collection, J. Walter Thompson Company Archives, Hartman Center for Advertising History, Duke University Library.

56. "Lifebuoy Advertising 1918–1920," Account File (November 24, 1944), Information Center Records, Lever Bros., box 3, 1916–1959, J. Walter Thompson Company Archives, Hartman Center for Advertising History, Duke University Library.

57. "The World's Progress and Soap," *Soap Gazette and Perfumer* (November 1, 1908): 345.

58. *Printers' Ink* (June 21, 1917): 9.

59. Johnson & Johnson Company, *Household + Handbook*, booklet (1916), Hagley Library, Wilmington, Delaware.

60. Palmolive Soap, *Palmolive Beauty Culture*, booklet (n.d.): 13, 60: Soap, box 3, folder: Johnson, B. J. Warshaw Collection of Business Americana, Archives Center, National Museum of American History, Smithsonian Institution Collection.

61. "Early History of Palmolive," *Soap Gazette and Perfumer* (May 1, 1928): 140.

62. *Printer's Ink* (June 9, 1910): 30.

63. Ibid., pp. 30–35.

64. *Soap Gazette and Perfumer* (May 1, 1928): 140.

65. Ibid., p. 141.

66. On "pre-emptive claim" technique, see Claude Hopkins, *Scientific Advertising* (1927; reprint, Lincolnwood, Ill.: NTC Books, 1986).

67. Palmolive, advertisements, *Ladies' Home Journal*: "luxury-loving Greeks" (August 1916), "Cleopatra's Vision" (April 1917), and "3000 years ago" (July 1917).

68. Kathy Peiss, *Hope in a Jar: The Making of America's Beauty Culture* (New York: Owl Books, 1999), pp. 147–48.

69. David R. Foster, *The Story of Colgate-Palmolive: One Hundred and Sixty-Nine Years of Progress* (New York: Newcomen Society, 1975), p. 16.

70. Woodbury's Facial Soap, *The Story of Woodbury's Facial Soap*, booklet (n.d.) p. 11, Account Files, Andrew Jergens Company, box 1, J. Walter Thompson Company Archives, Hartman Center for Advertising History, Duke University Library.

71. Ibid.

72. "$25,000": Woodbury's Facial Soap, *The Story of Woodbury's Facial Soap*; "Appropriation": "The Andrew Jergens Company—Woodbury's Facial Soap " (April 12, 1926): 1, Account Files, Andrew Jergens Company, Account Histories 1916–1926, box 1, J. Walter Thompson Company Archives, Hartman Center for Advertising History, Duke University Library.

73. Ibid.

74. "Women in Advertising," advertisement, *Printers' Ink* (August 23, 1917): 8–9, J. Walter Thompson Company Archives, Hartman Center for Advertising History, Duke University Library.

75. Jennifer Scanlon, *Inarticulate Longings: The Ladies' Home Journal, Gender, and Promises of Consumer Culture* (New York: Routledge, 1995).

76. "Women in Advertising," advertisement, *Printers' Ink* (August 23, 1917): 8, J. Walter Thompson Company Archives, Hartman Center for Advertising History, Duke University Library.

77. "The Andrew Jergens Company—Woodbury's Facial Soap" (April 12, 1926): 2, Account Files, Andrew Jergens Company, Account Histories 1916–1926, box 1, J. Walter Thompson Company Archives, Hartman Center for Advertising History, Duke University Library.

78. Ibid.

79. "Woodbury's Facial Soap National Campaign 1926": 7, Account Files, Andrew Jergens Company, Account Histories 1916–1926, box 1. See also "Woodbury's Facial Soap" (n.d.), Account Files, Andrew Jergens Company, Account Histories 1946–1950, box 1, Account Files, J. Walter Thompson Company Archives, Hartman Center for Advertising History, Duke University Library.

80. "Pond's Spring 1921 newspaper," memo, January 6, 1921, Research

Reports, reel 52, J. Walter Thompson Company Archives, Hartman Center for Advertising History, Duke University Library.

81. "The Andrew Jergens Company—Woodbury's Facial Soap" (April 12, 1926): 2, Account Files, Andrew Jergens Company, Account Histories 1916–1926, box 1, J. Walter Thompson Company Archives, Hartman Center for Advertising History, Duke University Library.

82. The ad, which appeared in the May 6, 1911, *Saturday Evening Post* is thought to be the earliest form of the slogan "A skin you love to touch."

83. "A-skin-you-love-to-touch," Woodbury, advertisement, *Ladies' Home Journal* (September 1916).

84. *JWT News Bulletin* (April 1923): 12–13. Newsletter Collection, J. Walter Thompson Company Archives, Hartman Center for Advertising History, Duke University Library.

85. Peiss, *Hope in a Jar*, p. 122.

86. "The Story of Woodbury's Facial Soap" (January–February 1930): 5, J. Walter Thompson Company Archives, Hartman Center for Advertising History, Duke University Library Account Files, box 1, folder: Andrew Jergens Company 1930.

87. "Phrase sings itself": *Atlantic* (October 1919).

88. Quoted in Fox, *Mirror Makers*, p. 81.

89. Goodrum and Dalrymple, *Advertising in America*, p. 69.

90. "Not the look of the shower" (1917) and "Come on in, the water's fine" (1918): Ivory, advertisements, reproduced in ibid., p. 53.

91. "The Soldier's Equipment," *Saturday Evening Post*, July 6, 1918, p. 48.

92. Ibid., p. 52.

93. Ivory, advertisement (1916), reproduced in Goodrum and Dalrymple, *Advertising in America*, p. 53.

94. Ivory, advertisement, *Saturday Evening Post*, April 19, 1919.

95. *Soap Gazette and Perfumer* (February 1, 1920): 56.

CHAPTER 5: NEW SHRINES OF CLEANLINESS, 1920 TO 1940

1. Crane advertisement, *Ladies' Home Journal* (February 1925).

2. Standard Sanitary Mftg. Co., advertisement, *Ladies' Home Journal* (March 1928).

3. "The Shrine of Cleanliness," *House Beautiful* (October 1925): 422.

4. The motivation to consume for the sake of consuming was first discussed by the social analyst Thorstein Veblen at the turn of the twentieth century. Veblen coined the term "conspicuous consumption" to refer to people's desire to provide prominent visible evidence of their ability to afford luxury goods. Veblen criticized

the decorative role women were often forced to play as they were bestowed with expensive clothes, pretentious homes, and a life of leisure as a way to advertise the wealth of their husbands. Thorstein Veblen, *The Theory of the Leisure Class* (1899; reprint, New York: New American Library, 1953), p. 45.

5. In 1904, George Simmel first proposed the relationship between product adoption and class structure, one of the most influential approaches to understanding fashion. First, dominant styles originate with the upper classes and trickle down to those below. Those people in the dominant groups are constantly looking below to ensure they are not imitated; they respond by adopting even newer fashions. These two processes create a self-perpetuating cycle of change that drives fashion. George Simmel, "Fashion," *International Quarterly* 10 (1904): 130–55.

6. William B. Hansen and Irwin Altman, "Decorating Personal Places: A Descriptive Analysis," *Environment and Behavior* (December 1976): 491–504.

7. Richard A. Peterson, "The Production of Culture: A Prolegomenon," in *The Production of Culture*, ed. Richard A. Peterson (Beverly Hills, Calif.: Sage, 1976): pp. 7–22.

8. E. S. Turner, *The Shocking History of Advertising!* (New York: E. P. Dutton & Company, 1953), p. 213.

9. Typical movies of the 1920s with opulent bath scenes include *Male and Female*, *Dynamite*, and *Sign of the Cross*. On DeMille, see Gabe Essoe and Raymond Lee, *DeMille: The Man and His Pictures* (New York: Castle Books, 1970); Charles Higham, *Cecil B. DeMille* (New York: Charles Scribner's Sons, 1973); and Gene Ringold and Dewitt Bodeen, *The Films of Cecil B. DeMille* (New York: Citadel Press, 1969).

10. Essoe and Lee, *DeMille*, p. 69.

11. Quoted in Ringold and Bodeen, *The Films of Cecil B. DeMille*, p. 207.

12. *Kohler of Kohler News* (December 1927): 3.

13. "Color Charm Enters the Bathroom," Kohler, trade catalog (1928): 2, Hagley Library, Wilmington, Delaware.

14. "How much does a Modern bathroom cost?" Kohler, advertisement, *Liberty* (April 6, 1929).

15. "You pay so little more for this new color beauty," Kohler, advertisement, *Liberty* (June 29, 1929).

16. "A $5000 bathroom—and a $500 one," Kohler, advertisement, *Liberty* (March 9, 1929). See also advertisement in *Liberty* (April 6, 1929); Kohler Colorware ready-to-install lavatories from $35 to $800, bathtubs $70 to $500, and toilets $65 to $150.

17. "The first coming of beauty," Standard Sanitary Mfg. Co. advertisement, *Ladies' Home Journal* (March 1928).

18. American Standard, *Planning Your Plumbing Wisely*, trade catalog (1935): 7. Hagley Library, Wilmington, Delaware.

19. Crane Plumbing Company, *Crane Co. 1855–1975*, company publication (New York: 1975), p. 23, Hagley Library, Wilmington, Delaware.

20. "Rainbow Bathrooms," *House and Garden* (June 1928): 750.

21. "Old-fashioned": *Planning Your Plumbing Wisely*, American Standard,

trade catalog (1935): 3; "quiet water closet" and "lavatory": "Planning Your Plumbing," p. 11, Hagley Library, Wilmington, Delaware.

22. *Reeves Journal* (May 1934).

23. Beth Austin, "From the Outhouse to Your House: How the Bathroom Sink Became a Fixture in Our Lives," *Chicago Tribune*, November 23, 1986, Home section, p. 1, zone C.

24. "And Here is Your Bathroom," Kohler, advertisement, *Saturday Evening Post*, May 12, 1923.

25. Quoted in "From Haphazard to Hip," *Reeves Journal* (January 1996): 42.

26. *Printers' Ink Monthly* (August 1928): 86.

27. *Printers' Ink Monthly* (August 1928): 30, 86; *Printers' Ink* (February 17, 1927): 196.

28. "New Orders of the Bath," *Vogue* (November 15, 1927): 140.

29. Veblen, *The Theory of the Leisure Class*.

30. Simmel, "Fashion," pp. 130–55.

31. Ninety percent of all soaps selling through groceries sold for twenty-five cents a cake or less. Among these, most of the soaps retailed for ten cents. See "A Summary of Conclusions: Based upon the study made of the toilet soap and lotion market" (July–September 1929): 149, Account Files, box 1, folder: Andrew Jergens Co., The Story of Woodbury Soap, J. Walter Thompson Company Archives, Hartman Center for Advertising History, Duke University Library.

32. Piggly Wiggly, the first major self-service grocery chain, opened its first store in Memphis, Tennessee, in 1916, while the first use of term "supermarket" in a trade name was Albers Super Markets in 1933. On grocery retailing, see James M. Mayo, *The American Grocery Store: The Business Evolution of an Architectural Space* (Westport, Conn.: Greenwood, Press, 1993). On drugstores, see Exhibition catalog, American Pharmaceutical Association, *Pharmacy Through the Ages* (Washington, DC, 1996), Hagley Library, Wilmington, Delaware; and Jane Mobley, *Prescription for Success: The Chain Drug Story* (Kansas City: Hallmark Cards, 1990).

33. "Report on Trade, Lifebuoy Consumer Investigations," November 1919, p. 13, Research Reports, reel 197, J. Walter Thompson Company Archives, Hartman Center for Advertising History, Duke University Library.

34. Robert Staughton Lynd, *Middletown* (New York: Harcourt, Brace and Co., 1929).

35. Michael R. Solomon, *Consumer Behavior*, 4th ed. (Upper Saddle River, N.J.: Prentice-Hall, 1992), p. 166.

36. *Printers' Ink* (May 15, 1919): 86.

37. Ibid.

38. Carl G. Jung, "The Archetypes and the Collective Unconscious," in *Collected Works*, ed. H. Read, M. Fordham, and G. Adler (Princeton: Princeton University Press, 1959), vol. 9, part 1.

39. Ibid.

40. *Printers' Ink* (August 11, 1927): 40.

41. Representatives' meeting (February 17, 1931): 5. Staff Meetings 1930–1931, Minutes of Representatives, box 3, J. Walter Thompson Company Archives, Hartman Center for Advertising History, Duke University Library.

42. Stephen Fox, *The Mirror Makers: A History of Advertising and Its Creators* (New York: Vintage, 1983), p. 86.

43. Vincent Vinikas, *Soft Soap, Hard Sell: Personal Hygiene in the Age of Advertisement* (Ames: Iowa State University Press, 1992), p. 14.

44. Quoted in John Braeman, ed., *Change and Continuity in Twentieth Century America: The 1920s* (Columbus: Ohio State University Press, 1968), p. 351.

45. *Ladies' Home Journal* (May 1929): 35.

46. Katherine Fishburn, *Women in Popular Culture: A Reference Guide* (Westport, Conn.: Greenwood, 1982), p. 163.

47. Around the turn of the century large bureaucratic organizations developed and required cooperation well into the twentieth century. On the movements away from nineteenth-century culture, see David Riesman, Reuel Denney, and Nathan Glazer, *The Lonely Crowd* (New Haven, Conn.: Yale University Press, 1950); and William H. Whyte Jr., *The Organization Man* (New York: Simon and Schuster, 1956).

48. Charles Goodrum and Helen Dalrymple, *Advertising in America: The First 200 Years* (New York: Abrams, 1990), p. 37.

49. In 1915, H. L. Mencken coined the term "flapper" for the new American woman. Gilbert M. Ostrander, "The Revolution in Morals," in *Change and Continuity in Twentieth-Century America: The 1920s*, p. 335.

50. Clifton Daniel, ed., *Chronicle of America* (Mount Kisco, N.Y.: Chronicle Publications, 1989), p. 620.

51. Jennifer Scanlon, *Inarticulate Longings: The Ladies' Home Journal, Gender, and Promises of Consumer Culture* (New York: Routledge, 1995), p. 225.

52. R. A. Wicklund and P.M. Gollwitzer, *Symbolic Completion Theory* (Hillsdale, N.J.: Erlbaum, 1982).

53. *National Markets and National Advertising* (New York: Crowell, 1929), p. 9.

54. Roland Marchand, *Advertising the American Dream: Making Way for Modernity* (Berkeley: University of California Press, 1985), p. 52.

55. Ibid., pp. 52–61.

56. Amy Janello and Brennon Jones, *The American Magazine* (New York: Henry N. Abrams, 1991), p. 62.

57. *Printers' Ink Fifty Years 1888–1938* (New York: Printers' Ink, 1938), p. 346.

58. Ostrander, "Revolution in Morals," p. 346.

59. *Printers' Ink Fifty Years*, pp. 174–75.

60. Here Marchand refers to this form as the "Parable of the First Impression"; Marchand, *Advertising the American Dream*, pp. 208–17.

61. "Scare copy": *Fifty Years*, p. 362. "Whisper copy": Copywriter Milton

Feasley coined the term "whisper copy," referring to a series of ads for Listerine that used advertising by fear. See Fox, *Mirror Makers*, p. 329.

62. William F. Aarens, *Contemporary Advertising*, 7th ed. (Burr Ridge, Ill.: Irwin McGraw-Hill, 1999), p. 397.

63. Listerine, advertisement, *Cosmopolitan* (November 1921).

64. Vinikas, *Soft Soap, Hard Sell*, p. 33.

65. "Mothers" and "The Kind of Bath That Just Tops Off a Holiday"(1923); "Train": "The Danger in Dirt" (1923); and "Isn't Health Worth Guarding, too?" (1925): Lifebuoy, advertisements, Research Reports, reel 197, J. Walter Thompson Company Archives, Hartman Center for Advertising History, Duke University Library.

66. "Wise Daddy Wash Up": Lifebuoy, advertisement (1926), Research Reports, reel 197, J. Walter Thompson Company Archives, Hartman Center for Advertising History, Duke University Library.

67. "Poor Uncle Ed" Lifebuoy, advertisement (1928), Research Reports, reel 197, J. Walter Thompson Company Archives, Hartman Center for Advertising History, Duke University Library.

68. Marchand, *Advertising the American Dream*, p. 13.

69. "Personal daintiness" and "Nothing Has More" (December 1922), "His unspoken thoughts" (September 1921), "All around you" (December 1922): Wood-bury's Facial Soap, advertisements, *Ladies' Home Journal*.

70. Harold Ernest Burtt, *Psychology of Advertising* (New York: Houghton, 1938), p. 71.

71. Michael L. Ray and William L. Wilkie, "Fear: The Potential of an Appeal Neglected by Marketing," *Journal of Marketing* 1 (1970): 54–62.

72. Brian Sternthal and C. Samuel Craig, "Fear Appeals: Revisited and Revised," *Journal of Consumer Research* (December 1974): 22–34.

73. "Milestones in the Love Affair That Last a Lifetime," Palmolive Soap, advertisement, *Ladies' Home Journal* (May 1928).

74. Palmolive, advertisement, *Ladies' Home Journal* (August 1928).

75. Michael S. LaTour and Tony L. Henthorne, "Ethical Judgements of Sexual Appeals in Print Advertising," *Journal of Advertising* (September 1994): 81–90.

76. Palmolive, advertisements (1938), Domestic advertisement collection, J. Walter Thompson Company Archives, Hartman Center for Advertising History, Duke University Library.

77. "Milestones in the Love Affair That Last a Lifetime," Palmolive Soap, advertisement, *Ladies' Home Journal* (May 1928).

78. "History of Lux Toilet Soap, 1925–1951," Account files, box 12, folder: Lever Brothers Account History 1925–1957, J. Walter Thompson Company Archives, Hartman Center for Advertising History, Duke University Library.

79. Lever Brothers, *Lever Standard*, p. 8.

80. Account Histories: Lever Brothers—Lux Toilet Form (January 30, 1926): 2. Information Center Records, box 3, folder: Lux Case History 1923–1973. For value for the money, see the 1919 market study for Lifebuoy; it reported that women

in the homes of skilled industrial workers, unskilled laborers, or foreign districts considered "toilet soap, a luxury, and used laundry soap for all purposes." Report on New York Office Investigation for Floating Lifebuoy Soap" (September 1919), memorandum for tables 65 and 66, Research Reports, reel 197, J. Walter Thompson Company Archives, Hartman Center for Advertising History, Duke University Library.

81. A. F. Countway, Lever Brothers Company, correspondence, January 27, 1925. Information Center Records, box 3, folder: Lux Case History, 1923–1979, J. Walter Thompson Company Archives, Hartman Center for Advertising History, Duke University Library.

82. "Lever Brothers Company Account History": 4. Information Center Records, box 3, folder: Lux Case History, 1923–1979, J. Walter Thompson Company Archives, Hartman Center for Advertising History, Duke University Library.

83. "Please" and "So Captivating": Lux advertisements in Lever Brothers, *Lever Standard*, company publication (1950), p. 8. "Made as women asked": Lux, advertisement, Domestic Advertisements, Lever Brothers, box 2, J. Walter Thompson Company Archives, Hartman Center for Advertising History, Duke University Library.

84. "History of Lux Toilet Soap 1925–1951": 5. Account files, box 12, folder: Lever Brothers Account History 1925–1957, J. Walter Thompson Company Archives, Hartman Center for Advertising History, Duke University Library.

85. "It has captivated" and "My entire family": Lux advertisements in Lever Brothers, *Lever Standard*, p. 8.

86. Creative Staff Meeting Minutes (May 24, 1932): 7–8. Information Center Records, box 3, folder: Lever Brothers 1916–1959, J. Walter Thompson Company Archives, Hartman Center for Advertising History, Duke University Library.

87. Esty on drawings and photography: see Representatives' Meeting (September 19, 1928): 1. See also Staff Meetings 1927–1929, Minutes of Representatives' Meetings, box 1, J. Walter Thompson Company Archives, Hartman Center for Advertising History, Duke University Library.

88. Lever Brothers, *Lever Standard* .

89. Representatives' Meeting (April 9, 1928): 7. Staff Meetings 1927–1929, Minutes of Representatives, box 2, J. Walter Thompson Company Archives, Hartman Center for Advertising History, Duke University Library.

90. Representatives' Meeting (April 9, 1928): 6. Staff Meetings 1927–1929, Minutes of Representatives, box 1, J. Walter Thompson Company Archives, Hartman Center for Advertising History, Duke University Library. See also "Danny Danker," *Advertising Age* (July 10, 1944, December 7, 1964).

91. Lever Brothers, *Lever Standard*, p. 12.

92. "Sales doubled": Lever Brothers, *Lever Standard*, p. 1.

93. "Graceful silver swan": Lux Toilet Soap, advertisement, *Ladies' Home Journal* (March, 1928). On Gaynor, Ralston, and Haver, see Lux Toilet Soap, advertisements, *Ladies' Home Journal* (January–May, 1928).

94. Representatives' Meeting (September 19, 1928): 1, 2. Staff Meetings

1927–1929, Minutes of Representatives, box 1, J. Walter Thompson Company Archives, Hartman Center for Advertising History, Duke University Library.

95. Andrew Jergens Company, *The Story of Woodbury's Facial Soap* (1930), p. 7. Account Files, box 1, Andrew Jergens Company. See also Representatives' Meeting (February 28, 1928): 1–2. Staff Meetings 1927–1929, Minutes of Representatives, box 1, J. Walter Thompson Company Archives, Hartman Center for Advertising History, Duke University Library.

96. Palmolive, advertisements: *Ladies' Home Journal* (May 1929, July 1929) and August 1929).

97. Campaign included stars' advice on how to be alluring in your thirties and forties, the importance of proper make-up removal, how to pass the "Close-Up Test," and closeup photos of "Lux Girls." Lux advertisements in Lever Brothers, *Lever Standard*, p. 12–13.

98. In a study on movies and conduct, led by sociologist Herbert Blumer in the late 1920s and 1930s, three-fourths of the "delinquent girls" said they heightened their sex appeal by imitating movie stars' clothes, hair, and cosmetics. Herbert Blumer, *Movies and Conduct* (New York: Macmillan, 1933): pp. 30, 31; Herbert Blumer and Philp M. Hauser, *Movies, Delinquency, and Crime* (New York: Macmillan, 1933), pp. 100–101, 115.

99. Creative Staff Meeting Minutes (May 24, 1932): 4. Information Center Records, box 3, folder: Lever Brothers 1916–1959, J. Walter Thompson Company Archives, Hartman Center for Advertising History, Duke University Library.

100. "Women's angle" and "Four girls speak out": Camay, advertisements, *Ladies' Home Journal* (April 1929); "something" and "I discovered a complexion secret in 24 basins of water": Camay, advertisement, *Ladies' Home Journal* (May 1929).

101. *J. Walter Thompson News Bulletin* (April 1929): 6. Newsletter Collection, J. Walter Thompson Company Archives, Hartman Center for Advertising History, Duke University Library.

102. Fox, *Mirror Makers*, p. 89.

103. *J. Walter Thompson News Bulletin* (April 1929): 3.

104. Ibid.

105. *Printers' Ink* (April 11, 1929): 115.

106. *J. Walter Thompson News Bulletin* (April 1929): 5.

107. Everett M. Rogers, *Diffusion of Innovations,* 3rd ed. (New York: Free Press, 1983).

108. Jung, "The Archetypes and the Collective Unconscious," part 1.

109. *Advertising and Selling* (March 31, 1932).

110. *Printers' Ink* (March 24, 1932).

111. Quoted in Fox, *The Mirror Makers*, p. 166.

112 Patricia Johnston, *Real Fantasies: Edward Steichen's Advertising Photography* (Berkeley: University of California Press, 1997), p. 217.

113. Goodrum and Dalrymple, *Advertising in America*, p. 73.

114. Creative Organization Staff Meeting (November 9, 1937): 7, JWT Staff

Meetings, March 1933 to March 1938, Meetings of Representatives, boxes 6, 7, 8, J. Walter Thompson Company Archives, Hartman Center for Advertising History, Duke University Library.

115. Creative Organization Staff Meeting (November 9, 1937): 7, JWT Staff Meetings, March 1933 to March 1938, Meetings of Representatives, boxes 6, 7, 8, J. Walter Thompson Company Archives, Hartman Center for Advertising History, Duke University Library.

116. "Adstrips": *Advertising & Selling* (May 11, 1933): 23.

117. Ibid., p. 55.

118. Creative Organization Staff Meeting (March 12, 1932): 1, JWT Staff Meetings, March 1932 to March 1933, Meetings of Representatives, box 5, J. Walter Thompson Company Archives, Hartman Center for Advertising History, Duke University Library.

119. Ibid.

120. Ibid.

121. *Printers' Ink* (January 13, 1938): 25.

122. *Advertising & Selling* (May 11, 1933): 23.

123. Palmolive, advertisements, 1938, Domestic advertisement collection, J. Walter Thompson Company Archives, Hartman Center for Advertising History, Duke University Library.

CHAPTER 6: SOAP, SEX, AND SOCIETY, 1920 TO 1940

1. *Printers' Ink* (October 14, 1937): 12.

2. Ibid.

3. "Purchasing agent": *Printers' Ink* (February 18, 1926): 2. On "80 to 85 percent," see *Printers' Ink* (February 18, 1926): 2; *Ladies' Home Journal* (May 1929): 35; and *Advertising and Selling* (February 2, 1933): 20.

4. "How It Was in Advertising: 1776–1976," in *Advertising Age* (Chicago: Crain Books, 1976), p. 31.

5. Here Marchand references *Who's Who in Advertising* (1931) and notes that the directory had included sketches of only 125 women but gave profiles of 5000 advertising men. See Roland Marchand, *Advertising the American Dream: Making Way for Modernity* (Berkeley: University of California Press, 1985), p. 33.

6. Charles Goodrum and Helen Dalrymple, *Advertising in America: The First 200 Years* (New York: Abrams, 1990), p. 38.

7. Christine Frederick, "Historical Introduction," in *Advertising Careers for Women*, ed. Blanche Clair and Dorothy Dignam (New York/London: Harper & Brothers Publishers, 1939), pp. xiii–xix. See also Cynthia M. Lont, *Women and Media: Content, Careers, and Criticism* (Belmont, Calif.: Wadsworth, 1995), p. 111–13.

8. M. M. McBride, *How to Be a Successful Advertising Woman* (New York: Whitlesey House, 1948), p. 203.

9. Ibid., p. 204.

10. "Contribution of Dorothy Dignam, Writer" in Helen Rosen Woodward, *It's an Art* (New York: Harcourt, Brace and Co., 1938), p. 214.

11. *Printers' Ink* (July 5, 1928): 76.

12. On copy addressed to women, typical of the period were two articles. From a woman's view, *Printers' Ink* (January 31, 1924): 105–10; *Printers' Ink* (November 18, 1926): 97–100. From a man's perspective, *Printer's Ink* (February 18, 1926). On copy addressed to men, *Printers' Ink* (July 24, 1924): 109–12.

13. Frederick, "Historical Introduction," pp. xiii–xix.

14. On Frances Maule as a suffragist, a note written by Helen Resor in Maule's personnel file recommended hiring her by highlighting her suffrage activities. Maule was a member of Heterodoxy in New York City; the group included feminist Charlotte Perkins Gilman, lawyer and social activist Crystal Eastman, and radical black leader and NAACP member Grace Neil Johnson. See Jennifer Scanlon, *Inarticulate Longings: The Ladies' Home Journal, Gender, and Promises of Consumer Culture* (New York: Routledge, 1995), pp. 187–89.

15. *J. Walter Thompson News Bulletin* (January 1924): 7. Newsletter Collection, J. Walter Thompson Company Archives, Hartman Center for Advertising History, Duke University Library.

16. Christine Frederick, *Selling Mrs. Consumer* (New York: Business Bourse, 1929), p. 51.

17. *J. Walter Thompson News Bulletin* (December 1924): 18–19. Newsletter Collection, J. Walter Thompson Company Archives, Hartman Center for Advertising History, Duke University Library. Also see "The Women Appeal," *Printers' Ink* (January 31, 1924): 105–10.

18. "Vocabulary": *Printers' Ink* (November 18, 1926): 97; "technically minded": 100.

19. *Printers' Ink* (November 15, 1928): 17–20.

20. Jackson Lears, *Fables of Abundance: A Cultural History of Advertising in America* (New York: Basic Books, 1994), p. 4.

21. Although Christine Frederick does not identify herself as a suffragist in *Selling Mrs. Consumer*, she makes several points that support the feminist doctrine. On equality, Frederick acknowledges that women are born "as second fiddle to man" (44), with "inferiority bred in her because of her subjugation by man" (48). On representations of women in mass media, Frederick criticizes advertising for using "pretty women as bait . . . the artificial doll type, for whom man, in his crass ignorance and uncritical susceptibility, so commonly 'falls'!" (349–50). Also, Frederick was a pioneering businesswoman for her time as founder and director of Applecroft Home Experiment Station, consultant to manufacturers on marketing home goods, home economics textbook author, and former household editor for *Ladies' Home Journal*. In 1911, she also founded the first women's advertising club in New York City, since

women could not attend the meetings of the New York Advertising Men's League. On the club, see Clair and Dignam, *Advertising Careers for Women* pp. xvi–xvii

22. Frederick, *Selling Mrs. Consumer*, p. 21.

23. In 1939, women spent an estimated $500 million on beauty aids. Elizabeth Colt Kidd, "How to Advertise Cosmetics and Toiletries," in *Advertising Careers for Women*, p. 87.

24. *Soap Gazette and Perfumer* (November 1937): 21.

25. "The Woman Appeal," *Printers' Ink* (January 31, 1924). For examples of the woman's viewpoint, see Carl A. Naether, *Advertising to Women* (New York: Prentice-Hall, 1928).

26. Kidd, "How to Advertise Cosmetics and Toiletries," p. 87–88.

27. Lois W. Banner, *American Beauty* (Chicago: University of Chicago Press, 1980).

28. Michael R. Solomon, *Consumer Behavior*, 4th ed. (Upper Saddle River, N.J.: Prentice-Hall, 1999), pp. 132.

29. On mediated gender images, see Fred Fejes, "Masculinity as Fact: A Review of Empirical Mass Communication Research on Masculinity" in *Men, Masculinity, and the Media*, ed. S. Craig (Newbury Park, Calif.: Sage, 1992), pp. 9–22. See also Ellen McCracken, *Decoding Women's Magazines: From Mademoiselle to Ms.* (New York: St. Martin's, 1993).

30. *J. Walter Thompson News Bulletin* (January 1924): 1–2, Newsletter Collection, J. Walter Thompson Company Archives, Hartman Center for Advertising History, Duke University Library. Also see "The Women Appeal," *Printers' Ink* (January 31, 1924): 105–10.

31. The home as a haven is an important theme of Christopher Lasch's *Haven in a Heartless World: The Family Besieged* (New York: Basic Books, 1977).

32. Kathy Peiss, *Hope in a Jar: The Making of America's Beauty Culture* (New York: Owl Books, 1999), p. 142.

33. "The Business Girl Knows," Palmolive, advertisement, *Photoplay* (November 1927).

34. *Advertising & Selling* (February 2, 1933): 20.

35. Frederick, *Selling Mrs. Consumer*, pp. 349–50.

36. "The Male Face," *Fortune* (May 1937).

37. *J. Walter Thompson News Bulletin* (December 1924): 16, Newsletter Collection, J. Walter Thompson Company Archives, Hartman Center for Advertising History, Duke University Library.

38. Fels-Naptha, advertisements: *Survey* (April 1928, July 1928, April 1931, and May 1934).

39. *Soap Gazette and Perfumer* (February 1, 1929): 44.

40. "Urges Lindbergh Bathtub," *New York Times*, June 24, 1927, p. 3.

41. Ibid.

42. *Advertising & Selling* (January 25, 1928): 23.

43. *Soap Gazette and Perfumer* (January 1, 1927): 18.

44. Representatives' Meeting (November 15, 1927): 1, Staff Meetings, 1927–1929, Meetings of Representatives, box 1, J. Walter Thompson Company Archives, Hartman Center for Advertising History, Duke University Library.

45. Suellen Hoy, *Chasing Dirt: The American Pursuit of Cleanliness* (New York: Basic Books, 1995), p. 142.

46. "Soapmakers Aim to Widen Market," *Advertising & Selling* (January 15, 1928): 74.

47. Vincent Vinikas, "Lustrum of the Cleanliness Institute, 1927–1932," *Journal of Social History* 22 (1989): 613–14.

48. Frederick, *Selling Mrs. Consumer*, pp. 110–11.

49. *Advertising & Selling* (January 25, 1928): 23.

50. *Soap Gazette and Perfumer* (August 1, 1927): 234.

51. Ibid., p. 235.

52. Platform of the Cleanliness Institute, in ibid., pp. 234–35.

53. "Take-A-Bath' Week Starts," *New York Times*, July 10, 1927, p. 7.

54. *Advertising & Selling* (January 24, 1928): 76.

55. *New York Times*, June 24, 1927, p. 3.

56. *Advertising & Selling* (January 15, 1928): 76.

57. *Soap and Perfumer Gazette* (January 1, 1928): 13.

58. Representatives' Meeting (November 15, 1927): 2, Staff Meetings, 1927–1929, Meetings of Representatives, box 1, J. Walter Thompson Company Archives, Hartman Center for Advertising History, Duke University Library.

59. Cleanliness Institute, advertisements. "Hoboes": *Advertising & Selling* (January 25, 1928): 23. "At 3 months": *Ladies' Home Journal* (October 1928). See also Representatives' Meeting (November 15, 1927): 1, Staff Meetings, 1927–1929, Meetings of Representatives, box 1, J. Walter Thompson Company Archives, Hartman Center for Advertising History, Duke University Library.

60. "What do the neighbors think of her children?" Cleanliness Institute, advertisement, *Ladies' Home Journal* (April 1928).

61. He had to fight himself hard to put it over," Cleanliness Institute, advertisement, *American Magazine* (February 1927).

62. "He had to fight himself hard to put it over," Cleanliness Institute, advertisement, *American Magazine* (February 1927). "If the wife": see Cleanliness Institute campaign, Representatives' Meeting (November 15, 1927), Staff Meetings, 1927–1929, Meetings of Representatives, box 1, J. Walter Thompson Company Archives, Hartman Center for Advertising History, Duke University Library.

63. "A kit for climbers," Cleanliness Institute, advertisement, *Ladies' Home Journal* (October 1928).

64. *Cleanliness Journal* (July 1927).

65. "Mental health": *Cleanliness Journal* (April 1932); "workers": ibid. (October 1931).

66. *Soap Gazette and Perfumer* (January 1, 1930): 1.

67. "As guardians of its health," Cleanliness Institute, advertisement, *Survey* (April 1, 1930)

68. *Soap Gazette and Perfumer* (January 1, 1930): 17.

69. Cleanliness Institute, advertisement, *American Magazine* (August 28, 1928): 149.

70. Newell-Emett Company, *Coupon Returns: One Advertiser's Experience* (New York: Newell-Emmett, 1932), pp. 5–6, 60–61.

71. Cleanliness Institute, "The Book About Baths," booklet (1930), 60, Soap, folder: Cleanliness Institute, p. 93. Warshaw Collection of Business Americana, Archives Center, National Museum of American History, Smithsonian Institution Collection.

72. Ibid., inside front cover.

73. Radio talk shows: Hoy, *Chasing Dirt*, p. 148; Vincent Vinikas, "Lustrum," in *Soft Soap, Hard Sell: American Hygiene in the Age of Advertisement* (Ames: University of Iowa Press, 1992), pp. 628–29.

74. *Soap Gazette and Perfumer* (August 8, 1931): 5.

75. Grace T. Hallock, *A Tale of Soap and Water: The Historical Progress of Cleanliness* (New York: Cleanliness Institute, 1928), p. 90.

76. *Soap Gazette and Perfumer* (November 1, 1927): 333–34.

77. Vinikas, "Lustrum," p. 619.

78. "Carry on at Home," Lifebuoy advertisement, 1933.

79. Editorial, *Soap Gazette and Perfumer* (August 1, 1934).

80. Quoted in Sydney Head and Christopher Sterling, *Broadcasting in America: A Survey of Electronic Media* (Boston: Houghton, 1987), p. 67.

81. Stephen Fox, *The Mirror Makers: A History of Advertising and Its Creators* (New York: Vintage, 1983), p. 159.

82. Procter & Gamble, *Ivory 75* (Cincinnati: Procter & Gamble Company, 1954), p. 35.

83. David Powers Cleary, *Great American Brands: The Success Formulas That Made Them Famous* (New York: Fairchild Publications, 1981), p. 177.

84. *Advertising and Selling* (October 13, 1932): 28.

85. Palmolive: Irving Settle, *A Pictorial History of Radio* (New York: Grosset, 1960), p. 59; Lux: ibid., pp. 102–104.

86. Representatives' Meeting (November 9, 1937): 1–4, Staff Meetings, 1935–1938, Meetings of Representatives, box 6-8, J. Walter Thompson Company Archives, Hartman Center for Advertising History, Duke University Library.

87. *Advertising Age* (January 13, 1941).

88. *Soap Gazette and Perfumer* (April 1939): 13–14.

CHAPTER 7: WHITE SOAP AND BLACK CONSUMER CULTURE

1. African Americans did not call themselves "African Americans" in the nineteenth or early twentieth centuries. As a group, they called themselves "Negro," "colored people," or "Colored Americans," as evidenced in the black press of the period.

2. On rights of African Americans, see Jay A. Sigler, *Civil Rights in America: 1500 to the Present* (Detroit: Gale, 1998), pp. 87–128.

3. In 1910, the city council of Baltimore approved the first ordinance designating the boundaries of African American and white neighborhoods; other cities followed. Starting in 1915, rulings in the U.S. Supreme Court began to chip away at the Jim Crow laws. In 1915, the Supreme Court supported the position that the Oklahoma law denying the right to vote to any citizen whose ancestors had not been enfranchised in 1860 was unconstitutional. In 1917, the Supreme Court declared the Louisville, Kentucky, ordinance and all other forms of housing segregation to be unconstitutional. But the first major blow against the Jim Crow system of racial segregation was the Supreme Court decision in 1954, which declared segregation in the public schools unconstitutional. See ibid., pp. xvi–xvii. On the history of America's civil rights movement, see also Jack M. Bloom, *Class, Race, and the Civil Rights Movement* (Bloomington: Indiana University Press, 1987); and Robert Weisbrot, *Freedom Bound: A History of America's Civil Rights Movement* (New York: Norton, 1990).

4. Throughout the 1900s and 1910s, the Chicago newspaper prominently reported the accomplishments of African American women in society columns. In the 1920s, black magazines and newspapers set out to highlight African American women and emphasized what they termed racial beauty, printing photographs of not only socially prominent women but also women who had sent in their pictures. Typical of the period were the *Messenger* (August 1924): 248, and *Half-Century* (June 1919).

5. On the history of African American business in America, see Shelley Green and Paul Pryde, *Black Entrepreneurship in America* (New Brunswick, N.J.: Transaction Publishers, 1990); Kilolo Kijakazi, *African American Economic Development and Small Business Ownership* (New York: Garland, 1997); and Juliet E. K. Walker, *The History of Black Business in America: Capitalism, Race, Entrepreneurship* (New York: Macmillan Library Reference USA; London: Prentice Hall International, 1998).

6. Robert Higgs, *Competition and Coercion: Blacks in the American Economy, 1865–1914* (Cambridge: Cambridge University Press, 1977), pp. 97, 100.

7. Ibid.

8. Herbert J. Bass, George A. Bilias, and Emma Jones Lapsanky, *American and Americans* (Morristown, N.J.: Silver Burdett Company, 1983), vol. 2, p. 150.

9. "Manufacturing Toilet Articles: A Big Negro Business," *Messenger* (December 1923): 937.

10. Ibid.

11. St. Clair Drake and Horace Cayton, *Black Metropolis* (New York: Harper & Row, Torchbook Edition, 1945), pp. 430–69.

12. "Beauty Culture and Colored People," *Messenger* (July 1918): 26.

13. Letter to Editor, *Colored American* (August 12, 1837), Accessible Archives, item #2721, University of Delaware.

14. "For the Colored American. Who would be loved?" *Colored American* (16 March 1839), Accessible Archives, item #4775, University of Delaware.

15. No provision of cleanliness: "Fear of Slaves on Plantations," *North Star* (April 26, 1850); "want of": "Woman-Whipping on Plantations," *North Star* (May 10, 1850); Accessible Archives, item #21914, University of Delaware.

16. Edward H. Beardsley, *A History of Neglect: Health Care for Blacks and Mill Workers in the Twentieth-Century South* (Knoxville: University of Tennessee Press, 1987), p. 12.

17. Frank G. Bruner, "Racial Differences," *Psychological Bulletin* 11 (1914): 384–86. See also George O. Ferguson, "The Psychology of the Negro—An Experimental Study," *Archives of Psychology* 36 (1916): 1–138; Ida Mitchell, Isabel R. Rosanoff, and Aaron Rosanoff. "A Study of Association in Negro Children," *Psychological Review* 26 (1919): 354–59.

18. Stephen Jay Gould, *The Mismeasure of Man* (New York: Norton, 1981). On the origins of racial stereotypes, see Jordan Winthrop, *White over Black: American Attitudes Toward the Negro, 1550–1812* (New York: Norton, 1977).

19. Dreydoppel Soap, *Light and Shade*, booklet, (Philadelphia, 1892), 60: Soap, box 209, folder: Dreydoppel. Warshaw Collection of Business Americana, Archives Center, National Museum of American History, Smithsonian Institution Collection.

20. "Better Health and Better Homes for Negroes by Negroes," *Survey* (May 15, 1915): 158–59. See also Beardsley, *History of Neglect*, pp. 102–103.

21. Booker T. Washington, *Up from Slavery: An Autobiography* (New York: Doubleday, Page, 1901), p. 58.

22. *Southern Workman* (May 1875): 36.

23. Carl N. Degler, *At Odds: Women and the Family in America from the Revolution to the Present* (New York: Oxford University Press, 1980)

24. Beardsley, *History of Neglect*, pp. 104–12.

25. Nannie H. Burroughs, "Not Color but Character," *Voice of the Negro* (July 1904): 277.

26. Kathy Peiss, *Hope in a Jar: The Making of America's Beauty Culture* (New York: Owl Books, 1999), p. 205

27. "Rough Sketches: A Study of the Features of the New Negro Women," *Voice of the Negro* (August 1904): 325.

28. On displays of African American bodies in beauty contests and fashion shows, see Shane White and Graham White, *Stylin': African American Expressive Culture from Its Beginnings to the Zoot Suit* (New York: Cornell University Press, 1998), pp. 180–219.

29. The *Defender* had become the largest-selling African American newspaper in the United States by World War I. See James R. Grossman, *Land of Hope: Chicago, Black Southerners, and the Great Migration* (Chicago: University of Chicago Press, 1989), p. 81.

30. Higgs, *Competition and Coercion*, p. 113.

31. Ibid., p. 110.

32. James D. Anderson, *The Education of Blacks in the South, 1860–1935* (Chapel Hill: University of North Carolina Press, 1988).

33. "Exalting Negro Womanhood," *Messenger* (January 1924): 7.

34. Alain Locke, ed., *The New Negro: Voices of the Harlem Renaissance* (1925; New York: Antheneum, 1992), p. 15.

35. David Levering Lewis, *When Harlem Was in Vogue* (1981; reprint, New York: Oxford University Press, 1989), p. 117.

36. Melville J. Herskovits, "The Negro and American Tradition," in *The New Negro*, p. 366.

37. Burroughs, "Not Color but Character," p. 277.

38. Guy B. Johnson, "Newspaper Advertisements and Negro Culture," *Journal of Social Forces* (1924–1925): 706–709; Paul K. Edwards, *The Southern Negro as a Consumer* (New York: Prentice Hall, 1932), pp. 185–87.

39. Chandler Owen, "Good Looks Supremacy," *Messenger* (March 1924): 81.

40. "Negro Incomes and How They Are Spent," *Sales Management* (June 15, 1945).

41. Stanley Lieberson, *A Piece of the Pie: Blacks and White Immigrants Since 1880* (Berkeley: University of California Press, 1980), pp. 381–83.

42. "Selling to Harlem," *Advertising & Selling* (October 11, 1928): 17.

43. Elise Johnson McDougald, "The Task of Negro Womanhood," in *The New Negro*, p. 369.

44. A full account of a remarkable group of black entrepreneurs in the cosmetics business, including Madame C. J. Walker, Annie Turbo Malone, Anthony Overton, and Claude Barnett, is contained in Peiss, *Hope in a Jar*. Also see White and White, *Stylin'*, for an interpretation of two centuries of black style as dress, hair, body language, and dance.

45. A'Lelia Perry Bundles, *Madame C. J.Walker* (Philadelphia: Chelsea House Publishers, 1991), p. 38.

46. "Exalting Negro Womanhood," *Messenger* (January 1924): 7.

47. "History of the Mme. C. J. Walker Mfg. Co." (n.d.), Mme. C. J. Walker Papers, box 12, folder 7, Indiana Historical Society.

48. "You, too, may be a fascinating beauty," Walker Mftg., advertisement, Mme. C. J. Walker Papers, box 11, folder 6, Indiana Historical Society.

49. "Some Problems You May Meet," company newsletter, *Walker News* (February 1930): 2, Mme. C. J. Walker Papers, Indiana Historical Society.

50. Bundles, *Madame C. J. Walker*, p. 39.

51. Phil A. Jones to F. B. Ransom (April 22, 1918), Mme. C. J. Walker Papers, box 11, folder 4, Indiana Historical Society.

52. "A Million Eyes Turned Upon It Daily," Walker Mftg., advertisement, *Crisis* (1919).

53. "Glorifying Our Womanhood," Walker Mftg., advertisement, *Messenger* (1925).

54. "Soap and Water and the Skin," company newsletter, *Walker News* (December 28): 3, Mme. C. J. Walker Papers, Indiana Historical Society.

55. "Anthony Overton," obituary, *Pittsburgh Courier*, August 20, 1929.

56. "Negro Business," *Messenger* (October 1927): 321.

57. "Beauty Hints," *Half-Century* (August 1916): 14.

58. High-Brown Soap, advertisement, *Half-Century* (August 1916): 14.

59. Anthony Overton, *Encyclopedia of Colored People*, Overton Hygienic company publication (1921), p. 11.

60. "Anthony Overton," obituary, *Pittsburgh Courier*, August 20, 1929.

61. Commission on Chicago Historical and Architectural Landmarks, *Black Metropolis Historic District* (March 7, 1984), p. 15, Chicago Historical Society.

62. Kashmir Chemical company, *Nile Queen for Hair and Skin*, brochure (1919): 1, Claude A. Barnett Papers, box 262, folder 3, Chicago Historical Society.

63. Ibid., pp. 3, 9.

64. "From boudoir to beach," Walker Mftg., advertisement, *Messenger* (September 1924).

65. White and White, *Stylin'*, p. 209

66. Edwards, *The Southern Negro as a Consumer*, p. 242.

67. Ibid., pp. 11–12.

68. "Plough Chemical Repackages Entire Line as 1929 Campaign Breaks," *Sales Management* (April 13, 1929): 73.

69. Ibid.

70. "Rough, dark skin," Black and White, advertisement, *Pittsburgh Courier*, August 4, 1928.

71. Attachment, S. Holsey to Barnett, February 24, 1933, CAB, box 251, folder: Beauty Products Correspondence, Chicago Historical Society.

72. "Plough Co. Opens $5,000,000 Plant," Associated Negro Press, News Release (June 25, 1951), Claude A. Barnett Papers, box 251, folder "Beauty Products News Clippings," item 41.120, Chicago Historical Society.

73. F. B. Ransom to Kashmir Chemical Company, March 20, 1920, Claude A. Barnett Papers, box 262, folder 4, Chicago Historical Society.

74. Edwards, *The Southern Negro as a Consumer*, pp. 185–87.

75. W.B. Ziff Co., *The Negro Market*, booklet (1932), p. 24, Claude Barnett Papers, box 131, folder 5, Chicago Historical Society.

76. Ibid., pp. 16, 18.

77. Ibid., p. 37.

78. Peiss, *Hope in a Jar*, p. 237.

AFTERWORD

1. *Soap Gazette and Perfumer* (April 1939): 13.

2. Ibid.

3. Ibid., p. 14.

4. Jib Fowles, *Advertising and Popular Culture* (Thousand Oaks, Calif.: Sage, 1976), p. 47.

5. In 1934, the FTC filed complaints against Lifebuoy and Lux soap alleging false and deceptive advertising, issuing orders for these soap advertisers to drop many of their most popular claims of recent years. Lifebuoy had to drop its basic B.O. theme. According to clinical tests and scientific opinion, the single application of Lifebuoy soap or any other soap could not effect the permanent elimination of perspiration or any body odor. Also, the ability of Lux Toilet Soap to "keep skin flawless" could not be relied upon to keep the skin "clear" without reasonable evidence, unless the ad limited the promise to such conditions as were due to dirt, cosmetic residue, epithelial debris, or foreign materials. See Minutes of the Meeting of the Young Women's Apprentice Group (October 7, 1938); Staff Meetings, box 6, J. Walter Thompson Company Archives, Hartman Center for Advertising History, Duke University Library. See also "Rigid Rules on Soap Advertising," *Soap Gazette and Perfumer* (August 1938): 9–10.

6. David Riesman, Reuel Denney, and Nathan Glazer, *The Lonely Crowd: A Study of Changing American Character* (New Haven, Conn.: Yale University Press, 1950).

7. Warren Susman, "Personality and the Making of Twentieth-Century Culture," in *New Directions in American Intellectual History*, ed. John Higman and Paul K. Conklin (Baltimore: Johns Hopkins University Press, 1979), pp. 212, 221–22.

8. Grant McCracken, "Culture and Consumption: A Theoretical Account of the Structure and Movement of the Cultural Meaning of Consumer Goods," *Journal of Consumer Research* (June 1986): 71–81.

9. *Business Week* (January 27, 1992): 84.

10. Diane Barthel, *Putting on Appearances: Gender and Attractiveness* (Philadelphia: Temple Press, 1988).

11. Jane Trachtenberg, "It's Become Part of Our Culture," *Forbes* (March 23, 1987): 134–35.

12. For a summary of Colgate-Palmolive's market research report, "Body Care Habits and Practices in the United States," see *Chicago Sun-Times*, September 26, 1993, p. 61, Medlife.

13. American Standard Bathroom Study [online], http://www.us.amstd.com/scripts/trade/update [August 1, 1999].

14. On cleanliness in Japan, see "Cleaning Up on Hygiene Mania," *Los Angeles Times*, November 21, 1996 p. 1, Part A, Foreign Desk; "The Dirt on Disinfectant," *Newsweek* (October 12, 1998): 56, Pacific Edition.

A WORD ABOUT SOURCES

1. Henry Vance Davis, "A Critique of the Influence of the Socioeconomic Environment on the Black Press, 1900–1928," *Black Scholar* (fall 1992): 19.

Bibliography

SPECIAL COLLECTIONS

Accessible Archives, University of Delaware.

Claude A. Barnett Papers, Chicago Historical Society.

D'Arcy, Masius, Benton & Bowles, John W. Hartman Center for Sales, Advertising, and Marketing History, Duke University.

Foote Cone Belding Collection, State Historical Society of Wisconsin, Madison.

Hagley Library, Hagley Center for the History of Business, Technology, and Society, Wilmington, Delaware.

J. Walter Thompson Company Archives, John W. Hartman Center for Sales Advertising, and Marketing History, Duke University.

Madame C. J. Walker Papers, Indiana Historical Society, Indianapolis, Indiana

N. W. Ayer Collection, National Museum of History, Smithsonian Institution, Washington, D.C.

Outdoor Advertising Association, John W. Hartman Center for Sales, Advertising,and Marketing History, Duke University.

Warshaw Collection of Business Americana, National Museum of History, Smithsonian Institution, Washington, D.C.

Winterthur Library, Wilmington, Delaware.

Joseph Downs Collection of Manuscripts and Printed Ephemera Collection, the Winterthur Library, Wilmington, Delaware.

PERIODICALS

Advertising & Selling, 1911–1940
Judicious Advertising, 1885–1910
Printers' Ink Weekly, 1890–1940
Printers' Ink Monthly, 1890–1940
Profitable Advertising, 1891–1909
Soap Gazette and Perfumer, 1890–1940

BLACK PRESS

Chicago Defender, national edition, 1905–1940
Colored American magazine, 1900–1909
Half-Century magazine, 1900–1909
Messenger, 1917–1928
North Star, 1807–1891
Pittsburgh Courier, national edition, 1910–1940
Voice of the Negro, 1904–1906

WORKS CITED

Published before 1950

Allen, Mary Wood. *What a Young Woman Ought to Know*. Philadelphia: Vir Publishing Co., 1905.

Baird, James. *The Management of Health: A Manual of Home and Personal Hygiene*. London: Virtue & Co., 1867.

Beecher, Catherine E. *A Treatise on Domestic Economy*. Boston: Marsh, Calipen, Lyon, and Webb, 1841.

Bennett, Helen Christine. *American Women in Civic Work*. New York: Dodd, Mead, 1915.

Blumer, Herbert. *Movies and Conduct*. New York: Macmillan, 1933.

Blumer, Herbert, and Philip M. Hauser. *Movies, Delinquency, and Crime*. New York: Macmillan, 1933.

Bruner, Frank G. "Racial Differences," *Psychological Bulletin* 11 (1914): 384–86.

Burroughs, Nannie S. "Not Color but Character." *Voice of the Negro* (July 1904).

Burtt, Harold Ernest. *Psychology of Advertising*. New York: Houghton, 1938.

Clair, Blanche, and Dorothy Dignam, eds. *Advertising Careers for Women*. New York/London: Harper & Brothers Publishers, 1939.

Clark, Sir James. *The Ladies Guide to Beauty*. New York: Dick & Fitzgerald, 1858.

Drake, St. Clair, and Horace Cayton. *Black Metropolis: A Study of Negro Life in a Northern City*. New York: Harper & Row, Torchbook Edition, 1945.

Edwards, Paul K. *The Southern Negro as a Consumer*. New York: Prentice-Hall, 1932.

Ferguson, George O. "The Psychology of the Negro—An Experimental Study," *Archives of Psychology* 36 (1916): 1–138.

Frederick, Mrs. Christine. *Selling Mrs. Consumer*. New York: Business Bourse, 1929.

———. "Historical Introduction." In *Advertising Careers for Women*, edited by Blanche Clair and Dorothy Dignam. New York/London: Harper & Brothers Publishers, 1939.

Freese, John Henry. *Aristotle with an English Translation: The Art of Rhetoric*. London: W. Heinemann; Cambridge, Mass.: Harvard University Press, 1926.

Freud, Sigmund. *Introductory Lectures on Psycho-Analysis*. New York: Carlton House, 1933.

Gunn, John. *Gunn's Domestic Medicine*. 1830. Reprint, Knoxville: University of Tennessee Press, 1986.

Hallock, Grace T. *A Tale of Soap and Water: The Historical Progress of Cleanliness*. New York: Cleanliness Institute, 1928.

Harland, Marion. *The Modern Family Receipt Book: Containing Great Variety of Valuable Receipts Arranged*. London, 1833.

———. *Common Sense in the Household: A Manual of Practical Housewifery*. New York: Charles Scribner's Sons, 1871.

Herskovits, Melville J. "The Negro and American Tradition." In *The New Negro: Voices of the Harlem Renaissance*, edited by Alain Locke. 1925. Reprint, New York: Antheneum, 1992.

Holland, Marion. *Eve's Daughters or Common Sense for Maid, Wife and Mother*. New York: J. R. Anderson & Henry S. Allen, 1882.

Johnson, Guy B. "Newspaper Advertisements and Negro Culture." *Journal of Social Forces* (1924–1925): 706–709.

Jordan, David Starr. "The White Man's Burden," from "A Blind Man's Holiday." In *Imperial Democracy*. New York: D. Appleton and Co., 1899.

Kidd, Elizabeth Colt. "How to Advertise Cosmetics and Toiletries." In *Advertising Careers for Women*, edited by Blanche Clair and Dorothy Dignam. New York/London: Harper & Brothers Publishers, 1939.

Kilburn, C. L. *Notes on Preparing Stores for the United States Army; and on the Care of the Same, etc., with few rules for detecting adulteration*. 2d ed. Cincinnati: Steam Printer and Stationer: 1963.

Lamb, Ruth deForest. *Chamber of Horrors: The Truth About Food and Drugs*. New York: Grossett & Dunlap, 1936.

Lémery, N. *New Curiosities in Art and Nature: or, A Collection of the Most Valuable Secrets in All Arts and Sciences*. London: Printed for John King, 1711.

Locke, Alain, ed. *The New Negro: Voices of the Harlem Renaissance*. 1925. New York: Antheneum, 1992.

Lyman, Abbott. *The House and Home, a Practical Book*. 2 vols. New York: Charles Scribner's Sons, 1896.

Lynd, Robert Staughton. *Middletown*. New York: Harcourt, Brace and Co., 1929.

McBride, M. M. *How to Be a Successful Advertising Woman*. New York: Whitlesey House, 1948.

McDougald, Elise Johnson, "The Task of Negro Womanhood," *The New Negro: Voices of the Harlem Renaissance*, edited by Alain Locke. 1925. Reprint, New York: Antheneum, 1992.

Mitchell, Ida, Isabel R. Rosanoff, and Aaron Rosanoff. "A Study of Association in Negro Children." *Psychologal Review* 26 (1919): 354–59.

Moody, Eleazar. *The School of Good Manners*. 1715.

Naether, Carl A. *Advertising to Women*. New York: Prentice-Hall, 1928.

National Markets and National Advertising. New York: Crowell, 1929.

Owen, Chandler. "Good Looks Supremacy." *Messenger* (March 1924).

Pancoast, S. *The Ladies Medical Guide*. Philadelphia: John E. Potter & Co., 1859.

Platt, Sir Hugh. *Delightes for Ladies*. 1609. Reprint, Herrin, Ill.: Trovillion Press, 1939

Printers' Ink Fifty Years. New York: Printers' Ink Publishing Company, 1938.

Presbrey, Frank. *The History and Development of Advertising*. Garden City, N.Y.: Doubleday, Doran & Co., 1929.

Revised United States Army Regulations of 1861. With an Appendix containing the Changes and Laws Affecting Army Regulations and Articles of War to June 25, 1863. Washington, D.C.: Government Printing Office, 1863.

Reynolds, Reginald. *Cleanliness and Godliness*. New York: Doubleday and Co., 1946.

Richardson, Samuel. *Sir Charles Grandison* (1753–54).

Riesman, David, Reuel Denney, and Nathan Glazer. *The Lonely Crowd: A Study of Changing American Character*. New Haven: Yale University Press, 1950.

Simmel, George. "Fashion." *International Quarterly* 10 (1904): 130–55.

Thomas, J. *The Book of Health & Beauty, or the Toiletries of Rank and Fashion*. London, 1837.

Tomes, Robert. *The Bazar Book of Decorum: The Care of the Person, Manners, Etiquette and Ceremonials*. New York: Harper & Bros., 1877.

Valuable Secrets in Arts and Trades: Or, Approved Directions from the Best Artists, Containing Upward of One thousand Approved Receipts. London: Printed for J. Barker and J. Scatherd, circa 1797.

Veblen, Thorstein. *The Theory of the Leisure Class*. 1899. Reprint, New York: A. M. Kelly, 1965.

Washington, Booker T. *Up from Slavery: An Autobiography*. New York: Doubleday, Page, 1901.

Webster, Thomas, and Mrs. Parkes. *The American Family Encyclopedia of Useful Knowledge*. New York: Derby & Jackson, 1859.

Wesley, John. "Sermon XCII—On Dress." In *Sermons on Several Occasions*. Vol. 2. 1788. Reprint, New York, 1829.

White, Martha E. D. "The Work of the Woman's Club." *Atlantic Monthly* (May 1904): 614–15.

Wilcox, Estelle Woods. *Practical Housekeeping: A Careful Compilation of Tried and Approved Recipes.* Minneapolis: Buckeye Publishing Co., 1883.

Woodwarol, Helen Rosen. *It's an Art.* New York: Harcourt, Brace and Co., 1938.

Published after 1950

Aarens, William F. *Contemporary Advertising.* 7th ed. Burr Ridge, Ill.: Irwin McGraw-Hill, 1999.

Advertising Age, eds. *How It Was in Advertising: 1776–1976.* Chicago: Crain Books, 1976.

———. *Procter & Gamble: The House That Ivory Built.* Lincolnwood, Ill.: NTC Business Books, 1988.

American Pharmaceutical Association. *Pharmacy Through the Ages.* Washington, D.C.: APA, 1996.

Anderson, James D. *The Education of Blacks in the South, 1860–1935.* Chapel Hill: University of North Carolina Press, 1988.

Armstrong, Ellis L., Michael Robinson, and Suellen M. Hoy, eds. *The History of Public Works in the United States, 1776–1976.* Chicago: American Public Works Association, 1976.

Banner, Lois W. *American Beauty.* Chicago: University of Chicago Press, 1980.

Banks, Joseph A. *Prosperity and Parenthood: A Study of Family Planning among the Victorian Middle Classes.* London: Routledge & Paul, 1954.

Barthel, Diane. *Putting on Appearances: Gender and Attractiveness.* Philadelphia: Temple University Press, 1988.

Bass, Herbert J., George A. Billias, and Emma Jones Lapsanky. *America and Americans.* Vol. 2. Morristown, N.J.: Silver Burdett Company, 1983.

Beardsley, Edward H. *A History of Neglect: Health Care for Blacks and Mill Workers in the Twentieth-Century South.* Knoxville: University of Tennessee Press, 1987.

Belk, Russell W. "Possessions and the Extended Self." *Journal of Consumer Research* (September 1988): 139–68.

Belk, Russell W., Melanie Wallendorf, and John F. Sherry. "The Sacred and Profane in Consumer Behavior: Theodicy on the Odyssey." *Journal of Consumer Research* (June 1989): 1–38.

Blair, Karen J. *The Clubwoman as Feminist: True Womanhood Redefined, 1868–1914.* New York: Holmes & Meier, 1980.

Bloom, Jack M. *Class, Race, and the Civil Rights Movement.* Bloomington: Indiana University Press, 1987.

Boorstin, Daniel J. *The Americans: The Democratic Experience.* New York: Vintage, 1973.

Booth, Dottie. *Nature Calls: The History, Lore, and Charm of the Outhouse.* Berkeley, Calif.: Ten Speed Press, 1998.

Braeman, John, ed. *Change and Continuity in Twentieth Century America: The 1920s.* Columbus: Ohio State University Press, 1968.

Briefer, Gert H., ed. *Theory and Practice in American Medicine: Historical Studies from the Journal of the History of Medicine & Allied Sciences.* New York: Science History Publications, 1976.

Bloom, Jack. M. *Class, Race, and the Civil Rights Movement.* Bloomington: Indiana University Press, 1987.

Bundles, A'Lelia Perry. *Madame C. J. Walker.* Philadelphia: Chelsea House Publishers, 1991.

Bushman, Richard L. *Refinement of American Persons, Houses, Cities.* New York: Knopf, Random House, 1992.

Bushman, Richard L., and Claudia L. Bushman. "The Early History of Cleanliness in America." *Journal of American History* (March 1988).

Carson, Gerald. *The Old Country Store.* New York: Oxford University Press, 1954.

Carson, Mina. *Settlement Folk: Social Thought and the American Settlement Movement, 1885–1930.* Chicago: University of Chicago Press, 1990.

Cawelti, John G. *Adventure, Mystery, and Romance: Formula Stories as Art and Popular Culture.* Chicago: University of Chicago Press, 1976.

Cleary, David Powers. *Great American Brands: The Success Formulas That Made Them Famous.* New York: Fairchild Publications, 1981.

Cogan, Frances B. *All-American Girl: The Ideal of Real Womanhood in Mid-Nineteenth-Century America.* Athens: University of Georgia Press, 1989.

Commission on Chicago Historical and Architectural Landmarks. *Black Metropolis Historic District.* 1984.

Crocker, Ruth Hutchinson. *Social Work and Social Order: The Settlement Movement in Two Industrial Cities, 1889–1930.* Urbana: University of Illinois Press, 1992.

Daniel, Clifton, ed. *Chronicle of America.* Mount Kisco, N.Y.: Chronicle Publications, 1989.

Davis, Henry Vance. "A Critique of the Influence of the Socioeconomic Environment on the Black Press, 1900–1928," *Black Scholar* (fall 1992): 17–28.

Degler, Carl N. *At Odds: Women and the Family in America from the Revolution to the Present.* New York: Oxford University Press, 1980.

Dempsey, Mike, ed. *Bubbles: Early Advertising Art from A. & F. Pears Ltd.* London: Fontana, 1978.

Douglas, Mary. *Purity and Danger: An Analysis of Concepts of Pollution and Taboo.* New York: Praeger, 1966.

Douglas, Mary, and Baron Isherwood. *The World of Goods.* New York: Basic Books, 1979.

D'Souza, Giles, and Ram C. Rao. "Can Repeating an Advertisement More Frequently Than the Competition Affect Brand Performance in a Mature Market?" *Journal of Marketing* (April 1995): 32–42.

Erwin, Paul F. *With Lotions of Love.* Cincinnati: Andrew Jergens Company, 1965.

Essoe, Gabe, and Raymond Lee. *DeMille: The Man and His Pictures.* New York: Castle Books, 1970.

Fagan, Garrett G. *Bathing in Public in the Roman World.* Ann Arbor: University of Michigan Press, 1999.

Fejes, Fred. "Masculinity as Fact: A Review of Empirical Mass Communication Research on Masculinity." In *Men, Masculinity, and the Media,* edited by S. Craig. Newbury Park, Calif.: Sage, 1992.

Fieldhouse, David Kenneth. *Unilever Overseas: The Anatomy of a Multinational 1895–1965.* London: Croom Helen; Stanford, Calif.: Hoover Institution Press, 1978.

Fish, Stanley. *IsThere a Text in this Class? The Authority of Interpretive Communities.* Cambridge, Mass.: Harvard University Press, 1980.

Fishburn, Katherine. *Women in Popular Culture: A Reference Guide.* Westport, Conn.: Greenwood Press, 1982.

Foster, David R. *The Story of Colgate-Palmolive: One Hundred and Sixty-Nine Years of Progress.* New York: Newcomen Society in North America, 1975.

Fox, Stephen. *The Mirror Makers: A History of Advertising and Its Creators.* New York: Vintage, 1983.

Fowles, Jib. *Advertising and Popular Culture.* Thousand Oaks, Calif.: Sage Publications, 1976.

Garland, Robert. *Daily Life of the Ancient Greeks.* Westport, Conn.: Greenwood Press, 1998.

Garvey, Ellen Gruber. *The Adman in the Parlor: Magazines and the Gendering of Consumer Culture, 1880s to 1890s.* New York: Oxford University Press, 1996.

Gere, Ann Ruggles. *Intimate Practices: Literacy and Cultural Work in U.S. Women's Clubs, 1880–1920.* Urbana: University of Illinois Press, 1997.

Goetz, Hans-Werner. *Life in the Middle Ages: from the Seventh to the Thirteenth Century.* Notre Dame, Ind.: University of Notre Dame Press, 1993.

Goodman, Susan. "Simple Story of Personal Hygiene." *Current Health* (January 1992).

Goodrum, Charles, and Helen Dalrymple. *Advertising in America: The First 200 Years.* New York: Abrams, 1990.

Gould, Stephen Jay. *The Mismeasure of Man.* New York: Norton, 1981.

Green, Harvey. *Fit for America: Health, Fitness, Sport, and American Society.* New York: Pantheon, 1986.

———. *Light of the Home: An Intimate View of the Lives of Women in Victorian America.* New York: Pantheon, 1983.

Green, Shelley, and Paul Pryde. *Black Entrepreneurship in America.* New Brunswick, N.J.: Transaction Publishers, 1990.

Grossman, James R. *Land of Hope: Chicago, Black Southerners, and the Great Migration.* Chicago: University of Chicago Press, 1989.

Halttunen, Karen. *Confidence Men, Painted Women: A Study of Middle-Class Culture in America, 1830–1870.* New Haven, Conn.: Yale University Press, 1982.

Hansen, William B., and Irwin Altman. "Decorating Personal Places: A Descriptive Analysis." *Environment and Behavior* (December 1976): 491–504.

Head, Sydney, and Christoper Sterling. *Broadcasting in America: A Survey of Electronic Media*. Boston: Houghton, 1987.

Herskovits, Melville J. "The Negro and American Tradition." In *The New Negro*, edited by Alain Locke. 1925. New York: Antheneum, 1992.

———. *Cultural Anthropology*. New York: Knopf, 1963.

Higgs, Robert. *Competition and Coercion: Blacks in the American Economy, 1865–1914*. Cambridge: Cambridge University Press, 1977.

Highman, Charles. *Cecil B DeMille*. New York: Scribner's Sons, 1973.

Hill, May Brawley. "Making a Virtue of Necessity: Decorative American Privies." *The Magazine Antiques* (August 1998).

Holmberg, Carl B. *Sexualities and Popular Culture*. Thousand Oaks, Calif.: Sage Publications, 1998.

Hopkins, Claude. *Scientific Advertising*. 1927. Reprint, Lincolnwood, Ill.: NTC Books, 1986.

Hoy, Suellen. *Chasing Dirt: The American Pursuit of Cleanliness*. New York: Basic Books, 1995.

Hunt, John A. "A Short History of Soap." *Pharmaceutical Journal* 263, no. 7076 (1999): 985–989.

James, Edward T., Janet Wilson James, and Paul S. Boyers, eds. *Notable Women, 1607–1950*. Cambridge: Harvard University Press, 1971.

Janello, Amy, and Brennon Jones. *The American Magazine*. New York: Henry N. Abrams, 1991.

Johnston, Patricia. *Real Fantasies: Edward Steichen's Advertising Photography*. Berkeley: University of California Press, 1997.

Jones, Duane. *Ads, Women and Boxtops*. Pleasantville, N.Y.: Printers' Ink Books, 1955.

Jones, Robert. "The Basics of Making Soap." *Countryside and Small Stock Journal* (March 1995): 38.

Jung, Carl G. "The Archetypes and the Collective Unconscious." In *Collected Works*, edited by H. Read, M. Fordham, and G. Adler. Princeton: Princeton University Press, 1959.

Kane, Joseph N. *Famous First Facts*. New York: Wilson 1950.

Kijakazi, Kilolo. *African-American Economic Development and Small Business Ownership*. New York: Garland, 1997.

LaTour, Michael S., and Tom L. Henthorne. "Ethical Judgements of Sexual Appeals in Print Advertising." *Journal of Advertising* (September 1994): 81–90.

Laird, Pamela. *Advertising and Progress: American Business and the Rise of Consumer Marketing*. Baltimore: Johns Hopkins University Press, 1998.

Larkin, Jack. *The Reshaping of Everyday Life, 1790–1840*. New York: Harper & Row, 1998.

Lasch, Christopher. *Haven in a Heartless World: The Family Besieged.* New York: Basic Books, 1977.

Leach, William. *Land of Desire: Merchants, Power, and the Rise of a New American Culture.* New York: Pantheon, 1993.

Lears, Jackson. *Fables of Abundance: A Cultural History of Advertising in America.* New York: Basic Books, 1994.

Lerner, Gerda. "Early Community Work of Black Club Women." *Journal of Negro Education* (April 1974).

Lewis, David Levering. *When Harlem Was in Vogue.* 1981. Reprint, New York: Oxford University Press, 1989.

Lieberson, Stanley. *A Piece of the Pie: Blacks and White Immigrants Since 1880.* Berkeley: University of California Press, 1980.

Lief, Alfred. *It Floats: The Story of Procter & Gamble.* New York: Reinhart, 1958.

Lissak, Rivka Shpak. *Pluralism & Progressives: Hull House and the New Immigrants, 1890–1919.* Chicago: University of Chicago Press, 1989.

Loeb, Lori Anne. *Consuming Angels: Advertising and Victorian Women.* New York: Oxford University Press, 1994.

Lont, Cynthia M. *Women and Media: Content, Careers, and Criticism.* Belmont, Calif.: Wadsworth, 1995.

Lowenstein, Eleanor. *Bibliography of American Cookery Books, 1742–1860.* Worcester, Mass.: American Antiquarian Society, 1972.

Lynch, Edmund C. "Walter Dill Scott: Pioneer Industrial Psychologist." *Business History Review* (summer 1968): 149–70.

Marchand, Roland. *Advertising the American Dream: Making Way for Modernity.* Berkeley: University of California Press, 1985.

Martin, Theodora Penny. *The Sound of Our Own Voices: Women's Study Clubs, 1800–1910.* Boston: Beacon Press, 1987.

Mayo, James. *The American Grocery Store: The Business Evolution of an Architectural Space.* Westport, Conn.: Greenwood Press, 1993.

McCracken, Ellen. *Decoding Women's Magazines: From Mademoiselle to Ms.* New York: St. Martin's Press, 1993.

McCracken, Grant. "Culture and Consumption: A Theoretical Account of the Structure and Movement of the Cultural Meaning of Consumer Goods." *Journal of Consumer Research* (June 1986): 71–84.

———. *Culture of Consumption.* Bloomington: Indiana University Press, 1988.

Miller, Ernestine G. *The Art of Advertising.* New York: St. Martin's Press, 1982.

Miner, Harold. "Body Ritual Among the Nacirema." *American Anthropologist* 58 (1956).

Mitchell, Stephen. *Freud and Beyond: A History of Modern Psychoanalytic Thought.* New York: Basic Books, 1995.

Mobley, Jane. *Prescription for Success: The Chain Drug Story.* Kansas City, Mo.: Hallmark Cards, 1990.

Muir, Frank. *An Irreverent and Almost Complete Social History of the Bathroom.* Briarcliff Manor, N.Y.: Stein and Day, 1982.

Neverdon-Morton, Cynthia. "Self-Help Programs as Educative Activities of Black Women in the South, 1895–1925: Focus on Four Areas." *Journal of Negro Education* (summer 1982).

———. *African-American Women of the South and Advancement of the Race, 1895–1925.* Knoxville: University of Tennessee Press, 1989.

Nyerges, Christopher. "Naturally Clean: How to Find and Use Some of Nature's Most Common Soaps; Herbal Remedies." *Mother Nature News* (August 18, 1997).

Olsen, Kirstin. *Daily Life in 18th-Century England.* Westport, Conn.: Greenwood Press, 1999.

Ostrander, Gilman M. "The Revolution in Morals." *Change and Continuity in Twentieth-Century America: The 1920s.* Columbus: Ohio State University Press, 1968.

Otnes, Cele, and Linda M. Scott. "Something Old, Something New: Exploring the Interaction Between Ritual and Advertising." *Journal of Advertising* (spring 1996).

Peiss, Kathy. *Hope in a Jar: The Making of America's Beauty Culture.* New York: Owl Books, 1999.

Peter, J. Paul, and Jerry C. Olsen, *Understanding Consumer Behavior.* Burr Ridge, Ill.: Richard D. Irwin, 1994.

Peterson, Richard A. "The Production of Culture: A Prolegomenon." In *The Production of Culture*, edited by Richard A. Peterson. Beverly Hills, Calif.: Sage, 1976.

Pope, Daniel. *The Making of Modern Advertising.* New York: Basic Books, 1983.

Procter & Gamble. *Ivory 75.* Cincinnati: Procter & Gamble, 1954.

Randel, William Pierce. *The Evolution of American Taste.* New York: Routledge, 1976.

Ray, Michael L., and William L. Wilkie. "Fear: The Potential of an Appeal Neglected by Marketing." *Journal of Marketing* 1 (1970): 54–62.

Reader, W. J. *Fifty Years of Lever, 1930–1980.* London: Heinemann, 1980.

Richmond, Phyllis Ann. "American Attitudes Toward the Germ Theory of Disease (1860–1880)." In *Theory and Practice in American Medicine: Historical Studies from the Journal of Medicine & Allied Science*, edited by Gert H. Brieger. New York: Science History Publications, 1976.

Ringold, Gene, and Dewitt Bodeen. *The Films of Cecil B. DeMille.* New York: Citadel Press, 1969.

Rogers, Everett M. *Diffusion of Innovations.* 3rd ed. New York: Free Press, 1983.

Rook, Dennis W. "The Ritual Dimensions of Consumer Behavior." *Journal of Consumer Research* (December 1985): 251–64.

Scanlon, Jennifer. *Inarticulate Longings: The Ladies' Home Journal, Gender, and Promises of Consumer Culture.* New York: Routledge, 1995.

Scheffel, Richard L., ed. *Discovering America's Past: Customs, Legends, History and Lore of Our Great Nation.* Pleasantville, N.Y.: Reader's Digest, 1993.

Schisgall, Oscar. *Eyes on Tomorrow: The Evolution of Procter & Gamble*. Chicago: J. G. Ferguson Publishing Company; New York: Doubleday, 1981.

Schlereth, Thomas J., ed. *Material Cultural Studies*. Nashville, Tenn.: AASHL Press, 1982.

Schramm, W. "How Communication Works." In *The Process and Effects of Mass Communication*, edited by W. Schramm. Urbana: University of Illinois Press, 1954.

Schudson, Michael. *Advertising, the Uneasy Persuasion*. New York: Basic Books, 1984.

Scott, Ann Firor. *Making the Invisible Woman Visible*. Urbana: University of Illinois Press, 1984.

Settle, Irving. *A Pictorial History of Radio*. New York: Grosset, 1960.

Sigler, Jay A. *Civil Rights in America: 1500 to the Present*. Detroit: Gale, 1998.

Sillings, Dennis, and Nancy Roth. "When Electroquackery Thrived." *IEEE Spectrum* (November 1978): 56–61.

Sims, William Lee. *150 Years—and the Future! Colgate Palmolive (1806–1956)*. New York: Newcomen Society in North America, 1956.

Singman, Jeffrey L. *Daily Life in Medieval Europe*. Westport, Conn.: Greenwood Press, 1999.

Sivulka, Juliann. *Soap, Sex, and Cigarettes: A Cultural History of America Advertising*. Belmont, Calif.: Wadsworth, 1998.

Sklar, Katherine Kish. *Catherine Beecher: A Study in American Domesticity*. New York: Norton, 1975.

Sobel, Robert, and David B. Sicilia. *The Entrepreneurs: An American Adventure*. Boston: Houghton Mifflin, 1986.

Solomon, Michael R. *Consumer Behavior*. 4th ed. Upper Saddle River, N.J.: Prentice-Hall, 1992.

Spurlock, John C., and Cynthia A. Magistro. *New and Improved: The Transformation of American Women's Emotional Culture*. New York: New York University Press, 1998.

Starring, Charles H. "Julia Bartlett Crane." In *Notable Women, 1607–1950*, edited by Edward T. James, Janet Wilson James, and Paul S. Boyers. Cambridge, Mass.: Harvard University Press, 1971.

Sternthal, Brian, and C. Samuel Craig. "Fear Appeals: Revisited and Revised." *Journal of Consumer Research* (December 1974): 22–34.

Storr, Anthony. *Freud*. Oxford; New York: Oxford University Press, 1989.

Strasser, Susan. *Never Done: A History of American Housework*. New York: Pantheon Books, 1982.

Susman, Warren. "Personality and the Making of Twentieth-Century Culture." In *New Directions in American Intellectual History*, edited by John Higman and Paul K. Conklin. Baltimore: Johns Hopkins University Press, 1979.

———. *Culture as History: The Transformation of American Society in the Twentieth Century*. New York: Pantheon, 1984.

Tardiff, Olive, and Marcia Ray. "The Larkin Idea." *Spinning Wheel* (March 1975).

Tebbel, J. *The American Magazine: A Compact History*. New York: Hawthorn Books, 1969.

Tedlow, Richard S. *New and Improved: The Story of Mass Marketing in America*. New York: Basic Books, 1990.

Temkin, Owsei. *Galenism: Rise and Decline of a Medical Philosophy*. Ithaca, N.Y.: Cornell University Press, 1973.

Tomes, Nancy. *The Gospel of Germs: Men, Women, and the Microbe in American Life*. Cambridge, Mass.: Harvard University Press, 1998.

Trachtenburg, Jane. "It's Become Part of Our Culture." *Forbes* (March 23, 1987): 134–35.

Turner, E. S. *The Shocking History of Advertising!* New York: E. P. Dutton & Company, 1953.

Vigarello, George. *Concepts of Cleanliness: Changing Attitudes in France Since the Middle Ages*. Cambridge/New York: Cambridge University Press, 1988.

Vinikas, Vincent. *Soft Soap, Hard Sell: American Hygiene in the Age of Advertisement*. Ames: University of Iowa Press, 1992.

Walker, Juliet E. K. *The History of Black Business in America: Capitalism, Race, Enterpreneurship*. New York: Macmillan Library Reference; Prentice-Hall International, 1998.

Weistbrot, Robert. *Freedom Bound: A History of America's Civil Rights Movement*. New York: Norton, 1990.

Werther, Hans. *Life in the Middle Ages: From the Seventh to the Thirteenth Century*. Notre Dame, Ind.: University of Notre Dame Press, 1993.

White, Shane, and Graham White. *Stylin': African American Expressive Culture from Its Beginnings to the Zoot Suit*. New York: Cornell University Press, 1998.

Whyte, William H., Jr. *The Organization Man*. New York: Simon and Schuster, 1956.

Wicklund, R. A., and P. M. Gollwitzer. *Symbolic Completion Theory*. Hillsdale, N.J.: Erlbaum, 1982.

Wightman, Richard, and T. J. Jackson Lears, eds. *The Culture of Consumption: Critical Essay in American History, 1880–1980*. New York: Pantheon Books, 1983.

Wilkie, Jacqueline S. "Submerged Sensuality: Technology and Perceptions of Bathing." *Journal of Social History* (summer 1986).

Williams, Marilyn T. *Washing the Great Unwashed: Public Baths in Urban America, 1840–1920*. Columbus: Ohio State University Press, 1991.

Wilson, Charles Henry. *The History of Unilever: A Study in Economic Growth and Social Change*. New York: Praeger, 1968.

Winthrop, Jordan. *White over Black: American Attitudes Toward the Negro, 1550–1812*. New York: Norton, 1977.

Wolf, Naomi. *The Beauty Myth: How Images of Beauty Are Used against Women*. Toronto: Vintage Books, 1991.

Wood, James Playsted. *Story of Advertising*. New York: Ronald Press Co., 1958.
Woodward, Helen. *The Lady Persuaders*. New York: Ivan Obolensky, 1960.

Index